BACKS
TO THE WALL

G.D. Mitchell on the Western Front, 1917,
just before he won the Military Cross

G. D. MITCHELL

INTRODUCED BY ROBERT MACKLIN

BACKS TO THE WALL

A larrikin on the Western Front

ALLEN&UNWIN

First published in 2007

Allen & Unwin
83 Alexander Street
Crows Nest NSW 2065
Australia
Phone: (61 2) 8425 0100
Fax: (61 2) 9906 2218
Email: info@allenandunwin.com
Web: www.allenandunwin.com

National Library of Australia
Cataloguing-in-Publication entry:

Mitchell, G. D. (George Deane), 1894-61.
  Backs to the wall : a larrikin on the Western Front.

  ISBN 978 1 74175 205 2.

  1. Mitchell, G. D. (George Deane), 1894-61. 2. World War,
  1914-1918 - Campaigns - Western Front - Personal narratives,
  Australian. I. Macklin, Robert, 1941- . II. Title.

940.4144

Text design by Kirby Stalgis
Set in 10.5/13 pt Adobe Garamond by Midland Typesetters, Australia
Printed in Australia by Griffin Press

10 9 8 7 6 5 4 3 2 1

Contents

Preface

While researching my biography of Albert Jacka, the quintessential Australian hero of World War I, I found myself continually stumbling upon references to George Deane Mitchell, an Anzac whose words had the power to capture the sweep of history or the horror of combat in a single, indelible phrase. He leapt from the pages of Bill Gammage's classic work *The Broken Years* through the diaries he kept at Gallipoli. As the carnage began, with Mitch and his mates in the 10th Battalion preparing to charge into the teeth of the Turkish guns, he wrote: 'We rejoiced as we gripped our rifles. The long waiting should be terminated in one last glorious dash, for our last we knew it should be, for no man could live erect in that tornado for many seconds.'[1]

The order to charge never came. Mitch survived Gallipoli; indeed he survived the war on the Western Front, and all along he kept one of the most remarkable diaries in military history. For many hours at the Australian War Memorial I leafed through the grubby pages with their tens of thousands of rough-hewn words, their big bold letters perfectly legible in pencil, written as he awaited yet another German barrage or slumped in nervous exhaustion behind the lines.

They are a national treasure. They form the basis of the book he wrote many years later and published in 1937 as *Backs to the Wall*, the title an indicator of the fierceness of the struggle in France and Belgium against the advancing Germans.[2]

The timing of its publication could hardly have been more inopportune. World War I was history; the struggle for Empire no longer set the colonial pulse racing. On the contrary, in the interim the Great Depression had ravaged the country and many blamed the British for its worst excesses. Besides, the promise of the League of Nations and a mood of accommodation and demilitarisation had swept through the parliaments of the democracies. No one wanted to revisit the horror of the Somme and the Hindenburg Line. The result was that the book quickly faded into obscurity.

But when I found a rare copy of the hardback—at a time when the deadline for my own book was pressing—I was instantly captured and held by the power of the writing and the raw, uncompromising honesty of the author. *Jacka VC* was put aside until I had finished it. For it is the most powerful account of war in all its obscenity, its futility, its madness and its wild camaraderie that I have read.

Mitch went on to command a company of volunteers in World War II known as 'Mitchell's Maniacs'. It was a remarkable group that contained such conservative bastions of later years as Corporal Ninian Stephen, who would become Governor-General of Australia, Captain Nigel Bowen, later Commonwealth Attorney-General and Chief Justice of the Federal Court, and Captain Frank Packer, a media tycoon in the making. The afterword covers Mitch's remarkable adventures with his units in the Western Australian outback and in New Guinea.

Preface

I would particularly like to thank Bill Gammage for his assistance and Anthony Staunton for his guidance in developing the project. Major-General Professor John Pearn, author of *Watermen at War* (among many other distinguished works) was very generous in granting his permission—albeit to a fellow Brisbane Grammarian—to quote from the book that details Mitch's World War II military career. He was also most helpful in providing leads for additional research. In this respect, my thanks to former 'watermen' Ken Telfer and Don Hacker.

I am indebted, once again, to the staff of the Australian War Memorial, the National Archives of Australia, the National Library, my publisher Ian Bowring, and particularly to my editor Angela Handley, the calm comptroller within the eye of the storm.

Robert Macklin
Canberra, 2007
robert@robertmacklin.com

Introduction

Backs to the Wall was George Deane Mitchell's first published work, which he began writing in the mid-1930s. It opens only after the disaster of Gallipoli, probably because Mitch spent only three of the eight horrific months on the peninsula with his fellow Anzacs.

By contrast, he fought through the nightmare of the Western Front from 1916, after the AIF was blooded at Pozières until the eleventh hour of the eleventh day of the eleventh month of 1918, and it is these years that form the basis of *Backs to the Wall*.

However, he chronicled his war from the time his small boat approached Anzac Cove on the morning of 25 April 1915 and the power of his observation and his prose is captured for all time. Until then he had known only the flat horizons of the Australian countryside and the imperial patriotism of its citizenry. The experience he was about to undergo would change him utterly.

Mitch was born in Caltowie, a small town in South Australia's farmland east of Port Pirie, on 30 August 1894. His father—also George—was a humble railway porter at the town's station, at the junction of the lines heading north and west from Victoria and New South Wales. Mitch's early schooldays were spent there and as a teenager he struck out for Adelaide where, at the outbreak of war at the beginning of August 1914 he was a 20-year-old clerk.

On 6 August the Australian Government offered to send an expeditionary force of 20,000 men to Europe in the form of an infantry division and a light horse brigade. The division would be representative of all Australian states and by 10 August recruiting had commenced in Adelaide with Colonel Stanley Price Weir in command of the 10th Battalion.[1]

Mitch joined up on 5 September at the Adelaide suburb of Thebarton. The battalion was in full training in a camp at nearby Morphettville, an 80-acre farm beside the famous racetrack. Mitch had enlisted earlier in the 76th Infantry battalion of the local militia so when he joined the AIF he carried with him the rank of corporal.

By now uniforms, rifles and kits were arriving and musketry practice was undertaken in the sandhills north-west of the camp. Regular route marches took them through the suburb of Glenelg, where they swam in the ocean and returned to the applause of the locals. The governor-general, Sir Ronald Munro Ferguson, inspected the troops and addressed the assembly. 'The whole future of the Empire depends upon the defeat of a strong, arrogant and unscrupulous foe,' he said. 'The fate of free institutions is in the balance against military tyranny.'[2]

However, he declared, prospects were good. 'You will find when you reach the front a high standard of personal leadership and of efficient organisation,' he said. 'You will find that we have got the generals, we have got the troops, and we shall have the victory.'

The commander of the 1st Division, General William Bridges,

accompanied the vice-regal party and confided his own assessment to the local press. 'I am more than pleased with the show put up by the South Australian contingent today,' he said. 'I think they will uphold the reputation held by corps from the Mother Country.'

A week later came the first route march through the city of Adelaide by all AIF troops training at Morphettville. Government offices were closed and the governor of South Australia, Sir Henry Galway, took the salute as 2193 men and 725 horses paraded past Parliament House. The crowds cheered and the soldiers responded with military vigour and discipline. The governor handed over the blue and gold regimental flag designed by a committee of prominent Adelaide matrons. 'I know every man will do his utmost to guard and keep it clean,' he said. 'It should be carried high, upholding those traditions which have made the British Empire. I trust you will all return with peace in your helmets [*sic*] and victory in your eyes.'[3]

The troops responded dutifully. However, once they reached the outskirts of town they fell upon the free beer supplied by Landlord Tolley at his Half-Way House on Bay Road.

Finally on 19 October the men packed their kitbags and first thing next morning the battalion boarded the train for the Outer Harbour of Port Adelaide. The 10th was ready for the fray. According to Colonel Weir, 'My men are second to none and my officers are of the first water.'[4]

They embarked on HMAT *Ascanius* and at 4.30 p.m., after an emotional speech by Sir Henry Galway, the ship pulled away from the docks. According to the battalion war diary, 'Many of the men of the 10th looked towards the Adelaide Hills for the last time, some with feelings of hope that they would eventually return; but the die in the great game had been cast, and some never returned, and on that occasion viewed their native hills with leave-taking recollections.'[5]

Their destination was Britain, the heart of empire, where they would train for the terrible conflict underway in Europe. The Germans had swept through Belgium and were threatening Paris. The British Expeditionary Force was on the Continent fighting to halt the seemingly implacable advance while the French armies to the south, seeking to drive through Alsace and Lorraine to the heart of Germany, had been stopped in their tracks. The need for new blood was urgent.

Meantime, Mitch and his mates were giving evidence of the larrikin nature that bubbled just beneath the surface of the Australian volunteers. When the *Ascanius* berthed in Fremantle on 25 October two companies were granted leave and immediately began to take Perth apart. After two days all further shore leave was cancelled. When the *Ascanius* departed on 2 November two men were still missing.

On board, the officers were issued with textbooks on the French, German and Austro-Hungarian armies, notes on the military geography of France and Belgium, notes on night operations in Europe and a glossary of English, French and German military terms. Soon afterwards they joined a convoy of ships emanating from other Australian ports and for a time were escorted by the allied Japanese cruiser *Ibuki*.

A few days later they watched as the HMAS *Sydney* gave chase to the German raider *Emden* and cheered when the message from the *Sydney* was relayed: '*Emden* beached and done for.'

Shortly after leaving Colombo (where all shore leave remained cancelled) the *Ascanius* accidentally rammed another convoy vessel, the *Shropshire*, and Mitch, along with the other members of his company, was hurled out of his hammock. The hull of the *Ascanius* was badly torn and the commander of the *Hampshire*, who inspected the damage, bellowed through his bullhorn to the *Ascanius*'s captain: 'In my whole career of navigation I have never seen anything so careless. You are not fit to be in charge of a ferry boat.'[6] However, the ship was sufficiently watertight to continue and reached Aden for repairs on 26 November.

The colonel of the Australian Light Horse Brigade, Harry Chauvel, had gone ahead to inspect the training facilities in Britain and pronounced them overcrowded and inadequate. So, on his recommendation both the 1st Division under General William Bridges, the former commandant of Duntroon, and his own Light Horse were to be diverted to Egypt, which was under the control of the British Government. The Australians would combine with the New Zealanders to form a corps under the British general, William Riddell Birdwood, and would travel to the Western Front from there.

At 7 a.m. on 5 December the *Ascanius* arrived at Alexandria and over the next two days the men disembarked and entrained for Cairo and Mena camp, set up in the shadow of the great pyramids. By now Mitch had somehow contrived to lose both stripes and then to be reinstated as a lance corporal. It was a pattern that would be repeated several times over the next few months during a training regime conducted in the shit, sand, sin and syphilis of Egypt, well before he confronted the hellfire of Gallipoli.

There was something about military discipline that rankled with Mitch, and his adventures in Cairo's red light area, Haret el Wasser—which the Australians immediately nicknamed 'the

Wozzer'—were fairly typical. After a few drinks, he and his mates hired donkeys from the locals and raced them down the narrow lanes with little regard for the trinket vendors' displays on either side. They gambled and fought, laughed and sang their raucous ballads. They went out of their way to ignore the British officers, who took umbrage at these uncouth colonial upstarts when they doggedly refused to salute.

But at the same time they trained hard and by the end of January they were routinely handling extended marches across the desert sands in full kit. Mitch was now in C Company and on one such occasion his platoon, under the command of Scottish-born Lieutenant 'Jock' Hamilton, was reprimanded for talking too much. As punishment the company commander, Captain Robert Jacob, ordered Hamilton to take the platoon further into the sand dunes. However, neither the platoon commander nor Mitch and his mates were impressed by this and they simply marched till they were out of sight, halted and broke out the rations. Hamilton said, 'Gentlemen, today you dine with me.'[7] In due course they marched back to Mena camp where they were dubbed 'The Lost Platoon' much to their delight and the chagrin of the company commander.

Then in February came news that instead of proceeding to the Western Front, the Australians and New Zealanders would become part of an assault on the straits of the Dardanelles designed to knock Turkey out of the war. The Gallipoli campaign—the brainchild of Winston Churchill as First Lord of the Admiralty—was initially planned as a naval exercise in which Britain's Mediterranean fleet would crash through the Turkish defences and sail up the Sea of Marmara to Constantinople. With their capital under British guns the Turks would soon capitulate.

The British, Australian and French troops would 'mop up' any resistance on their triumphal march to the heart of the tottering Ottoman Empire.

Suitably reinforced, the troops would then surge through the Balkans to overwhelm Germany's Austro-Hungarian allies. The Germans would be surrounded and victory for the Entente would follow as day followed night.

However, Churchill's plans went seriously awry when, on 18 March, the fleet under Britain's Admiral de Robeck was not just repulsed by the Turkish guns and mines, it was seriously crippled. By the end of the day 700 Allied lives were lost and three ships sunk. De Robeck had no stomach for a second assault and the emphasis of the campaign turned towards a massed landing of troops under the command of the British general Ian Hamilton, whose battlefield experience until this point had been confined to Indian and South African skirmishes. Both he and his forces were woefully under-prepared for the mission at hand.

The plan was to attack on a wide front, with the French providing a diversion on the southern side of the Dardanelles, the main British forces striking at the northern tip and the Anzacs under General Birdwood attacking further up the peninsula. It was not a good plan. The front was far too wide and the expedition's most potent strike force, the Anzacs, were to be landed in an area that could hardly have been more favourable to the defenders. Moreover the Turks, under the German general Liman von Sanders, were waiting for them.

Meanwhile, Mitch's 10th Battalion arrived at Lemnos Island just out from the Gallipoli peninsula on 12 March and began practising landings and other battle exercises. Lieutenant Colonel

Weir was impressed. 'By Jove, my men are a good lot of fellows,' he wrote. '[They] are just longing to get under fire, although they must know that many of them will fall in the first "scrap", but it is the sporting instinct that leads them on, and I am quite sure they will give a good account of themselves.'[8]

The orders for the 10th Battalion arrived. As part of the 3rd Infantry Brigade of the 1st Division, they would serve as the landing or covering force for the invaders. General Hamilton sent a message to the troops: 'Before us lies an adventure unprecedented in modern war. Together with our comrades of the Fleet, we are about to force a landing on an open beach, in the face of positions which have been vaunted by our enemy as impregnable. The landing will be made good by help of God and the Navy. The positions will be stormed, and the war will be brought one step nearer to a glorious close. The whole world will be watching our progress. Let us prove ourselves worthy of the great feat of arms entrusted to us.'[9]

Birdwood's orders were slightly more practical. 'We are going to have a real hard and rough time of it,' he said. 'You must not waste [ammunition] by firing away indiscriminately at no target.'[10]

That would not be a problem. There would be plenty of targets—on both sides. Mitch opened his diary, 'Here goes death or glory,' he wrote. 'So long all.' But then, as he waited in his rowing boat to be towed towards the shore, a more complex response stirred him. 'I think that every emotion was mixed,' he wrote, 'exultation predominating. We had come from the New World for the conquest of the Old.'[11]

Introduction

The landing was hellish. When Mitch and his company hit the narrow shoreline at about 10 a.m. it was under blistering fire. 'Fierce we expected it to be,' he wrote, 'but fierce as it was we never dreamed.' The dead and dying lay all about. He rushed forward into the low brush at the base of the cliffs that rose through gullies and blind alleys up towards a rim of fire from the Turkish gunners and riflemen.

'All the time the snipers were at me,' he wrote. 'Not knowing where they were, it was impossible to use cover as one did not know on which side of it to get.

'Then came another shock to the system—there was a weird shrieking note somewhere in the air which increased in volume every fraction of a second. It culminated in a deafening report and a cloud of smoke some 30 yards on my right and 30 feet high. Simultaneously there was a swishing sound as the bullets beat down bushes and swept the earth and a devilish scream as large pieces of the case spun through the air.'

Still he pressed forward. 'Continually in my progress I came across groups of men all going ahead, but as our opinions differed as to the easiest route we were constantly split up.

'After climbing a precipice I came upon the real meaning of war. A sturdy Australian lay on his face, congealing blood flowed from a ghastly wound in the head, streaking his face and forming a crimson pool. His flesh was the waxy colour I was to grow so familiar with. Lt Col Hallcombe stood by studying the situation ahead. He gave no heed to the dying soldier. All round our unprotected bodies the bullets thrashed through the barely concealing bushes.'

Mitch found a depression that gave some cover and dug further into the stony ground with his hands and bayonet. 'We settled down to a musketry duel,' he wrote later. 'The men began to get hit. A terrible cry was wrenched from the bravest as the nickel demon ripped through flesh, bone, sinew . . . Alec Gilpin [was] fatally wounded in the stomach. All day he begged to be shot.'

Later, 'No stretcher bearers could approach our position without being shot down. The wounded and dying had to lie in their own blood and ask for things they could not have. Some begged to be shot. Others asked their mates to load and pass the rifles so they could end themselves.'

The day dragged on endlessly. Colonel Weir described it in detail in the Battalion War Diary. 'We had desperate fighting all day long, the shrapnel shell being very deadly, but our men were game and dug in for all they were worth with their entrenching tools.'[12]

In the front line, Mitch welcomed a newcomer. 'One man dropped beside me laughing, 'You've got yourself into the hottest corner you'll ever strike.' He fired a few shots and again I heard the sickening thud of a bullet. I looked at him in horror. The bullet had fearfully smashed his face and gone down his throat rendering him dumb. But his eyes were dreadful to behold. And how he squirmed in his agony.

'There was nothing I could do for him but pray he might die swiftly. It took him about 20 minutes and by then he had tangled his legs in mine and stiffened. I saw the waxy colour creep over his cheeks and breathed freer.

'I felt thirsty after that but not caring to deplete my water bottle so early in proceedings, I unhitched the dead man's, had a long drink and passed it on. Between the incidents that occupied my attention I actually dozed.'

There was a brief respite when a British reconnaissance aircraft flew overhead and attracted the Turkish gunners.

However, such was the intensity of the fusillade from the heights that the Anzacs realised the massive strength ranged against them. Their only consolation was that from the sea their own naval artillery was similarly alerted. Mitch wrote, 'Every now and again above the fiendish din of battle came the WOOM-PAH at which ground, sea and sky seemed to get up and sit down again. It was Big Lissie[13] arguing with her 15-inch toys. And when her shells landed—suffering sinner, they shifted a hill—arms, legs and other curios flying in all directions . . .'

According to the battalion's war diary, 'At 4pm the enemy fire died down under ship's fire and spotting by aeroplane. At 6pm all were ordered to entrench and dig in for the night. All night counter-attacks and sniping by the enemy followed.'

Colonel Weir recorded in his diary, 'The night was cold and rain fell but we never moved from the positions taken up on Sunday afternoon until Wednesday night and were under fire night and day during the whole of that time.'

By then, Mitch and his mates were utterly exhausted. Casualties included 13 officers and 453 other ranks. However, after two days' spell on the beach they returned to the trenches.

In May they were transferred to the extreme right flank of the ANZAC position to relieve the 9th Battalion. They joined a raid on Gaba Tepe led by Captain R.L. Leane of the 11th Battalion. It was Mitch's first association with the soldier who would play a pivotal role in his military career. The Turkish defenders retained the heights. On 5 May the battalion relieved the 11th, which took a well-deserved rest behind the lines.

Then on 19 May came the massive Turkish counter-attack designed to sweep the Anzacs back into the sea. Mitch and his mates in the 10th were in the thick of it. The heaviest fighting was at Quinn's Post and nearby at Courtney's Post[14] where acting lance corporal Albert Jacka won the first Victoria Cross to be awarded to an Australian soldier in the war. A dozen Turks had hurled themselves into the Australian trenches and Jacka went in after them, shot five, bayoneted two and sent the remainder fleeing.

At Mitch's trench to the right, 'The Turks showered our [position] with bullets and their big guns played havoc. They rushed to within twenty yards but our lads mowed them down like grass.'[15]

According to Mitch, one Turk died on his knees about 25 metres from the trench line and remained in an upright position. Colonel Weir noted in his diary, 'Capt. Nott would not believe it possible until he went up this morning and saw for himself.'

Mitch wrote, 'All morning one of the heaviest bombardments that I have ever experienced has been raging. A pall of smoke from the bursting shells continuously hangs over this gully . . . there were terrific bursts of rifle fire, so loud was it that one had to yell into a man's ear to make himself audible.

'The Turks came up six and seven deep and every time were repulsed by our fire . . . just outside the opening trench were 12 men of the 10th—stark in death. Four of them were pals of mine and one belonged to my section: Glorious war.'

The anger and irony are clear. By now it was obvious that the Gallipoli expedition was not only ill-conceived and badly led, it had all the makings of a military disaster. Mitch's contempt for 'the heads' who had put them in this position was growing. He was torn between his battlefield mateship and a powerful sense that they had been placed in an unwinnable position. According to historian Bill Gammage, Mitch was 'a vain man, but a good soldier . . . whose outlook [typified] the irreverence and valour of the A.I.F. [He was] commended for bravery and fined or imprisoned for indiscipline with almost equal regularity.'[16]

On 25 May 1915 he copped his first combat 'field punishment'—one day in irons—for being absent from duty. The punishment was ordered by Colonel Weir and once again, it seems, he lost his single lance corporal's stripe.

By the end of May, dysentery was beginning to strike at the men who had been fighting for weeks in fetid conditions among the clouds of flies attracted by rotting corpses from both sides. Colonel Weir wrote, 'Since 19 May the enemy has been very quiet—hasn't made any fresh attacks. They continue to shell us every day, but with very little effect.'

June saw 'the summer heat becoming oppressive, and flies existed in their countless millions.'[17] The 10th Battalion was given the unenviable task of burrowing tunnels designed to undermine the Turkish trenches and blow them up while others were assigned to 'digging parties' to construct 'Artillery Road' up Shrapnel Valley.

This was not the kind of soldiering that appealed to Mitch. He was more interested in the canteen stores that arrived in the *Seeang Bee* for purchase by the troops—pickles, sauce, tinned fruit, biscuits, condensed milk, chocolate and cigarettes. However, the rush was so great that, according to the official unit diary, 'not many of the 10th Battalion were fortunate enough to procure their requirements before the "sold out" signs went up'.

This may well have been the start of Mitch's career as a 'liberator' of the little luxuries that made life bearable in the front lines, and perhaps even of the political instincts that would later see him elected to State Parliament. His diary records his pleasure in 'trading' for the delicacies, and the delight of his mates on his return from a 'treasure hunt'.

In July they were given three days' rest at nearby Imbros Island—'a perfect holiday picnic'—but on their return they went back into the line, relieving Captain Leane and his men of the 11th Battalion. The front lines were always fraught with danger and the nervous tension was unremitting. More deadly, however, was the dysentery, which by now was becoming acute. On 21 July Mitch had his first bout and was admitted to field hospital on Gallipoli.

He was back in action a week later but relief was short-lived. On 1 August he collapsed; now the dysentery had become enteric[18] and he was transferred to the hospital ship *Reva* for transportation to Alexandria. Once in Egypt complications set in and he was diagnosed with a life-threatening fever that refused to respond to treatment.

Though he did not realise it at the time, Mitch had seen the last of Gallipoli. His diaries were neglected for long periods as the illness took its course but it is hard to believe that he regretted leaving the killing fields above Anzac Cove. Like the vast majority of the Australian volunteer force, he had formed strong bonds with his mates and his battalion. He left many close friends in the stony soil of the peninsula; many others remained behind to carry on the fight. But he had done all that was asked of him, and more; and now he was struggling simply to survive the sweats and tremors that were shaking his body and stripping the flesh from his bones.

On 2 October he embarked with other casualties on the hospital ship *Leticia*, and arrived in London ten days later, where he was immediately admitted to the Royal Victoria Hospital.

He would spend the next four months recuperating there and in December he would hear of the ignominious withdrawal of the Gallipoli expedition with almost 8000 young Australian lives sacrificed in vain.

'All that sacrifice,' he wrote, 'all that labour, all that suffering, for nothing at all. No advantage gained and the flower of Australia's manhood lies on and below the earth which is not even in our own hands. I feel bitter about it.'[19]

In February 1916, still convalescent and with the bitterness of Gallipoli still rankling just beneath the surface, Mitch was posted to a training unit at Abbey Wood and then to Weymouth on Britain's southern coast. There he underwent light infantry training, but it is apparent that he took every opportunity to blow off steam and as a 21-year-old soldier far from the restrictions of home he found plenty of ways to get himself into trouble.

In March he was admitted to hospital suffering a mild venereal infection that cleared up after ten days. In May he had his pay stopped for 'damage to barracks' and the following month he went AWOL for three days and was confined to barracks for a week with three days' loss of pay. Transferred to Westham Camp in August, according to his personnel file he managed to lose his kit on the way from there to the camp at Perham Downs and had to repay its value with another loss of pay.

Finally in September he was officially 'taken on strength' of his 10th Battalion[20] and ordered to France where, with a big contingent of reinforcements, the battalion had reassembled for the war of attrition in the killing fields of Flanders and the Somme. In his new kitbag Mitch carried all the usual accoutrements of soldiery. But to them he had added a supply of pencils and notebooks and as he crossed the Channel he resumed the diary that would provide the foundation of one of the most powerful stories of war ever penned.

Within it George Deane Mitchell found his true voice. And it speaks to all the generations of men and women who go to war, to the politicians who send them, and to the families who wait—all too often in vain—for their safe return.

BACKS
TO THE WALL

1

To sunny France

Gallipoli, that tale of disaster, was closed and done. New and
terrific, at closer view, loomed the battles of Flanders and
France.

The wild winds of the autumn of 1916 were blowing the
bright-coloured leaves from the trees before I was put on draft for
France. I held the rank of full private. Twice while standing on
parade with the draft, fully equipped to the last detail, my name
was called, and I was taken from its strength. 'No enteric cases to
be sent to France yet,' was all they told me. On 4 September 1916
I was finally equipped for draft to France.

In the camp at Perham Downs we rejoiced at the news of a
Zepp raider brought down in flames, red-handed.

The train loped through the English countryside. The hop-
fields of Kent, then the chalk cliffs of Folkestone.

We packed on to the sharp-bowed cross-channeller *Invicta*,

which plunged into the rough grey seas. From my diary comes the following:

Ere many lengths were traversed the *Invicta* was in her full stride of 20 knots. The sea is choppy. Destroyers edge in to escort us. Many ships dot the waters—troopers, destroyers, patrol boats, and cargo vessels. One bears the inscription on her side in great letters, 'Belgian relief-ship'.

Neutrals have their flags blazoned on their hulls.

It is 4.30 p.m. The day is overcast with the mists of autumn. It is raining.

The last I saw of England was two grey lines. The nearer dark grey and the farther overhanging—a dim, misty grey. Then the fog shut England out. Boulogne takes shape. Cathedral spires and towers rise out of the formlessness of distance.

Alongside us at the wharf is a transport of Scotties. They give us sprigs of heather. We march up a long hill to a camp of bell-tents. One blanket each is issued. The night is windy and it is raining. The mud outside is ankle-deep. Now to get something to eat.

Then to Etaples, and through the sweatshop of the 'bull-ring'.

After a few days we were entrained again—Boulogne, Calais, St Omer, then Hazebrouck. We eagerly watched the green countryside as it slipped by. In the cattletruck the thirty-six of us sang, and we drank wine and beer as we could wangle it.

A party of us, all destined for the 10th Battalion, messed together. Our united efforts produced some wonderful food and drinks at different stopping-places. Our money was a common pool.

We burrowed into wheat stooks in the fields outside Hazebrouck, and slept in perfect comfort through two nights of rain and hail.

On 19 September we marched into the silent, deathly region that was the Ypres salient. The world of life and light was behind us. Here all was still, and we moved under the shadow of death.

A subtle difference pervaded everything. The rough crosses by the road told the tale of the days.

Shattered, mouldering ruins were new to us of Anzac. The chill, still stink of death pervaded everything. 'All hope abandon' seemed to be the message of that region as we marched stolidly over the cobbles in strung-out groups of ten.

We rejoined the 10th at an old ruined barn, its headquarters. For a few minutes we mingled and looked for men we knew. I found some, but very few. The men who marched through Egypt and survived the heights of Anzac had been raked through the hell of Pozières. The reunion was in keeping with the vast graveyard we occupied.

That night, in lashing rain, we marched over shell-pocked fields. We entered shattered Ypres, and saw the abomination of desolation by the reflection of wavering Very lights. Masses of transports rumbled through the darkness. From cellars came streaks of light that denoted some military office. We glanced through the yawning window space of a tall, roofless building. There, by the light of candles, was a group of Diggers playing two-up. A more powerful star shell caused the gaunt ruins to outline stark against the dim, weeping skies.

Out of the town of death and across the bridge—a railway bank, on which there was a duckboard track.

Our heavy kits dragged mercilessly, as we stumbled along the broken boards. The sweat on our faces mingled with the drifting rain. Exhaustion was squeezing us tightly. The oily water of a canal below us gleamed fitfully in the intermittent light. Odd shells crashed far and near into waterlogged fields.

Across a field on broken duckboards, and then—worst of all—a long communication trench. Most of the duckboards were a foot under water. Some were broken, some did not meet. We reeled with exhaustion, stumbled, rose and stumbled again. Now a wire would catch us across our faces; now tangle our feet.

Beyond even cursing, we blundered on. At last we came to a set of dugouts along a hedge. The three of us allotted to a small one crawled through the narrow entrance and collapsed. As our strength was slowly coming back a sergeant splashed up outside, poked his head through the doorway, and said apologetically, 'You chaps have to go on fatigue till daylight.'

We crawled out, cursing with our returning breath. But a crescent moon had come from behind a cloud. With only rifle and bandolier, in the cold night wind, we found that we were good for much more. A string of machine-gun bullets hissed through our ranks as we heaved duckboards. No one was hit. We returned to our dugout at daylight, and slept well. That was the morning of 20 September.

Night after night we went out. Twice we tried to dig trenches in reeking, smashed Square Wood, a hundred yards behind the line. Water filled in what we dug. My shovel struck a twisted Vickers gun. I dragged it from the mud and slung it over the embryo parapet. Then a belt of ammunition snagged my shovel. That, too, went on the parapet. My shovel was again caught. I reached down into the cold, foul water to clear this latest obstruction, and felt a hand down there.

Moved over close to my neighbour on the right and commenced to dig there. 'Dig in your own bloody possie,' he said. 'Not on your life!' I told him. Strange groups of Boche lights would form and hang over us. We would watch with silent apprehension to see if these were to call artillery down on our defenceless heads. The wood behind us was an almost impenetrable maze of broken tree trunks, tangled wire, and dead men.

Great, sleek, corpse-fed rats ran in squads between our legs and over our feet as we stood. Their obscene squeaking could be heard at all times. Some men conceived an unmeasured hatred of these loathsome things, and were always trying to slaughter them. I wondered, as I stood, did they picture themselves as those scattered corpses—a prey to these. Imagination is decidedly not good for a soldier. It is one of the things Kipling forgot to tell us.

Sometimes shells came in a shower, unheralded, out of space. Men flung themselves into whatever cover there was—laughing. The flame and thunder continued a little while, and we went on with our work, cheerful for the break.

One afternoon we sheltered in the trench alongside our dugouts. A pale sun was setting. Five-point-nines were bursting in salvos, raking the ground and tearing chunks out of a weary-looking hedge. A man was being led away by his mates. His face was a mask of blood that dripped and made lines down his greatcoat.

A copy of the *Sydney Mail* was under my hand. Picked it up, and it came open at the society page. There was an account of a wedding. I read to a group of the boys, 'Mrs Blank looked charming in ninon over nunon.' Blistering comments mixed with the detonations of the shells. Over the page were racing reports. Futility on futility.

On 24 September we examined our rifles and equipments, and moved up through long winding saps to the deep dugouts behind Hill 60. Next morning we marched to the front line on fatigue, and set to work revetting the parapet with sandbags.

During the afternoon a chap looked over where the trench was shallow, and said, 'Look! I can see the German line!' But that was the last thing he saw. He slumped down in the trench, shot through the brain. During the night an original sergeant, out on patrol, was shot. We could see his body when we looked over the parapet.

On 26 September five of us were taken from the platoon to occupy a special listening-post. We filed through the sodden saps to the front line, and beyond the front line to the listening-post on top of Hill 60. The outgoing party whispered a caution that we were within five yards of the German advanced post.

The sap was shallow, and the post was in the state of decay and collapse that we would never have endured on Gallipoli. The sides were caving in, and offered poor cover. Barbed wire, pieces of clothing, smashed rifles, and beams protruded everywhere. But, here, where a spade of earth thrown over the top would bring down a shower of explosives, we had to endure it. No sooner had two of us established ourselves and noted where the bombs and ammunition were stacked than our guns opened.

For an hour we cowered against the back parapet. Our eighteen-pounders burst their shrapnel ten feet overhead. The pellets swept forward over the enemy positions. But portions of the shell-cases hissed and smacked into the earth round us. We trembled against the sodden ground, naked to the storm. The enemy guns took up the game, and the earth rocked to din indescribable. White clouds of resinous smoke from our shrapnel eddied round us, billows of stinking acid smoke from the German shells. The concussion jarred through us in wave upon wave of fury. Demoniac shrieks of descending shells, snarling of swarms of ragged fragments, blow upon blow of concussion. All the fiends of hell seemed to be struggling and wrangling round us.

With a hissing rush, swift beyond imagination, an eighteen-pounder shell fell short, into our parapet. All was squalling metal violence and thudding earth. We looked at each other, grey-faced, except where we bled from small cuts. The taste of death was very bitter.

'Look up!' said my mate. There through the air was a black shape like a rum jar, spinning and turning through a great arc. Now it reached its peak and commenced to rush down towards us. We watched as condemned men. Just as everything seemed finished we saw that its path would take it beyond us. The air shuddered and the earth rocked to an appalling explosion.

Through the air as we watched came from our lines a string of what appeared to be small sticks. One followed fast in the track of the other—fast as we could count. Swift came the flat crashes of the exploding bombs, swift followed fresh bombs as big Bill Montgomery's crew slammed them into the hungry Stokes gun-muzzles.

Spinning through the air, right into our post, came a German rifle butt. I stared at its broad-toed steel butt plate as it rested beside my foot. Now came a whistling sound as of wild ducks in flight, and I recognised long-shafted rifle-grenades. These burst with a howling noise. From our line went showers of Mills rifle-grenades, to burst with shrill detonations on the enemy lines.

Steadily the fire died down. Odd shells rushed viciously

overhead, as if to renew it all. Sergeant Doddridge pushed into our post to see if we were still alive.

'Just the usual evening strafe,' he said, casually.

'But do you think it is fair,' complained my mate, 'that we should get lashed by both bloody sides?'

Doddy laughed, and said that he would report the shells falling short. Tea was brought up to us. Many times I stopped in the middle of a bite, until the menace of some approaching missile was past. Certainly not good for nerves or digestion. No content could be with us when we knew that underfoot were mines and countermines, and that we lived only at the enemy's pleasure.

Through the long troubled winter night we stood our watches, one hour on and two off, bombs stacked close beside us, eyes just above the parapet. At intervals, strings of Maxim bullets squealed and spat around us. With the enemy so close, we had to keep a sharp look out.

Blighty was never like this, I thought, as I remembered the pretty girls I had taken out, the good meals I had eaten, the cosy fires and the warm beds. The crash of a Minnie or the howl of a grenade would call me from my delectable dreams to unpleasant realities. Greasy rats moved about in stinking platoons, sniffed our rifle-muzzles, and sometimes jumped on our shoulders as they came in from their feeding-grounds in No Man's Land.

We stood to arms while the grey dawn of 27 September hesitatingly revealed a world of torn earth, debris and unburied dead. Throughout the day the sun shone and warmed us. At three in the afternoon, while two of us were on duty in the post, Doddy brought up word that our guns were to open.

Again the tale was the same. Guns answered guns. Stokes

answered Minnies. Grenades spoke to grenades. Thunder, flame and smoke ruled the world. Two eighteen-pounders crashed into our post. We staggered into the sap, dazed and half blind, falling over the men who lay there. Another shell crashed the side of the sap, and we blundered out into the front-line trench. More shells landed round the trench. Overhead was a double arch of explosives in travel.

Sergeant Doddridge sent back word that our shells were dropping short. 'Just another evening strafe?' I asked him. 'That's all,' he said, and laughed.

To the right of us was the steep bank of the Ypres–Comines canal. Nearby ran a deserted sap into Fritz-land. There lay my pal James with his rifle ready. I visualised a helmeted Fritz at the other end in just such an attitude.

Darkness ushered in a still menacing night. On such a night as this could dead men walk, and speak to us who were out beyond the ways of life only awaiting the reaper. Dread and foreboding possessed me as I went on listening duty. The night seemed to be full of warning voices that made no sound, but formed their messages in the brain.

As Godfrey wrote in *The Anzac Book*:[1]

> This is indeed a false, false night,
> There's not a soldier sleeps,
> But like a ghost stands to his post,
> While death through the long sap creeps.

In that hour was born in me a fear that lasted throughout the whole winter. It was the dread of dying in the mud, going down into that stinking morass and though dead being conscious throughout the ages. It was probably a form of claustrophobia. Waves of fear at times threatened to overwhelm me, but that I kept tight rein on myself. A little weakness, a little slackening of control at times and I might have gone over the borderline. In the light of the sun, on firm ground, I could laugh at fate. But where the churned mud half hid and half revealed bodies, where dead hands reached out of the morass, seeming to implore aid—there I had to hold tight.

The long hour of duty came to an end at last. Two men relieved us. I stepped out of the post into the sap with a sigh of relief. The ground lunged beneath me, rose and fell. The trench crushed in and swung apart. A stunning wall of air battered against me. A few yards beyond the post stood a giant tower pierced through with swords of flame. A mine!

A rushing noise filled the air as the debris began to fall. My tin hat went. I covered my face and head with my arms. Something struck me a frightful blow on the shoulder and pitched me face down. An appalling weight fell across my loins. Clods of earth struck me everywhere.

'This is the end,' I said quietly. But the hail ceased. I groped blindly for my rifle. Found one, not my own. The strap was loose. Mine was tight; no matter. I reeled down the sap. As I bent to get under an arch of iron, a bayonet touched my throat and an excited voice challenged me. First pressure on trigger, I thought, as I answered. Sergeant Doddridge pushed past the sentry.

'Is the post wrecked?'

'No,' I told him.

'Do you know where the bombs are?'

'Yes.'

'Come with me then.'

I followed him to the empty post. Together we stood, eyes above the parapet, a bomb in each hand, waiting for a rush. Cool and still he was, as though no hail of bombs flamed around us, or stammering Maxims flailed the parapet. The calm of resignation was on me.

'Raggie' Holland sent reinforcements to the post. I went into the sap to rest. Men walked over me, but I was too dopey to protest. The following from my diary:

About 2 a.m. a feeling of sickness overcame me. Passed the word to the sergeant and staggered out into the more open air of the communication trench. I was in the throes of sickness when Lieutenant Don Chisolm found me. He was sympathetic and ordered me back to Infantry Tunnel to get some rest, and said that he would tell Sergeant Doddridge. So I made my way wearily to Infantry Tunnel, which is a deep drive in the hillside.

I could not rest, partly for a terrible thirst. Wandered through the timbered drive until I encountered a Canadian cook from whom I begged a drink of tea. Lay down in the main passage but could not rest.

At about 9 a.m. so exhausted that I could scarcely crawl. I went up and found the garrison of our little hell-post intact. After collecting my goods the journey to the doctor took me an hour and a half. Got down to the quack at last and sat on a box awaiting his pleasure. He sent me inside the medical dugout where I lay on a stretcher and fell asleep. The sound of voices woke me. Four men were having various wounds dressed. A rum jar had come over and caught seven of them. Three were dead. One had a slight wound in the arm, another the side of his face knocked about, the third had a shattered hand, and the fourth was prostrate after being dug out from beneath the debris. He had my sympathy.

The army must have run out of No. 9, for we were sent to Railway

Dugouts. Here a wagon took us along the shell-torn road to Ypres, from whence a motor ambulance took us to Poperinghe, where we entered a dressing-station. An orderly gave us biscuits and cocoa, and led us into a big room. With a stretcher and three downy blankets apiece, we slept.

We were sent on to another dressing-station. A doctor there examined me and placed me in a fever ward. I fell asleep trying to see the connexion between being jammed in a trench and fever. All night the rumbling of guns shook the hut. A little before noon of 2 October the quack rushed in and wrote all over my card. He said that I was to go down to the base, marked for Blighty by the midday train. But alas for dreams of the warmth of Blighty—no midday train ran that day.

By Red Cross train and motor, I drifted to a hospital outside Boulogne. At nights the lights of England winked across the tumbled waters. So near, yet so far. The doctor came in purposefully and wrote on my card. I persuaded the pretty, fair-haired nurse to translate it for me. She did so in two words: 'Castor oil'. On 8 October I was drafted to No. 1 Convalescent Camp by the Grand Army Tower. A week later I was in Etaples.

In a day the winter clamped down hard upon France—the coldest winter for forty years. The trees were bare to the icy blasts. The 'bull-ring' did not keep us long. Before the end of October we were pushed off in a draft for the 48th Battalion.[2]

We didn't think much of these new mushroom battalions. Had the weather been warmer, we would have worked up quite a lot of indignation and protest at the prospect of being pitchforked into one of these upstart, cheapjack units. Another 10th man— Arnold—was with me. He later acquired his commission, MC, DCM and MM. And he missed some that he should have got. He had been wounded at Mouquet Farm, and was now getting back to work.

2

The Somme

The train headed up the Somme Valley. 'Wait till you get on the Somme,' said men who had been through Pozières. 'The rest is a joke.'

We caught up with the 48th in Berteaucourt. Something about this crowd took my eye. As we marched through the streets we saw laughing groups of big, able-looking men. Here was a sing-song in progress. There in one billet came the voice of someone reciting 'The Man From Snowy River'. They reminded me of the 10th before the Landing, but the 10th with years of experience and discipline. There was certainly something about them that attracted me greatly.

We were lined up on parade. 'The Bull', a big soldierly figure, inspected us.[1] Then I began to understand. 'I find', he said, 'that there are some original members of other battalions among you. Step out those who are.' Three of us stepped forward, a 12th man, a 16th, and myself.

'I would not,' he said, 'keep any original man away from his own unit. I will arrange to send you back at once.' The other two beamed their thanks. I thought hard. Those who were gone from the 10th meant more to me than those who were left. Why live in the past? And there was something bright, strong and cheerful about this crowd. I took another pace forward.

'If you please, sir, I think I would like to stay.'

'Pleased to have you, my boy,' he said heartily, and for some reason I felt inordinately cheered.

We swiftly settled among the new crowd. They had a way of making us feel at home. The dags were there, the wild men, the conscientious soldiers, the lean hungry ones, and odd nerve-racked men who soldiered on in spite of themselves.

At the end of October we left the motor lorries and entered the squalid village of Dernacourt. Here was the edge of the zone of death, newer and fiercer than Ypres. We billeted in a barn from which most of the side wall was gone. Icy winds swept through the place and candles could not be kept alight. Mud was over all outdoors—soft, squelchy mud. But ere long we were to look back on those billets as on paradise.

And out of Dernacourt we marched along a road deep in mud, through an avenue of dead horses, mules, and wrecked wagons. Here, for the first time, I saw the appalling waste of modern war. Stacks of bombs sinking into the mud, all manner of abandoned munitions. 'Fricourt' was a notice on a signpost, but Fricourt had been completely razed.

We debouched into a field of soft mud, and put up canvas bivouacs.

There was a sound of tapping of wooden pegs by metal. Thinking to borrow the implement, I went over to the user. I was scandalised to find a new hand industriously hammering away with a dud shell. Gently I took it from him. Carefully I placed it in the bottom of a shell hole.

'Was it dangerous?' asked the recruit ingenuously.

In rain and wind, we slept the long night through. Evening and on our way again. No building save a few newly erected Nissen huts existed in this shell-blasted zone. No trees remained standing. No grass grew in the churned fields. But only signs of death more and more numerous as we went forward.

Off the road on each side was a morass dotted with bogged wagons and occasionally a wrecked gun. Now a duckboard track led off to the left through Delville Wood. Here was ruin and desolation beyond all compare.

In the darkness our strung-out line of heavily laden men trudged along the duckboards, the gloomy mass of the levelled wood on both sides. Great shell craters, water-filled, below us. The merciful darkness spared us the sight of that charnel house. But night and rain could not mask the stench that told its tale.

The dismal rain pattered bleakly on our tin hats, and little streams dropped on our faces. The man in front of me said, 'Always raining, when the bloody Joan of Arc battalion goes up the line.'

'Why Joan of Arc battalion?' I asked.

'Maid of Orleans,' he replied. 'Bull Leane, Ben Leane, Allan Leane, and a nephew of The Bull. Quite a family affair.'

Ahead in the distance were wavering Very lights, shown only by a glow in the fog, until thrusting themselves above the blanket of mist they shone bright in the clear air. After a second or so they fell back in to the fog-bank again, and died in diminishing sheets of white glow. At one point, high in the air, came a red wink which told of bursting shrapnel. Again and again this red eye gleamed in the same spot. Utter desolation was ahead of us, and the sense of it weighed heavily on our souls. We knew by now that Ypres had been a rest home compared to this.

The wood petered out on the forward slope. The duckboards ended at the edge of the valley. We plunged into mud from knee- to waist-deep churned to the consistency of pea soup. Here were our eighteen-pounders emplaced against the farther bank. A double team was attached to one gun which was above its hubs in mud. The muzzle barely cleared the slime. A sweating crowd of gunners laboured mightily at the wheels, and horses. The horses, mired to their shoulders, reared, plunged, snorted, and fell. A fit subject for a masterpiece by Doré.

The far bank was lined with dugouts. Fitful gleams of candlelight crept from the blanket-hung entrances. In one, we caught a momentary glimpse of a group of officers round a box on which there seemed to be a map. In another, a party of mud-covered men ate from their mess tins. With terrific effort we ploughed through the morass.

Long-legged Captain Allan Leane led the company up the far bank. A field gun lunged in sudden flame and roar beside us, and a shell rocketed away with a tearing sound. Followed the musical clink of the falling shell-case, and the click of the breach-block closing. A voice drifted up: 'No. 1 gun—ready.' Our troubles were commencing. The front line was about three miles away. It took us seven hours of constant struggle to reach it.

The guns were banging behind us as we tried to pick our way in the quick flash. Here shell craters were superimposed on shell craters. Water filled them to varying depths. The pulverised, soaked earth made every step a supreme effort. No two steps were ever on the same level. We fell, rose and fell again, soaked to our very hides.

'A man's a stupid big galoot to be here anyway,' growled Matthews, 'but there is one bloody comfort. After you fall three bloody times, you don't bloody well care. You can't get any bloody wetter.' Splash, as he found an extra deep shell hole. Sulphurous language burst out as he broke water like a seal. He seized my extended rifle-muzzle and climbed out. Then he became silent. The situation was beyond even his lurid expressions.

Every hundred yards or so strength failed as we tried to extricate a deep-sunk leg. Then we would collapse and lie inert in the soft mud. Our sweaty faces would become cold in the chilly wind and wet clothes press icy against our skins. With a despairing effort we would rise and battle on.

The slough of despond! I fought hard against an impulse to burst into childish tears. Hour succeeded hour, strength gone, hope gone, we struggled on automatically. Later, duckboards spanned this country in curving miles, but we unfortunates had no help. Minutes seemed hours long and the night an age.

'Even this will pass,' I whispered to myself to keep up my courage. The world of warmth, light and laughter was distant, almost beyond the power of imagination.

At length we reeled and tottered into derelict, shattered Flers. The shell-bitten road, a foot deep in slime, was grateful to our trembling legs. Here we halted a little time, lolling against the dugout riddled banks of the sunken road. Captain Leane in wonderful bursts of eloquence checked the assembled platoons. With his wind restored I heard Matthews say: 'A man would break his leg doing that in civvy life. But could he in the army?— Not on your tin-bloody-tack.'

Again the muddied, burdened line was moving ghostlike in the night. Sucking, squelching noises of mud underfoot. The flares were much nearer now. Up a long valley that men called the 'Valley of Death'. A tank, half sunk, loomed vaguely on our right. Up a gentle slope. A trench yawned at my feet. I could not see the farther side of it. 'Jump,' said someone on the farther side. I jumped. The strong hand of Major Ben Leane caught me as I tottered on the edge. He hauled me to safety. 'Jump,' I heard him say to the next man.

Two whizz-bangs shrieked to earth close by, sending up fountains of mud. We blundered into the forsaken confines of Cheese Road. A narrow sap led to the front line. The churned mud was knee-deep. In places, the arms and legs of dead men protruded from the trench wall, ghastly in the light of the flares. Where two men tried to pass they jammed.

About three hundred yards forward we came to an old German gun-pit. A deep dugout ran down at the side. Fritz's Folly, just beyond, was occupied by the enemy. We stood on a plank track, waiting our turn to go down. A German flare hissed up, and hung overhead. On its heels came a shell that burst redly on the bank. The shock toppled five of us into the mud alongside. I sank swiftly to my waist and was held firm.

A roar of other approaching shells filled the air. The men near the dugout entrance hastened down. The five of us were trapped like flies on a paper. The air was filled with the crash of shells bursting in and around the gun-pit. Red flames lit the place. Squalls of metal ripped and thudded. The men around me groaned and collapsed into the gripping mud.

Something tore my helmet away. I pressed the upper part of my body close along the mud. From the waist down I could not move. Someone groaned. This then was the culmination of all my fears. I lay helpless and passive beneath the hot hail, picturing myself as those others we had seen. No words can describe my feelings during the long minutes. Red-hot panic and cold clammy fear possessed me alternately. The shells ceased.

Major Ben Leane was the first out. He asked me if I was hit. 'No,' I said, 'but I can't get out.' I groped for my rifle and found it a foot below the surface. Extending it to him, and heaving and straining, reached the boards again. A board was laid out to the other four, and their heads were pulled clear of mud. A swift examination showed that three were dead. The survivor was placed on a stretcher. Only two stretcher-bearers were there. So I was detailed with another man to help them down. We had three hundred yards to go, but it took us about three hours.

At first we tried to enter the sap, all four on the stretcher, but it was too narrow. So we climbed out on top. For a few yards we went with the handles on our shoulders. Then a front bearer pitched into a deep shell hole. I missed my footing in another. Patient and bearers went down in a heap. Carefully we placed him back again. Then we held the handles in our hands, so that he would not fall far next time. A shell roared up behind and crashed at our heels. The blast blew us forward in a heap. Tenderly, we replaced the casualty.

We fell again and again. Decided to try the sap once more with one man at each end of the stretcher. The front man fell in a bad patch, and the patient slid over his head into the deep mud. As quickly as our exhaustion permitted, we lifted him out and placed him on the parapet. Again we staggered over the top. Another five-point-nine burst close, blanketed by the mud, and again we went down in a heap. Every few yards we had to rest, the wounded man lay still, his grey face to the weeping skies. At last we reached the dressing-station down past Cheese Road. We grounded the stretcher at the entrance to the curtained dugout, with the air of men who had done a good job of work. The MO came out and examined him swiftly. Then he looked at us. 'This man is dead!'

He looked at us more closely, and then said, 'Wait a minute,' and went into the dugout. He came out with four tots of rum. The stretcher-bearers quietly took our casualty off the stretcher and placed him beside three others who lay in the rain by the bank. Wordless, they folded the red-blotched canvas, and we moved off. Conviction came home to me that I was at the end of my tether.

A little trench led off the main sap. There sat a man with his head in his hands, glistening waterproof sheet over his shoulders. I sat beside him, and, leaning against him, slept. With broad daylight I woke. My neighbour's attitude was unchanged. Spoke to him. He did not answer. Looked at him closely. His face showed the familiar waxen colour of death.

I left the silent one, and waded through the mud of the sap towards the front line. The pale light of the foggy winter day could well have been spared. All ancient pictures of mud-bound hells, where lost souls floundered for ever, recurred to me. But all of them were feeble imitations beside the reality of the line beyond Flers.

I shrugged my shoulders to disclaim all responsibility, and announced, in passing, to a man built into the sap wall, 'C'est la blasted guerre, Fritz.'

But maybe I only wriggled my shoulders to dislodge some of the squirming, biting lice that congregated beneath the straps of my equipment. Instead of being satisfied to wander at large around our shirts, having a nip when the call for nourishment arose, these chats would assemble for their divisional sports, race-meetings and free fights, wherever a belt or strap bore heavily. Then, at any extra pressure, they would make concerted or spasmodic rushes. Many a true believer will spend a few extra thousand years in purgatory on account of these same chats. Too bad if they get chatty there also.

In the cold winter winds we were debarred from the Anzac national sport of 'reading our shirts', sometimes also called 'chatting by the wayside'. We had to bear them, but there was nothing in army regulations to make us grin at the same time.

We wore no overcoats. Men could not have made their way under the weight of mud that would have covered them. Sheepskin vests made up in part for the loss of warmth.

The faint gleam of candles came from the depths of the timbered dugout as I made my careful way down the stairs, steel hat bumping overhead at every step. Mud-covered men lay about in shapeless heaps. Lewis guns and rifles stood against the walls. Equipment hung from nails. In one corner sat a Lewis-gun crew, cleaning and oiling the separate parts of their dismantled gun, with a candle all to themselves.

In another corner were men cleaning cartridges and loading them back into magazines. Shadows flickered in grotesque outline on ceiling and walls. One man squatted in careful custody of a mess tin that was perched over the blue flame of a Tommy cooker. The light of day made a feeble showing a couple of feet beyond the foot of the stairway.

The walls shook at the impact of shells outside, and the explosions came to us as strange hollow booms. Here was security, and almost magical comfort—a haven beyond price. But at any moment a voice might hail us to go up to face the hazard and misery above.

Our platoon sergeant, George Foster, came down. 'Mitchell, report with all your gear, to the transport lines. You are to go to a Lewis-gun school at Le Touquet.'

I climbed the steps again in my newly acquired rubber thigh-boots. Matthews's voice followed me, 'Make your will before you come back, you stupid ———. You're as good as a stiff now they've got you in the suicide mob.'

It seems that N.G. Imlay, the Lewis-gun officer, had picked on me as a future gunner. Why, I never knew, nor did I worry, as I plodded my stolid way through and round shell holes.

Darkness was settling like a blanket over the flat featureless waste when I located and entered the transport dugout. A heavy tarpaulin made the roof. Inside was a profusion of stores. A corner was pointed out for me, and I slumped down, thanking the gods for a dry, warm resting place.

An unctuous NCO opened a large parcel from Blighty. A rich cake was revealed. A big slice was cut for the QM, another for the transport officer, and one for himself. I was the only other occupant of the dugout. Now, I thought, the next slice will be for me. I watched, hungry-eyed as any fox-terrier pup at a juicy bone. But there was no fourth slice cut. A mud-covered, lousy, hungry Digger from the front line did not carry enough weight for a slice of that incomparable cake. I remembered that incident in other and different days. To this day, my estimate of that man is dominated by that one incident. In the light of other after events my judgement seems to have been a fair one.

At dawn I was on my way into Albert of the leaning Virgin,

and soon entrained. I remember little of the journey through the bleak, wind-lashed countryside. I trudged, muddied, steel-hatted and long-booted through the little village of Le Touquet, down by Boulogne. Fried eggs and Malaga in a café transported me to another world—a world in which there was light, music, warmth and laughter. A world where clean, unwearied people could go their untroubled ways, not moving always beneath the shadow of death.

Debonair Tommy officers on back area duties, all pink and white, strolled round blithely with gloves and canes. They moved me to dark thoughts of murder. I would not salute them. Blast 'em anyway.

The chats, spurred to renewed activity by the warmth, did nothing to improve my temper. And the grey shadow of Flers—a few days away—hung over me as a cloud. But on arrival at the school I was referred most willingly by war-wise officers to the delouser. While the chats, their offspring and eggs were cooking I stood beneath a glorious warm shower, soaping my red-spotted hide. It was a good bath. It had to be, for it was more than a month before I got another. For a little spell I did not scratch, save from force of habit.

Over several brief days the guns blazed across short ranges. We stripped and assembled them. There was a little talk of cones of fire, and the train, filled with laconic, accoutred soldiery headed for the Somme. Across the shell-pocked bog I found the company in Switch trench, three thousand yards from the line.

Two big shells from high-velocity guns landed on each side of me to announce my return. A five-point-nine burst right in the trench as I stood on top looking down. The ground gave beneath my feet as the side of a dugout caved under my weight. 'Big splawfooted muckin' lookin' stoopid big ———' came in muffled tones from something that yielded spongily beneath my rubber boots.

Hollow-cheeked men told the usual tale of posts being wiped out in bloody fragments by the blast of big shells and men drowned in the mud of blown-in dugouts; of old hands and new hands, swept from the ranks of the callous living to the unheeding dead. 'We're half bloody dead, anyway,' said one, 'they might as well get it over in one lick.'

One morning we awoke before the hour of 'Stand to', shivering in the terrible cold beneath a souvenired tarpaulin. Daylight revealed a white, clean world. Unsullied snow lay thick on the tarpaulin, and unbroken to the far skyline. All the foulness and ugliness of war at its worst were hidden from sight. Only here and there an uncouth new-flung shell marked the surface with a round dark hole and widespread shower of debris. Five-point-nines, with amazing accuracy, burst along the trench at intervals.

A fussy little major from another battalion blew up, all beans and bounce. 'Where is company headquarters, my man?' he asked. The chats were nipping again. A five-point-nine landed in a thunderous flame-pierced blast of destruction.

'It was,' I answered, 'just where that shell landed. I couldn't say where it is now.' He gave me a dirty look, opened his mouth to say something, but changed his mind. 'If you go now, sir'—I improved the shining hour, respectfully—'you will arrive just as the next shell lands.' He gave me another black look, but took the hint and waited.

The snow melted beneath heavy rain in a cold, slushy mess that defies description. So naturally, that night our 'Joan of Nark' battalion moved forward to the front line. We blundered again through the darkness, slipping, sliding, and falling, wet to the bone. 'After this,' said Matthews, 'a man will be able to have a bonzer night's rest on a barbwire fence in a hailstorm.'

'If my old girl could see me now,' came another voice between gasps, 'she'd say, "Get out you big lousy mug ——." '

'Saviours of France! —— France!'

'Double up, those men at the rear,' came an officer's voice. 'Don't lose touch.'

'Double up!' said someone. 'When I double up it will be for bloody good.'

We sweated with the strain of movement. But when we stopped, the touch of our windbeaten clothing was as of ice.

Off Cheese Road ran a derelict collapsed trench, more gutter than earthwork. To one dugout three of us were allotted. We crawled through the foot of mud at the entrance and lit a candle. Inside was a pool of deep water. Around the walls, falling earth had made a ledge a few inches wide. On this soft mud we put our equipment, and sat, backs to the wall and feet in the water. Three rats splashed out into the night. A fourth man arrived. He crawled on hands and knees from the entrance to the middle of the pool. He was a new reinforcement.

He crouched there like a bemused animal, swaying his head from side to side. Tears made courses in the mud on his cheeks, glistening in the candlelight. 'I wish I could die,' he said.

We said nothing. Each man must bear his own cross. A shell thundered outside and the candle flickered out. As black as the grave was the dugout then. No man made any move to re-light the foul place.

Footsteps squelched outside. 'Come on, Mitch,' said Matthews, 'you're for fatigue, you lead-swinging black cow.' I went with them cheerfully enough from that black hole. Three strong men, they were, all marked for early doom—Joe Hyrons, cheerful big Tobin, and Ted Matthews.

Down Death Valley in the rain we went, past the wrecked tank, and on, until the broken brick-heaps of Flers loomed up. I smelt smoke, and followed my nose. A light gleamed in a cellar and I made my way down, the others following.

'Keep your eye on that black ——,' explained Matthews. 'If you don't, you're liable to miss something.'

The cooks gave us hot tea and lumps of boiled beef. We wolfed away in that smoky cellar. The shells that ramped through Flers troubled us not one bit.

Out again into the night we went, and collected each our two tins of water. The wind from up the valley drove the rain pattering onto our helmets and cold on our faces. Under the influence of the food I burst into unappreciated song. But perhaps my rendering of 'Beneath Thy Window' was not up to music-hall standard. Or maybe conditions were not just right.

We scrambled along the ridge of spoil thrown from a big impassable sap. At the very top the ground was almost hard. But we had many falls trying to keep on it. I caught up with the others as they stood grouped, looking down at a man lying in the bottom of the sap. 'Wasn't there when we came down,' said Tobin, 'he mightn't be a stiff.'

We examined him with searching fingers. He was alive, but we could find no sign of any wound. 'We'll send the bearers back,' I suggested. So we trudged on. Death Valley ran straight on to the German wire. Woe betide the stupid ones who blundered past, missing the entrance to Cheese Road.

Unfamiliar wire halted us, and we stopped for a whispered

conference. I arranged to go forward and have a look-see. I walked on warily a while. My foot was caught in something, and I fell. Mechanically, I reached back to free my foot. My back hair tingled when I encountered an arched, mummified dead hand, jammed over my instep—almost a warning from the dead.

If I were superstitious, I thought, I would take that as a hint to turn back. Mightn't be a bad idea, either. So I retraced my steps. 'Nothing up there,' I reported, 'except a lot of dead uns.' So we again picked up our burdens and moved back. Soon we found Cheese Road.

The sleep of exhaustion that is near to death was on all at company headquarters. Only a sentry stood at his post. We could wake no one else, nor find any bearers. The wind rattled the rain-gleaming oil-sheets on our shoulders as we stood in a foot of mud in wordless conference. The rain told its dismal, monotonous tale on our helmets. The hard, reflected glow of Very lights played on the features of the others. Odd shells raced overhead and crashed wetly to earth, but still we said no word until Tobin spoke: 'Couldn't leave a dog out on a night like this.'

We moved together to a folded stretcher and trudged off. We heaved our man out of the eight-foot sap with mighty labour, sinking waist-deep as we heaved, and struggled off through the mud. The casualty station had been shifted and we did not know its new location. So we had to take him back to Cheese Road. We put him under cover and ordered the sentry to hand him over to the bearers. Then we trudged off to our separate dugouts. Still vague shadows of the occupants showed as I crawled in.

I sat again with my feet in the water and back to the wall, thinking of the greatness of these, my mates. Their ideals, if they realised them, were hidden in jest and rough language. They would laugh at a high-sounding phrase, but time and time again I saw them rise above the ruck in some undemonstrative, self-sacrificing action to aid some fallen man. What if they did have to pull their guts out? Renewed strength would come at need. 'Couldn't leave a dog out on a night like this.'

The dawn light in the doorway did not then reveal to me the squalor that was there, but rather was the reflection of those great-souled, indomitable ones. Far removed from the surrounding sordidness, I fell into a happy sleep.

Our first job, with the assistance of daylight, was to find better quarters. I insinuated myself into a little low dugout on Cheese Road with Walter Webb, my stretcher-bearer cobber, Ted Matthews, and two others. We could not sit up, the roof being too low. The entrance was about two feet high by eighteen inches wide. We crawled in and out like muddy rabbits. All the day five-point-nines howled out of foggy space and burst with earth-shaking fury.

While Walter was heating some bully over a Tommy cooker the shells arrived every minute. As the first low whistle of approach could be heard, Walter would reach over and hold the mess tin firmly to prevent it from being upset. As the roar increased to the menacing howl that indicated a near burst, I sometimes wondered if fate would allow us to get outside again.

One night was enough in that dugout. We each had to lie on the same side jammed tight. When the assaults of chats and stiffness necessitated turning over, all hands had to be wakened and the turnover made together. Rats danced gaily over us and nibbled our hair. Two haversacks were bored into by them, to the detriment of rations (iron) 2.

At about midnight, judging by the shellfire, Walter crawled heavily over me and through the entrance.

'Where to?' I asked.

'Going outside for a rest!' he replied.

Next morning at the utterly dismal hour of 'Stand to' a delightful aroma of rum was in the air. But there was no rum issue. Inquiry elicited the facts: Sergeant Major Jim Ferrie had been carrying the jar containing the company's rum issue. A five-point-nine fragment had smashed the jar and left Ferrie untouched. 'Why the hell it couldn't have been the other way round, I dunno!' complained my informant bitterly.

The full hardship of the winter was now being felt. Each dawn revealed men hobbling to the rear on swollen, bag-wrapped feet. The corpse-impregnated mud was poisonous. Through constant falling, fingers split across the quick, as the mud dried on them. It was an unsafe proceeding to take boots off. Released from the pressure, frostbitten feet often swelled up so that it was impossible to put them on again.

The authorities were full of hobbies. Whale-oil applied to the feet was one of these. I, with most other Diggers, shared the opinion that while whale-oil might be most useful for the whale, it was no damn good to us. The only occasion on which my feet troubled me was, when in a weak moment, I applied the oil. Platoon commanders stood over us and watched with eagle eyes while we rubbed the oil in. My boss, Lieutenant Dick Caldwell, did not put very much faith in me, for a variety of excellent reasons, and he kept a specially good watch on me during these whale-oil parades. But I, diligently, and with a look of conscious virtue, would carefully pour the oil into one hand, and rub my feet with the other. Pounds of dubbin applied hot to my boots before each tour into the line kept my feet in good condition.

Profound and utterly true was a saying of the boys: 'The perfect infantry man takes size ten boots and size three hat.' This whale-oil came up in rum jars, and naturally was not so carefully guarded as the rum issue. Many a disgusted Digger took a long, surreptious swig and spluttered his disappointment all over the landscape.

Though the scenery was mostly water and mud, drinking water was scarce. Many a water-filled shell hole was a poison solution from gas shells. Many men who drank from these, against strict orders, promptly developed some marvellous pains in their little insides and went out feet first. But the thirst generated by the terrific labour of slogging through the mud broke down natural caution.

A volunteer from among a group of mates would sample the water from a selected shell hole. For the next hour or so he would be watched with frank interest and speculation. If he survived the observation period without throwing any 'sixers', that water would be pronounced good, and promptly utilised.

A great laugh went through the company on the next trip into the line. Members of a section headed back to a shell hole, from which they had continuously drawn a most excellent supply. But when they arrived on this occasion the water had drained off. Lying peacefully on the bottom was a large and very dead Fritz. 'And the water seemed so good,' said one. 'It was soup, you goat!' replied an unsympathetic onlooker.

I had found another dugout, and shared it with a man not long arrived in France. Though he had not been there for more than a couple of weeks, he had fully realised the error of his ways, and his sole ambition was to get back to Aussie quickly, and in one piece, to swing on the old garden gate again. A laudable intention, certainly, but difficult of execution. So he took his boots and socks off and slept with his feet outside. Mine were cold enough inside, lying as we were in the soft mud, with groundsheet over us for warmth.

Every time his shivering woke me I grinned and went to sleep again. But his feet were still in good order in the morning. He did not try that again. Late in the war he arrived at a spot at the same time as a whizz-bang, and went out like a soldier.

We moved forward to the front line. Again we occupied the old German gun-pit dugout. But there had been dirty work at the crossroads since we had last been there. A stream of mud was flowing down the steps. With bodies bent double, our heads just cleared the mud. The place had been pounded with delay-action shells. The roof timbers were all smashed and hanging down. The galleries were warped and distorted, and it seemed that another shell must cave the whole place in on us.

We were dozing through the day. The earth shook to occasional shell bursts. One came screaming from the skies, to burst like thunder right at the entrance, half closing it. A curl of smoke rolled down the stairway, sinister reminder of doom by suffocation. In utter silence the seconds went past. Then someone said, 'Close that.' 'My oath,' chorused every other occupant of the dugout. And I had thought that they had all been asleep!

At dawn we were standing to. In front we looked into a sunken road, parallel with our line. Growing daylight showed still, upright figures that puzzled me. Daylight soon revealed a line of men, facing forward, wearing the diamond patches of the 2nd Division. They had made an attack that had failed. They stood there, unrelieved, held erect by the mud, maintaining the watch that was no longer theirs.

Each night two of our men, of whom I think Tom Kirkpatrick was one, voluntarily went out, at great risk, and buried some of them.

The short days went by. The long nights on watch were eternities of suffering. Death from exhaustion and cold came very close to me at times. The awful hours that stretched from midnight to daylight were dreadful to endure. Flashes of guns and shells in the foggy night. Crashes, showers of falling mud. Word of death at large. Stretcher parties stumbling along with their silent burdens, and cold that paralysed will and body. A man near me sobbed with the pain of his feet.

One night my grip was slipping. At dawn, I thought, I would be as those 2nd Division men. I could hold on no longer. A man slid into our post and collapsed. 'First of your relief,' he said. 'Others are somewhere on their way.' The others arrived in ones and twos in utter extremity of exhaustion. We gathered our gear together and moved back to Cheese Road.

At times, horrid realisation would come to us that we were in an interminable night of hell. Fatigue beyond the bounds of endurance, yet endure it through endless ages we must. Dawn farther away than the aeons of time when the world would spin black and dead in space, even as the moon. Hearts would tug painfully at their strings. Lungs would hurt to the panting gasps. Not even did the strength remain with us to drop and lie in our tracks. Will and individuality gone. Only an imp that leaped round the brain on fiery feet, recording the restless pain of utter exhaustion. Strange thoughts and curses beyond expression in any known language, would form. And such a night was this!

At dawn, a few of us reeled into huts at Delville Wood. The others were strewn along the way. I walked to a corner and dropped in a heap, tin hat clanging against the wall. Finish, absolute dead finish. I had lain unmoving for perhaps ten minutes, when I heard Sergeant Foster say, 'Mitchell—you are to go back straight away to Flers for dixies.' Rot, I thought, I can't, and what's more, I blasted well won't even try. I'll lie on the duckboards, and they can carry me if they want to.

But I went. Someone else would have to go if I didn't. By daylight, without kit, it was not so bad. I sat against the bank of the sunken roadway through Flers. A man was coming from the line. He tottered on failing legs, and I expected each moment to see him pitch forward into the mud. His face was the grey colour that is full brother to death. His sunken eyes were expressionless with the pain of exhaustion. His head lolled uncontrolled at each halting step. His uniform was one complete sheath of mud. Mud clung to his eyebrows and cheeks. His hair was matted with it. He looked like some long dead cadaver, reanimated.

'Hey, Dig,' I called, 'you look like I feel.' And I wondered that those around me laughed.

That night we were settled snugly in the huts, and ready for sleep. A large, noisy shell burst nearby.

'That's a Fritzer,' said someone.

'Yes,' said another, 'it had a German accent.'

We drifted back to Flesselles for Christmas. I woke with not enough strength to face the day. I was settled. That curse of a soldier's life, early morning parade, was still being held. I decided that I would not get up for it. 'Why aren't you up?' asked the sergeant, sourly. 'Sick,' I said. If he had said 'What of?' I am sure I would have answered, 'The blasted army.'

So I went on sick parade. Might as well make a good job of it. So told the quack a good tale. I must have looked sick, for he gave me 'No duty', and seven hefty big pills. On the way back to billets I ran into Dick Caldwell. 'What have you got?' he asked, distrustingly. I was debating whether I should tell him that it was pleurisy, with a touch of hydatids, but decided to treat the question another way.

'These,' I said, 'seven of 'em,' and showed him the pills proudly. Poor old Dick thought of something sarcastic to say, then decided not to cast pearls before swine, and went off with a snort. If he could have sold me he would have given me away with a fiver to boot. And I don't blame him, either.

The next two days I paraded sick and got no duty, and began to pick up, so that I could take notice. On the fourth day I arranged with a cobber to go sick with me. We both got no duty, and both slid off to Amiens, where a pleasant time was had by all. But the following day I went sick again, to give myself time to recover. Do you wonder that poor Dick scowled every time he saw me, or that my official title at company headquarters was 'That bloody Mitchell'.

Christmas Eve came. I went to bed early. I thought that I had awakened in hell. The blankets were off me and icy winds were at large. A ring of wild drink-lit faces was round me, candles held high. Joe Hyrons led them in some ancient hymn which ran:

> For the lion of Judah
> Shall break ev'ry chain,
> And give us the vict'ry
> Again and again.

Pongo, entirely denuded of clothing, fastened a lighted candle to himself and dashed round the billet on all fours, shouting, 'Make way for Halley's comet.'

Sports were held on New Year's Day, but on 2 January we route-marched again towards the line. A strong wind blew. Flocks of ravens fluttered in the air like pieces of black paper. Footsore, we drifted into Franvilliers. I scored a nice clean little pigsty in the corner of a stable for a billet, and was content.

The next day we marched by a long roundabout route, and arrived at stinking Dernacourt—hop-off point for hell. That evening I wandered back to Ribemont to see my cousin, a motor-transport driver. He and his mate entertained me in his heavily tarpaulined truck. Two bunks were rigged. They had eleven blankets each and an eiderdown, a primus stove, a box of provisions, and a Persian kitten. War as it should be!

It was midnight when I arrived home, wobbling wearily all across the road. The wind that roared through the broken wall made it impossible to keep a candle alight, so I made my bunk in the dark.

On 5 January came the order, 'Hand in overcoats and packs, and prepare to move out in fighting order.' That day the trail led to Fricourt, and huts. The old hands held a concert, but the new ones were very silent. Next day we set out on the march right to support in Cheese Road. The new duckboards finished at Flers. From then on it was the same old grind. Three of us shared a dugout. It was two feet six inches high, built up with boxes of live bombs, and the roof leaked continually. Just as we were settling down a crump landed near, putting out the candle.

But before we could settle properly, Sergeant Foster came up: 'Not enough infantry for fatigue. You gunners have to go as well.'

So we slugged back to Flers and brought back water. Then again we tried to settle down to sleep. But each time we were almost asleep a shell crashed near, rousing us fully.

3
The mud

On 7 January we slugged up to our post in the darkness. We had taken over the ghastly precincts of Fritz's Folly, recently captured by the 4th Battalion. All around were bodies, some stripped naked by the blast that destroyed them. All were sinking in the fetid morass. One of our party arrived without trousers, boots or socks. Several men of another battalion, stuck in the mud, had died while their friends worked throughout the night to extricate them. An officer, they tried to haul out with a mule. The strain broke his back.

Our post was a large watery, shallow shell hole. The gently sloping sides offered little shelter from the squalls of shell fragments that continually hissed through the night. We were wedged to our knees in mud.

The sunken road of Fritz's Folly was a level stretch of pea-soupy mud. Any man was lucky who got across without getting stuck. Gumboots were left behind by the wearer, and feet even pulled out of laced issue boots. Many a man got across the road by finding submerged corpses to tread on. The fear of dying in the mud and spending eternity there was on me again.

A football-shaped thing on a low ridge irritated me. Imagination conjured up visions of a leering death's head, watching those who were so soon to join it. For my peace of mind I clambered from the post to inspect it, and so destroy once and for all the images which so vividly formed in my mind. I knelt in the mud to look closely.

A Boche flare made of the fog an incandescent wall, mercilessly setting all things clear. It was the head of a man long dead and sunk upright into the mud. Hair had grown lank in a tangled mat, a travesty of humanity. Eyeless sockets seemed to look at me with terrible intensity. Lipless teeth gleamed in a sardonic grin. Quickly I went back to where men still moved and sometimes spoke.

The hours dragged so that night was an eternity. But at dawn we slogged down to a dugout. Soupy mud poured down the steps. We blocked it as well as we could. I piled my equipment so that it made a mound above the mud, sat on it, wrapped my wet blanket round me and slept.

Following is the diary entry of some typical days:

8 January 1917—As soon as I woke I heard Matthews saying, '—— was killed. A shell got their post last night and knocked the lot.'

'Who was killed?' I asked.

'Walter Webb,' he replied.

So this is how my little cobber went west. Could we all show such a clean sheet, we need have little fear of death. He lived straight and without fear. He hated war, but did a man's part in stretcher-bearing, making up for his lack of inches by the size of his heart. When, at Christmas-time, I was broke, he bought this diary for me in Amiens. Now he is dead. I will never again hear his laugh, see his face.

Our work for the day is a two-hour shift on observation. Each, as he goes to his post, has to sneak up carefully. If Fritz notices any move he will shell the place unmercifully. I sat in the position watching the shell-torn land that stretches about a mile into enemy territory. Then green fields commence. In the near distance is a ruined village into which our shells continually crash, further desolating complete desolation. Farther on is a village apparently untouched. On the skyline stands a row of tall poplars. Now and then the sunlight picked out the trees, then gradually came closer, so that for short periods the whole landscape was bathed in light. The near scene was evil, mangled and half-buried bodies everywhere.

The wind was terrifically cold. I watched the trees as the sun caught them, thinking and thinking. The war, Walter, Home, many things. After an age of physical endurance my shift came to an end, and I sneaked back to the dugout. We sat and talked and dozed. After dark they had a job for us, water carrying and duckboards: a back-breaking job. Back again to our leaky slushy dugout. An extra number of shells crumped round our dugout, one of which damaged the doorway.

9 January 1917—Gamlen woke us again before daylight. 'We've got to shift,' he said. So we all packed up and shifted to our new home. It was an old German dugout next to the one we camped in during our first stunt up here. But since then it had been shelled to a ruin. We were astounded that men should be asked to occupy the place. The doorway had been blown in. Mud poured down the steps leaving a foot clearance to get through. I went first and was freshly muddied to the armpits. In two bays only did the timbering hold. Everywhere else it was shattered and split.

The ceilings bulged downward. The others passed the Lewis gun and other impedimenta to me, then came down themselves.

We made ourselves comfortable by the light of my only candle. When that burned out the only thing to do was to go to sleep. Uneasily we rested. One fair-sized shell overhead and we would be buried alive. One crump landed in the doorway, almost filling it, and shaking the place. Since coming in to the line we had had no issue of rum, tea, or water, and very little rations.

Darkness came. We had to prepare our gun and selves for outpost, but it was useless to try to do so in the Stygian blackness that ruled down here. Luckily I remembered an abandoned spare parts bag that hung from a nail in the stairway. I felt for and removed the oil tin. A piece of cleaning rag made a wick and we had a good light. It is by this that I am now writing.

My first stunt was from 11 till 1 a.m. My feet were terribly painful. No wonder, for they are never dry. It was the same old watching game. When I would get too bored, I would look hard at three stumps. They were a sort of 'cheer-up' for freezing soldiers. After a while one would seem to sit on the ground. The other two would spar, hug, separate, then dance together. I am long past the stage when I would turn the Lewis gun on them.

10 January 1917—My second stunt was from 3.30 to 5.30 a.m. At the latter time we brought back our gun. I went down to Cheese Road and collected our rum and rations, and went back to the dugout. The entrance was a fearsome thing to see and worse to negotiate, but we were happy and comfortable in our two little chambers fifteen feet underground. The first thing we did was to have a feed. Rations were generous this day and we made a splendid meal of cold meat, bread, cheese, butter, and jam. Then we went to sleep.

On waking up at one o'clock we had another big feed. At dusk the first two went out with the gun. Two and a half hours later the next two went to relieve them. I fell asleep then. A strange feeling that all was not well woke me. I lit the slush lamp. I was alone. Was the entrance finally silted in, and was I cut off? I had just decided that this was the case and that I would have a good sleep before trying to get out, when one of our team came in. 'Position has been shifted. Every one to stand by the gun.' I went out with him into the noisy night.

11 January 1917—I followed him out to the new post which lay a lot nearer the German line. It was a waterway, and in no manner was it possible to get any protection from shellfire. Once already the party had had a terrible time of it. The cold was awful. We huddled together and waited. My mate whimpered occasionally at the pain of his feet.

Before very long we had our turn again. Whizz-bang! The shattering, fiendish roar of a big shell within thirty feet. My tin hat stopped a piece. Another shell, closer, blotting out the flare-lighted fog-bank in flame and smoke. Three more, and they had finished with us for a little while. But the devil's tattoo was being continually played in a narrow circle round us. To add to our other discomforts was thirst. For we had had nothing to drink for about eighteen hours.

A strange thing happened then. A chap who was digging a slight protection for himself unearthed an equipment on which was a full water bottle. We all drank. The long weary freezing hours in which time was only marked by the shell bursts, slowly passed.

I collected the rations and rum as usual. No sooner were we down in our dugout than we all gathered in cheerful mood and prepared a first-class breakfast. Our powers of endurance and recuperation surprise even ourselves.

There was a little inflammable mixture in a tin, and over this we heated two tins of meat and vegetable rations. This, with bread and butter, jam and cheese, went down well. No one seemed able to leave off. It was always: 'One more slice.'

We slept until 2 p.m. After this we packed up everything, for we are to be relieved this night.

As we made our way to the post I was in rear. In front of me was one of the relieving party, tottering and staggering over the heartbreaking ground. He got caught in a shellhole where the mud was a little heavier than usual, and collapsed, gasping: 'I'm done!'

I slipped round the lip of the crater and extended my rifle to him. He gathered his failing forces together and got out. I helped him to the front line. There he again slid to earth, and was barely distinguishable from the mud underfoot.

The relieving party had full possession when I arrived. Right glad were we to pack up our guns and leave. The trenches that used to be in this part are all smashed up or fallen in. It is 'Over the top!'

We made our way back to Cheese Road. This is a point always heavily shelled. Tonight was no exception. I was all in when I had covered the five hundred yards. Strugnell and I share a little wet dugout. After searching everywhere for drinking-water, 'Strug' filled my bottle at a shell hole. We took a risk and drank.

A man outside called: 'Where is Webb, the stretcher-bearer?'

I answered: 'Wasn't he killed?' 'No,' he answered. 'It was the other Webb.' Only my exhaustion prevented me from going out into the mud and night rain to rest my eyes on the resurrected Walter! The morning would do as well.

We turned in. The cold and damp seemed to pierce my bones. Lice in hundreds crawled over me. If I came out of this alive I shall be a bent up old man. And what a miserable old cow I will be!

Throughout the night five-point-nines screamed down from the skies at regular intervals. All burst close. The very regularity made them the more nerve-racking.

At the first faint sound of approach, one's guts would gather up in a ball, and nerves taughten till it seemed they would twang like violin strings. Louder and louder the roar would multiply upon itself as the steel would rush down on us cowering mortals. Strange devilish shrieks of triumph would mingle and culminate in the last frightful plunge to earth. Then the crash that seemed to shake soul loose from body, the wailing of hard-driven metal, and the hissing and thud of earth and fragments on dugout roofs and far and wide. Then, the acrid reek of the smoke that seemed to touch another chord of fear.

I know many better occupations than lying cold and wet in the mud, tormented by lice, wondering whether one would see the next grey cheerless dawn.

Morning, and news that the dugout we had left in the line had been blown in, not one of the occupants surviving.

Walter left his dugout to get our rations. In his absence it was blown in. The only occupant was dragged out bleeding at nose and mouth. Walter retrieved his goods with a shovel, and complained, dash it all, that this was the second time his domicile had been destroyed this trip.

'Time is the essence of the contract,' said someone. And there was no doubt at all about that. The art of continued existence lay in being absent from a particular piece of scenery just when it came unstuck.

Many men seemed to have a destined rendezvous with Fate. Every step and action from leaving Aussie seemed to conspire to lead them to the spot marked 'X' on their first trip into the line.

And many knew it. Call it what you will. Men who packed their haversacks with the food that they knew they would never eat. Kept their places in the ranks. Sometimes they made the announcement of their one-way trip with bravado. Sometimes in quiet tones to a mate, with a home letter to be sent on.

'Starve the blinking rats,' would say the other, 'do you think my chance is any better than yours?'

Big thermos containers were now in use. Tea and stew were brought up hot. These fitted on the back like a pack.

I was coming up from Flers in the dark, blundering over shell holes as usual, tottering with weariness. Tripped over something and plunged forward into a waterlogged shell hole. My outstretched arms encountered only the water and soft mud in the middle, and of course my face went under as I struggled beneath the weight of the container.

The water was icy. Steel hat fell off. Hot stew dripped from the defective lid on to the exposed back of my neck. All my timely eloquence reached the surface as bubbles. As I struggled out, righted by Matthews's strong arm, the others, on recovering their breath, started to laugh. What I told them would burn holes in asbestos.

At noon of 15 January, I was detailed with others to march out, as our relief would be completed that night. I buckled up my web equipment gleefully. Going out by daylight, under cover of the winter fog, was a very different proposition to the heartbreaking task of plunging through the shell holes by night. But Sergeant Foster saw me: 'You don't go, Mitchell,' he said, 'gunners stay till last.' Blast the war! I didn't start it.

After lunch, Starr and I were at each end of a duckboard, busily timbering in the collapsed sap to the front line. I heard the faint whistle of a far-flung whizz-bang coming high from extreme range. This was relief day, so I was taking no chances, and something in its note seemed to say that it would decorate the scenery close handy—so I crouched low.

A hissing rush and the world dissolved in chaos. Then a dead silence fell on the world, save only for a high-pitched pinging noise in my head. In the smoke where Starr had been came the sound of heavy coughing. 'He's not dead anyway,' I said with satisfaction.

The clearing smoke revealed that the duckboard we had been fitting was in matchwood. Starr, when he had coughed the smoke out of his lungs, found he was unhit. An engineer, feet beyond me, had his tunic ripped across the back. Just above my head where I had crouched, the U frame was riddled. Had I remained standing I would have collected the shell in the tummy. We looked around and burst out laughing—all except the engineer. He was grieving for good work spoiled.

I strolled down to company headquarters to tell the sigs that their lines were busted. There I encountered Sergeant Foster. 'Serg,' I said, 'if that shell had caught me, I'd have haunted you to your dying day for keeping me back.'

The silts soon had the line repaired. Then came a hail of shells that stopped all work. Men huddled into the best cover obtainable, while the untamed beasts of destruction snarled and roared round us. But, strangely enough, the psychological effect on me, of the shell that missed, was all to the good. If Fritzy could not hit me with a shell aimed directly at me, random shellfire could do me no harm. So, cocky as a bantam rooster, I felt quite at ease during the bombardment.

A man raced up the sap: 'Company headquarters blown in.

Get shovels and help to dig them out!' We ran down. A shell had landed at the entrance. Blood and shreds of clothing everywhere. Four men had been taken to the dressing-station.

'Find Sergeant Foster,' said Captain Leane as he took out his cigarette case. I timed it nicely so that he had the cigarette out, but not yet started towards his mouth. 'Thank you, sir,' I said, and held out my hand. He passed the fag to me without comment and selected another for himself.

High and low I hunted, but no sign of Foster. A fifth man was brought up from the dugout, wounded in arm and leg. I made the fourth on the stretcher. Lawson, our casualty, was concerned about us, and apologetic for the trouble he was causing.

'Put me down,' he said as we heaved our way through the knee-deep mud. 'I think I can walk.'

'Shut up,' we said when we could spare the breath. 'You're non-stop for Blighty.'

Five-point-nines hounded us on our way. At the dressing-station he thanked us. We laughed at him and offered to buy his wounds.

A dead man lay outside. The shelter was needed for the living. I examined his identity disk, commonly called 'cold meat ticket'. It was Sergeant Foster! So I reported back to the skipper in renewed hail of fire and promptly got another job for my pains.

Lieutenant Davis had had his leg shattered, Sergeant Major Jim Ferrie an eye knocked out and other wounds; Tobin—good old Tobin, who had been trotting out with wounded men on his back—died of his wounds. Several others were fatally injured.

At four o'clock, in a pregnant stillness we lined the duckboards ready to move back. Every ear was acock to hear the hated sound of an approaching shell that would again turn the road into a charnel house. Hours we waited. Evening grew into night black as a wolf's guts. Tension mounted higher and higher. At last out of the night came the wavering exhausted figures of the relief.

The relief company drifted up in parties of ones and twos. Like cattle, the strongest came first, and even they were in extremity. They crowded the one duckboard track, and stood there silently among us. The Lord alone knows what fears rode them in the hour and a half that we all had to wait, until the routine of handing over was complete.

But our fears in that still and starless foggy night were concrete enough. The five-point-nines were ranged on that shallow sunken road, and a shelling was long overdue. We had seen what had happened in the afternoon, when men were scattered and under cover. My imagination supplied all too vividly what would ensue if a shell landed among these crowded men.

But only there came the wavering glow of Very lights as they thrust themselves above the fog strata. And the scream of shells that burst with dull explosions in other places.

We cursed at the delay, while officers talked together and papers were signed. A great sigh of relief went up as we moved off from that marked place. Two filled panniers of Lewis-gun ammunition were dumped on to me, and the added weight made me stagger. The long, drawn-out line set off, Captain Leane leading. Sometimes we slipped off the duckboards into deep shell holes. Each time a Very light glowed we would all stop dead. The following blackness could be felt. But in the light we had mapped the next twenty or thirty paces and that helped a little. The first time I crashed into a shell hole I said to the two panniers, 'This is the end of your ride. We can't all get back.' So they stayed, and I went on.

The skipper was in a battling mood, and claimed the right of the duckboards for relieved troops. Long strings of cursing Diggers, laden with great sheets of iron, duckboards, and timber for the line, had to stand aside as we plunged along. A passer-by was questioning Captain Leane just as he executed a beautiful double somersault into a deep shell hole. His answer was terse. I was congratulating myself that I was up in front among the works. The stranger said severely, 'Next time you speak to an officer, speak civilly.' The skipper's reply, as he unwound his six feet from the clinging mud of that hole, brought joy to our tired hearts.

Flers was left behind, and we wended our way across the dreary plateau that stretches to the valley in front of Delville Wood. It seemed a little lighter, but it may have been that our eyes were not being alternately dazzled and blinded by the Very lights.

The terrible weariness was on me again. Screwed up my resolve to go a thousand paces without falling out. The whole of my consciousness was concentrated on that thousand. But when that thousand was at end, it was necessary to start on another thousand—another, and another—until I gave it up and blundered on automatically. But it helped.

Knee-deep in mud among the guns, we waded across the gully before Delville. A sudden gun would split the night with a lance of flame. Strange forms moved about in the sea of mud. Then our feet met the boards that led up the slope into Delville Wood. An eerie place it was—the shattered trunks standing in the swirling graveyard mists among the countless dead. A damp mouldering odour was all through that silent place. A whizz-bang crashed fair on the duckboards fifty yards ahead. The skipper halted, wondering whether to go ahead or wait. 'What do you think?' he asked us. But twin spouts of flame on each side of us clinched his decision for him, and he stepped out.

A crater glowed with phosphorescent light in the duckboard track. We picked our way round it, thanking the gods of time and chance. In several thousand years of constant duckboard walking, humanity might develop the faculty for walking along them without falling. But where they ended over a new shell hole, or turned suddenly, we fell without fail. But many of the falls were due to the weariness that made it impossible to walk straight ahead.

This happened to Joe Hyrons at the exit from Delville Wood, by the Comforts Fund 'joint'. An ice-covered shell hole lay eight feet below. It must have mesmerised him. He tottered a moment and crashed down on to the middle of it in a sitting position. The ice shattered, and Joe disappeared from our sight. A man descended the slope as Joe reappeared like a seal. He seized the muzzle of the proffered rifle and clambered out. His stony silence struck me as the most profane thing I never heard. That incident bucked me up enough to carry on a little farther. But I was flat out like a lizard drinking when we reached the hutted camp.

Just enough strength remained to take off wet boots and socks and curl up in my sodden blanket. We arrived at 2.30 a.m. Half an hour later I was detailed with two others to go back to Flers. And I can still remember the sensation of putting wet socks back on swollen feet. The others were of the same mind as I. The world was against us, and all NCOs were fair blanky cows of most indeterminate ancestry.

We had hot soup and cocoa at the Comforts Fund joint, and magnanimously acquitted the ancestors of our NCOs.

And so we drifted on our way. At Flers we were loaded to full capacity, and started back. On the way we encountered Bridley and Harding—original 10th men, now in the 50th—all neat, shaven and spotless, on their way back from leave. 'Been in the mud?' they asked. The only consolation that I could find was the thought of their appearance, a few days hence.

It was noon when we rolled in. On the way I had picked up two panniers of ammunition from beside a gun of another battalion, to replace the ones I had dumped. My shoulders ached, my feet pained, rheumatic pains were all up and down my legs. My head ached, my temperature was up from trench fever, and I would have sold out for fourpence.

At nine o'clock next day we were up again. There had been a snowfall, but there was not enough energy left in the whole battalion to throw a single snowball. The others were cleaning their rifles. I did not need to, as I had had the foresight to bring out the one belonging to Sergeant Foster.

4
The great frost

The weather grew colder and colder, the temperature climbed farther and farther below freezing-point. Vitality lowered by exposure had no chance of recuperation in this bleak treeless countryside, swept by arctic winds that seemed to have arisen in the complete cold of outer space beyond the stars. All things froze solid. The snow was dry and powdery. The road rang beneath one's feet.

A mocking travesty of the sun rose in a clear sky. The rays gave no warmth or cheer. We seemed to have been transplanted to another planet, wherein our lives would soon be blotted out, and ultimate stillness again rule.

On 19 January, I went to the MO. He said that I looked sick, and ordered me into the battalion hospital. This was just an ordinary hut, and was filled with trench feet cases whose feet were swollen to two or three times normal size, and many had burst open. Two orderlies laboured manfully all day, but could not catch up with the arrears of filth and neglect. There was no soap or water available, and not sufficient antiseptic dressings for these foot cases.

A battalion was in disgrace in having a large number of men evacuated sick, so these unfortunates were kept in this makeshift hospital, suffering agonies, instead of being sent to England. How the devil the 'heads' expected to man the Somme without a big sick list beats me, but I suppose the pain of those poor blighters made their honour white.

It had been said, in the autumn, that the Australians were to be taken out of the line for the winter and carefully nursed as shock troops. It was certain that we could not stand the rigours of winter, but we were put through it, only to discover that we were still shock troops. Occasionally some particularly bad case would be reluctantly evacuated. We were paying the penalty of the voluntary system. Units had to be kept up to strength with insufficient reinforcements. So the man who was in it had to stay in, so long as he could keep on his feet, and after.

But I was quite comfortable in there, sharing my two blankets with a man who had none. Slowly, in succeeding nights, the sensation of staring through closed eyelids wore off. This feeling was always with me after an extended period in the line. It usually took from three to six nights to wear off, according to the severity of the tour of duty. In spite of the deadly cold, barrages stormed throughout the nights. Even in our extremity, we could feel pity for those who were enduring the double terrors of cold and fire.

After a few days' rest the battalion moved back to Montauban, and we walking cases were packed back to our companies. Then came the real bitterness of the coldest winter for forty years.

The crowded huts had no chimneys, the windows did not open, and any discovered crack was stuffed with paper. Men massed round the braziers. Hoar-frost would form on the backs of the greatcoats of those men who were not immediately against the brazier. Men slept in pairs to get the greatest warmth from the pooled blankets.

The procedure of going to bed consisted of taking off boots and putting on all available pairs of socks. In addition to our underclothing, we usually wore an extra flannel shirt, a sheepskin vest, a muffler or two, and a balaclava cap that covered all but our eyes. Where our breath touched the wool, there icicles formed. On our hands were woollen gloves, and over these were fingerless leather ones. Our reissued overcoats were never off. All available newspapers were spread between the blankets. Equipments were stacked for pillows. And so we lay us down to sleep. In the morning it was useless to try to drink from the water bottle that had been a pillow. The water inside was always frozen.

I observed the dutiful Walter trying to write home one night. He heated the bottle of ink. Before he could write a single word the ink on the nib would be frozen. Whizz-bangs or field postcards were all I ever sent in those days. Everything crossed out except 'I am well, and hope to be discharged soon.' All this was inside the hut. Outside it was really cold.

Tea was taken by us in our dixies, boiling from the cookers. In the twenty paces that we hurried back to the hut, thin ice had formed round the edges. If the slightest wind was blowing men had to walk with head averted from the direction of the current. The pain caused by the moving air on the eyes made it impossible to look for more than a second or so to windward. Bare hands were numbed beyond use after five seconds' exposure. No use arguing—I know it was five seconds, because when one day I dropped a small gun part—too small to be gripped by the gloved hand—I missed the first grab and my fingers would not function for the second try. To cap it all, an epidemic of dysentery ran through the camp at the period of the greatest cold. A most unpopular complaint. A possie near the door was at a discount.

The only comments I remember were mostly regarding the effect of frostbite on the proverbial brass monkey.

There was a silver lining to the cloud; but not for us. The lice had a beautiful time and throve and multiplied on our emaciated frames. No baths were possible. Nights were times of hideous unrest, and only exhaustion finally induced sleep.

But in one of my prospecting expeditions I brought back a gallon tin of a treacly looking substance, the label on which guaranteed death to chats, or money returned. So that night I traced with it a lot of rings around my body. Upright lines converted my carcass into a number of squares. I reasoned that each chat would be bound to walk across the magic line at some place, and would die decently. But I reckoned falsely. Our old friend, the Chat, Army Issue, 4,000,000 PBI for the use of, was made of sterner stuff.

They raged in hordes round their restricted playgrounds, nipped furiously everywhere, and I was certain that I could hear thin squeals of rage at my liberty! But I was still willing to experiment. I had Walter subdivide each square into four, demanding that he be careful to leave no gates. But that night was even worse than the last. Then I smeared myself completely from head to foot with the sticky compound, and the result was absolute immunity for three days. Some reckoned that it was worse than the chats. I preferred to be sticky but unbitten.

The water fatigue parties would move off with picks and

sandbags, returning with loads of icicles. Some heroes occasionally shaved. Tin hats were always used for heating water over the braziers for washing purposes.

Then, to crown our woes, came a succession of road-making fatigues. The ground was like stone, and we barely had strength to raise our picks and let them fall by their own weight. On the first day, after carrying a few sleepers and rails, I got lost, and wandered till I found a dugout where I could make a fire. It was sheer self-defence. My vitality was so low that I had only the strength of a child, and a weak hold on that.

Odd entries in my diary recall the bitterness of those times. One dated 3 February 1917 reads:

It is a long lane that has no turning. Some day there will be warmth, light and laughter—some day—for some of us!

The French girl who said that the Australians had only three interests—wine, war and women— could not have been referring to this winter. But we still had only three interests—cold, food and chats.

Here I will take a few days out of my diary, scrawling pencilled pages, written by numb, gloved fingers:

6 February 1917—I was one of the mess orderlies for the day. So it fell to my lot to dish out grub to lines of hungry men. But we missed going out to Delville Wood. After each meal we took the dixies down to a big wooden tank and brought them back full of water.

The tank presents a queer sight with its sheathing of ice. Artesian water flows in through a pipe. Great blocks of ice float about in the tank, and the overflow freezes as it flows.

Word has been passed around that the Yanks have declared war on Fritz. Every one is cynical and unbelieving.

A big lot of reinstoushments has arrived, and the hut is overcrowded. They are all neat and fresh and tidy. They have a lot to learn, but they will soon find out.

7 February—Today we had to take the dixies to Delville. The cooks got a fire going. We chopped through sixteen inches of ice in a shell hole, and filled the dixies from the clear water below.

We had to wait until after dinner to bring the dixies back, and I had brought no grub. But a search through some empty dugouts produced the necessary. A tin of pork and beans, a tin of jam, and biscuits. After dinner we wasted no time getting back.

The full moon rising into a cold, soulless sky, above the blasted Delville trees, is a strange sight. Stars glitter harsh as diamonds, and a wind, bitter as death, sweeps the frost-bound earth.

8 February—Immediately after a meagre breakfast, our company headed again for the road job in Delville Wood. My head was muffled, only the tip of my nose showing. But even so, the piercing wind made walking an agony. Did not take me long to decide to give the fatigue a miss, having carefully placed myself on the rear of the party, with this contingency in mind.

I walked along the road towards Albert, the wind being on my back that way. But never once did I feel warm. The landscape is maddening. Everything is blasted and shattered. Not a whole tree, nor even a whole brick. Destruction can go no further. And the iron grip of the frost is on everything. In this part of the Somme, from Fricourt to the line, one seems to have passed beyond the gates of life.

For all the bustle of traffic, for all the labour of men, death seems to hover in the steely air. It seems that we can never return to pleasant paths and beautiful places. Our generation is being sacrificed on a bloody altar.

Our fathers, and our fathers' fathers went their ways, and lived to their allotted spans. We, in this mad world, are doomed to walk the red road, from which there is no turning back. Our friends fall beneath the hail of fire and steel. We go on, alone, among strangers who knew them not, with only our memories for company to the inevitable end, where we, too, fall and merge unheeded with earth again.

By the road (Albert-Bapaume) there is a single grave with about two hundred names on a board. Alongside it is a dead horse, with stiff legs pointing protestingly to the sky.

A little before Fricourt I turned back. Near where the fish-like observation balloons are moored, I had two tins of soup at the Comforts Fund joint. It was good. There being still a couple more hours to fill in before it was safe to go home, I wandered to another buckshee joint and had two more tins of soup. These stores are well run by unfit Diggers, on money provided by various funds, and are a very welcome reminder of Aussie.

Feeling more at peace with the world, I went home. A fire was going in the brazier, and the Nissen hut was filled with acrid smoke. A lousy tea, and so to bed.

9 February—Again the unwelcome morning march to Delville. Again I dropped out. Our rations are poorer now. Four men to a small loaf and bit of cheese. This time I found a deserted hut and made a fire, over which I read souvenired magazines. After dinner fuel ran out, and I had to go afield. But I discovered a mansion of a deserted dugout, complete with supplies of wood and coal, a fireplace, and even a door.

I soon transferred my belongings, including six tins of jam discovered at the last place. Soon a roaring fire was going, and I made tea and ate quantities of toasted bread and cheese and biscuits. Here I lie in comfort, like a sleek cat on a summer day. But the darkening streak of sky above the door tells of sunset. So I must out into the desolation again.

Later—Everything was as usual at home. A smoky fire inside, frost and snow outside.

Day after day the accursed fatigues of road-making in Delville Wood continued. Each time I planted myself on the end of the line farthest from the wood. When the order 'Left turn' was given, my only crime was to do a right turn. Each pace took me two from the party, and, if I was too dopey to find out that I was going the wrong way, well, it was not a very great sin, anyway. Officers and NCOs were too busy nursing their own vitality to look round in the searing wind. Huddled, misshapen, swathed to the eyes, they would lurch off to peck the iron-hard ground with feeble strokes.

But one day I received a little shock. No more than twenty paces of my retirement had been covered when I heard someone running, 'Hey! Wait a minute.'

'This is the end of my little game,' I thought. But it was Lane, a late reinjerkment.

'I knew you would have a snug possie for the day,' he explained, 'so I followed you.' He was learning all right.

'Aren't you ashamed of yourself,' I demanded, 'malingering on your poor blasted cobbers like this?'

'Yes,' he said, 'just as much as you are!'

That day was particularly good. Another oasis in a frozen desert.

We made porridge out of pounded biscuits, and a marvellous stew from souvenired ingredients. Some Tommies who wandered in to share our fire, gave us mutton. Grilled on the ashes, hot and greasy, we seized it two-handed, and ate to our great content. We shaved and washed in hot water and spread our underclothing out in the snow.

The heat of the fire warming them before we put them on did not revive the myriads of chats. They had passed out. In warm comfort the hours passed. We lolled on the bunks within range of the roaring fire. Life and strength seemed to be flowing back into our bodies.

'If I ever lose sight of you again,' said Lane, as we trudged homeward through the creaking snow, the bleak dusk wind hissing forlornly on the edges of our tin hats, 'May I be ——ed, photographed, and shot.'

The great salvage plan had come into operation. The Diggers took to it with abandon, almost as a game. It appealed to them with its scope for individual initiative. Strange and varied were the hauls. Much of the stuff, such as bags of coke, went by devious courses to our huts. I had some little difficulty explaining to one of our officers just how I had come by the carcass of a sheep that I had lifted off a GS wagon in transit.

I was putting up a wonderful tale about an abandoned cook-house and keeping the officer's attention occupied while the boys sneaked off with the evidence. There can be no postmortem without a corpse, so the case was dropped. Back at the hut my bed was unrolled and occupied. Now, I was not so dopey as to think that I was in bed when I was just stepping in the door. Investigation showed that that occupant was my old friend the frozen jumbuck.

That night the reek of grilling mutton brought envious crowds to the hut. 'Make it a flaming bullock next time,' ordered

Matthews, wiping his greasy chops with the back of his hand. With a mess tin and due ceremony they crowned me as Souvenir King.

Soon we were for the line again, and the crowd was working up to the necessary pitch. Joe Hyrons told the attentive reos at great length about the new German gun. Its shells would kill everything within five hundred yards, 'and what it doesn't kill, it takes prisoner'.

'That's nothing,' chipped in another, 'what about our new Pelter gun?'

'What is the Pelter gun?' asked a reo. 'What does it do?'

'You coots don't know nothing,' said the other. 'It puts a barrage of cow dung over the moon, so that we can raid in the dark.'

Under the cheering influence of good food, a roaring sing-song commenced. The program consisted wholly of hymns, among which were the 'Recessional', 'Lead, Kindly Light' and 'Onward, Christian Soldiers'. I know not whither their thoughts wandered as they sang. Our men do not tell of their innermost feelings. In all things a soldier keeps something intact, and sacred to himself alone. Sometimes a slight hint will escape, but the average Digger presented to the world and his mates an armour of chaffing and recklessness that hid, while pretending to reveal, his true self. But to us who have taken last messages from men on whom the cold hand of death was closing, who have talked with mates in tight places from which there seemed no escape, is a greater insight given.

Not always were we down in the dumps during this winter. But not often could we be cheerful. The little cheerful times were guiding lights in the darker hours. Far beyond the realms of our imagination were times of peace and plenty. All we would have asked of Fate at that time, were we given our choice, would have been a warm dugout, food and rest. Our spirits rose or fell in accord with our warmth, food and rest.

A slight thaw set in. The snow melted, and mud again clogged our boots. But under the layer of mud was still frozen ground.

5

Utmost test

The seventeenth of February was the day arranged for our return to the line. In the entry of that date is a verse culled from somewhere:

> A rudderless barque is drifting
> Through shoals and quicksands shifting,
> In the end will the night wrack lifting
> Discover the shores unknown.

A depression, heavy beyond imagination, gripped me that day. After the midday meal we moved forward laden for battle. Swirling grey mist swallowed us in Delville. At fifty yards a man was invisible. The grey splintered trunks looked deathlier in the strange half-light. So deaf had I become since the last near shell-burst that I could not hear the sound of footsteps, or ordinary conversation.

Past brigade, where lunging guns told us that we had come again beneath the flail of death, and on to Flers. Dead silence reigned over the thickening fog, broken only by an occasional muffled gun. To my keyed-up mind, the brooding powers of annihilation seemed to be crouched in the fog and silence, waiting to spring. Halfway between Flers and Cheese Road we were put into a derelict trench. After some grub and a smoke the depression lightened. But it came back in full force when we moved forward with the darkness. Beyond the duckboards at the old front line we entered upon treacherous ground—part mud, part frozen. Not until a few falls and complete wetness occurred did my spirits rise to normal. And the discomfort of body was a favourable exchange against the unrest of mind. Down Fritz's Folly we marched in ghostly file. Our feet found the frozen earth under four inches of mud, where it had previously been waist-deep.

We were now in new country. The flares lit up a landscape of sprawling dead. Through the wire we went with our picks and shovels and spread along an old crumbling German trench. We were to deepen it for occupation, from which to launch an attack. A screen of our men lay out in front, sharply outlined by every flare. Steady rain poured down. We started to dig to keep alive.

Most of my section was an ice-covered shell hole. I smashed the ice and lowered the pick to depth the water. But when my hand reached water level the head of the pick had still not reached bottom. So I resigned active operations, telling Lane, 'I'm no bloody submarine', and leaned against the parapet. Lieutenant Dick Caldwell, in his nice new trench boots, came along. Often thought I might pinch those boots when Dicky didn't need them any more. He stopped on the far side a while. Watched with interest to see him step into that hole, and pleasurably wondered how he would feel and what he would say when the water ran in the tops of his boots. But he lingered a long time, and finally asked, 'How deep is this?'

I answered truthfully enough, 'I don't know.'

'Well, depth it, then.'

'Tried,' I said, 'but it is deeper than the pick.'

'Why didn't you warn me?' he demanded.

Being a great believer in the soft answer that turneth away wrath, I replied, 'I wanted to see how deep it really is.'

'Damn and blast you!' he said, earnestly.

I was pained and disappointed, and felt that I had been entitled to hear something more original than that. Dick, a Rhodes scholar and all. Never did think much of this higher education, anyway.

A slight alarm there was in the night. Danger seemed to be creeping amid the myriad footsteps of the rain. It could be felt in the tingling of the hair of the neck, just enough to key us pleasantly above the furtive graveyard atmosphere of the place. Suddenly the rifles of the screen began to pop, sounding queerly wet and dull in the downpour.

'Stand to arms,' the word came down the trench. But we were already kicking footholds in the trench wall, and uncovering the breeches of our rifles.

It is strange how weariness and depression drop from one as a cloak is discarded at the first alarm. Soldiers once again, we stood unmoving, fingers on triggers, waiting for the stamping rush of our screen, when our rifles, too, would take up the chorus. The fire ahead slowed down till a final delayed shot put a period to it as a full stop.

By the light of a hurrying flare, one of the evenly spaced blobs arose, and with body bent, walked back to us. Like some great ape, he looked as he hunched low to avoid bullets. He flattened restfully on the parapet above me until our Richard came up. 'Fritzy fighting patrol,' he reported tersely, 'about thirty strong. They nicked off when we opened on 'em.'

With that, he picked himself up and ploughed back through the mud, finally to drop into place among the equally spaced blurs in front, an outpost of an outpost. Back to the pick and shovel again. No chance of a bit of fun. A rotten world. A pick is no good in pea soup. And fancy trying to shovel treacle! Every now and again I would drive the pick in, just to make a show of doing something.

A bomb crashed in the next bay. We again mounted the parapet, hoping to vent our accumulated spleen on some visible enemy. A wounded man blundered past, leaving behind him the hot raw smell of new blood. Dick came round the corner of the bay and said, wearily, 'Get back to work. He only put his pick into a stick bomb.' So I did not use my pick again. I could see no valid reason why I should blow myself up, trying to do exactly nothing.

One of the screen came weaving in, sliding into the trench by sitting on the parapet and letting the sodden earth break away with him. 'Stopped one in the back,' he said casually, by way of explanation, and, like a man carrying a very heavy burden, moved slowly towards our line.

Hour succeeded dreary hour. Only the sound of far-flung shells broke the monotony, and the occasional shuffling of men making a pretence of work.

At 4 a.m. the word came, 'Get back'. Again we moved in dreary file up Fritz's Folly. Now, on account of the thawing rain, we sank above our boot tops. In a few hours more our feet would be touching the dead, who lay so close below.

Once more we crossed Cheese Road and found our collapsing dugout already flooded by the rain. Water was dripping from the roof. We old hands stacked our equipment and rifles in the mud and sat on them, feet in deep water. But a reinforcement sat in the water without making even that effort.

His face, grey in the candlelight, was that of a man gone beyond the limits of endurance. This was his first turn in the forward area, and I knew that he had been unable to adjust his mind to the squalor and misery of it all. I tried to conjure up what preconceived ideas of the glory of war he had been compelled to discard. And now, after a winter's night of endurance, he was expected to sleep sitting in slimy cold water.

I almost grinned at how the future must have appeared to him then. I debated within myself whether I should tell him the sum of all that we old hands had learned. 'Even this will pass.' But the words would not have penetrated the mists of his misery; so I held my peace. Unless he could soon shake himself out of his torpor, and get a grip, he would be another burden for the slaving bearers, or a corpse in a shell hole.

When the dismal light of dawn filtered in, we wasted no time in searching for better quarters. Soon we found a dry one to hold two, so Lane and I entered into possession. We breakfasted on fried cheese and had a cigarette each; then decided that the world was not such a bad place after all.

But at that moment a five-point-nine landed on a spot about twenty feet away, and we were not so certain. There is always a promise of more shells following the path of the first from our methodical enemy.

Of course, some coot had to bring up the hoary query for the benefit of the new hands, 'Why do shells never land in the same spot twice?' For the edification of those innocents who have not been there, the reply is, 'Because the same spot just ain't.'

We had plenty to think about in the odd hours that the powers decided that we were too done up for any stray fatigue. We had seen a Guards regiment come up from good billets, do four days in the forward area, against our sixteen, and then disappear back to some comfortable billet. But their sick list was as long as ours, even in that short time.

Our commissariat was arranged, at the expense of terrific labour, to give us two hot meals a day. But the staff work of this Guards' mob was not equal to that. Their haversacks were crammed with four days' supply of bully and biscuits, and that had to see them through. We sometimes gave them hot tea, and I never remember anything more thankfully received.

Loud were the grousings from all hands, when they remembered our long spell in the forward area. 'Blasted "heads" think we're bloody labour battalions when there is no stoush on. But I betcha they give us a front flaming seat in the next hop-over, just the same.' You, Dig, the unremembered prophet, were perfectly correct, even as we anticipated.

The stutter of machine-gun fire overhead brought out all hands and the cook to watch a pretty little scrap between two planes. The watchers might have been barracking at a prize fight except that there was a little less lingual restraint. The black-crossed plane swinging aloft in dizzy single combat, was the focus of our intense dislike of the enemy who kept us in this mud bath.

For all the manoeuvring of the Fokker, the British plane sat at last on his tail with hammering twin guns. Close-spaced, the tracers ripped into the enemy machine. 'You little beauty—stick it in to the ———.'

The Fokker lurched and spun in a slow circle, swiftly increasing in tempo as the ground was neared. A mile away, over by Le Sars it crashed in a crumpled heap. The Sopwith spun and looped in a joyful gesture of victory.

What-ho—loot! Pistols—perhaps field glasses. So several of us started out. But I did not seem to be making any pace at all. So I took off my overcoat. Mud-caked and sodden, it weighed fully fifty pounds. Slinging it into a shell hole, I was able to do much better.

We gathered round the machine in disgust. The only part of the pilot that could be seen was the seat of his pants, five feet in the mud where the crash had sent him. The breeches of machine guns showed on each side of him. The plane was a splintered heap. We went back empty-handed.

That day we saw another aerial combat. The vanquished plane sped to earth as a flaming comet. The pilot climbed out from the flames and fell beside his machine, turning over and over in the rush to destruction. The victor again looped and flashed in joyous circles.

The mob cheered. But someone with sharper eyes suddenly said, 'You can save your cheers. That bloke up there has got black crosses on him.' Disgusted, the boys turned back to their interrupted pursuits.

Night closed in with pouring rain once more. We again lined the duckboards ready to move up to continue last night's job. It was bitterly cold without a greatcoat. Little streams of water were running down my legs from where the protection of the ground-sheet ended. It is never so dark as when it is raining heavily.

'Good night for a murder,' said someone, as we moved off with picks and shovels, rifles, bandoliers and gas masks. 'Too bloody right it is!' was my only contribution to the general gaiety.

Up the sap again. Velvety darkness and lashing rain. Red flashes where shells land. The flares make a radiance ahead which flickers and dies. Behind, the thud of guns that seem to curse the necessity of sticking their snouts into the rotten sodden night. Water lapping over the duckboards. Keep close to the man in front. Flatten into the collapsing trench wall while the stretcher party goes by; someone for hospital or a wooden cross. The rifle butt catches on a bearer's thigh as he forces his way past. His heavy panting recedes. Save your strength, laddies, the bad part is farther back.

'Wire overhead.' Hands guard the face against the strands. But it is down low, and meets the shins. Full-length on the boards, and cold, slimy water; steel hat rolling off. The stock of the slung rifle raps the back of one's head. Stars shoot in all directions. 'Don't lie there all night. You'll be late for the party.'

A searing roar, and a five-point-nine lands ten feet out. Flame, blast, singing metal and pattering mud. Breath-stopping, acid-tasting black smoke. 'Wire underfoot' comes back the warning. Feet are moved carefully to encounter the wire. But it suddenly jars across the bridge of the nose; tin hat drops and rolls, splashing and clanging.

'You will miss the party!'

'—— the party, —— you, —— the Kaiser, —— 'em all bar two, me an' me little dorg.'

You know it all, Diggers. I am just refreshing your memories. But next time you wander out into the yard at night and hit the clothesline with your face, don't go crook at wifey. Give her a squeeze and say, 'France was never like this.'

If she looks at you suspiciously and says, 'Drunk again, you brute. Another reunion, I suppose?' blame me. I am safe.

Where the boards end at Fritz's Folly we again entered the morass that we had all been dreading. The line of the sunken road called the Folly pointed straight towards the German line. Flares would light the dreary terrain as the ground sloped down to the middle of the old No Man's Land, and then rose gradually to where the trench that we were headed for was located.

Willow stumps showed vaguely in the hollow. There, in other days, ran a little stream. Grass probably grew on its banks. In summer there may even have been flowers, bees humming in warm sunlight. But the feet of war had stamped it into a sodden grey bog, littered here and there with things that had been men, broken guns, discarded equipment.

The front of our party was in the centre of the Folly, bogged to the thighs. Last night our boots were on frozen ground at ankle-depth. Struggling and sweating we fought our way to the right bank, where the ground was a little better. On hands and knees in most places, in order to spread our weight and get a better leverage. Every inch a fight. If a corpse gave a good foothold, that was so much gained. Never do I see a fly struggling on a paper but I feel a wave of brotherly sympathy. I have been there, too.

While we are still gasping and hearts yet pounding, the line moves on. We keep close to the man in front. Between the flares the darkness is appalling. If the man ahead disappears swearing, move round in a half-circle to miss what he fell into or over. You may encounter other obstacles, but that is all in the game. No two steps on the one level. If the devil designed a place, this is it. At the hardest parts the mud is halfway to the knee; at the worst, waist deep.

The rain and cold are forgotten in the fierce demands of movement. Four shining wet helmets in a shell hole, motionless men beneath, we are passing the last outpost, and are in No Man's Land.

'If Fritz is mug enough to come out on a night like this, it would be a mercy to shoot him,' said someone.

Idle thoughts wander aimlessly. This sort of thing must be hell for some pampered mothers' sons.

But probably the pampered ones were all at home.

In nearly every war picture I have seen, some long-haired coot, whose uniform did not fit him, starts waving his arms about squealing, 'I can't stand it.' Then very properly he dashes out of his cushy dugout or trench, and gets stonkered.

I am afraid that the histrionic gifts of the Diggers must have been very poor, for here and now I affirm that I have never seen anything of that sort. No blasted imagination. The best they could say was, '—— the war', or 'Home was never like this', and get on with the job.

After a long struggle we had descended the slope and climbed again, till the trench lay at our feet. The heat died out of our bodies, and the misery of the cold set in. Occasional rifle shots marked the slow march of the minutes. A bursting bomb would recall us from a state that was half coma, half sleep. In these times recurs the vivid memory of how often this sort of thing had been endured before. And how long those nights were when darkness set in at 4 p.m., and changed again to the feeble grey light that was called day at 8 a.m.

When at long last word came 'knock off', I set out alone to return, satisfied that I could, undelayed by the column, cut down the ninety-minute journey to cover the half-mile to our dugout, by an hour.

I was deaf, and did not know the password. A Digger challenged me from a shell hole at the front line, but I neither heard nor saw till I fell in beside him.

'Damn near shot you,' he said. 'Why didn't you give the password?'

'Deaf,' I said. 'What is the password, anyway?'

'Mutton chop,' he said.

I was drinking hot cocoa when the others drifted in, too weary to curse. 'Why didn't you tell me you were nicking off?' demanded Lane.

'Didn't care to be held up pulling a raw recruit out of all the shell holes he wanted to fall into,' I told him. He cussed comprehensively till Walter shut him up.

On 21 February we were warned to take over the outpost line that night. Four nights in a shell hole, how lovely! In full equipment I was sent down to Flers for a tin of tea. My feet ached with a dull, nagging pain. Fingers were split at the quick and intensely painful. My temperature was up from trench fever. The chats were raging round in hordes. Much of the protecting mist had been cleared away by the rain. Our line followed the duckboards till the derelict tank was on our right. 'Zipp', a bullet hit the mud. 'Zipp' again.

'Blasted sniper,' said a sergeant. 'Take cover under the bank.'

'Why shouldn't I be a little wounded hero like those other cows who are always getting cracked,' I thought, and kept on.

'Whizz-smack,' came the bullets. Pretty close. Hope he doesn't get me in the guts. An officer started yelling at me till I could not ignore him any longer. 'I'm deaf,' I told him, loudly, looking blank as I got under cover.

'Why didn't you come in with the others when the sniper started?' he yelled.

'Was there a sniper?' I asked him, looking stupid. He promised to put me under arrest, and gave up the unequal contest.

After a while we ventured out again. The bullets started once more, and I was left alone. Each bullet sizzled past as I trudged stolidly on. My deafness was to be my alibi. Five shots waist high. Not so good. Range altered, five shots round my feet. 'That's right, Fritzy, keep them there.' Five shots sizzling round my ears. Could picture the puzzlement of that sniper, as he could not even make his target duck, for all the alterations of range. The next clip varied between low and high, then he gave up in disgust, quite satisfied that none of his bullets went anywhere near me. By this time I was near Cheese Road. Other men were emerging from behind the tank.

Back to known ranges, Fritz gave up shooting at me, and started on them again. I do not yet know if I was relieved or disappointed.

The rest of the company awaited us. Grouped into our sections, we moved forward for the worst turn in the line, in that worst winter in memory.

Guides led each team forward to its respective post. We grunted and sweated as we fought our way through the mud that waited beyond the gun-pit dugouts.

The Folly, black and menacing, lay below us on our left. Flares lit up the stark unreality of No Man's Land. A scene from another world, it was—never our old and kindly earth! Even to this day every stump, every huddled heap, the crazy wire, the water that shone so silvery beneath the flares, are burned into memory. If I saw the place again I would look for the grim, sardonic death's head that watched our post, and all the thousand details there were.

We slid into the post, about five yards out from the sunken road that is Fritz's Folly. The relieved garrison gathered up their possessions and struggled silently and thankfully away into the darkness. Our Lewis gun was planted firmly on the parapet, loaded, and carefully sheeted. Never did I go into a post in the front line but my mind raced ahead, attempting to penetrate the hours to come. Life or death was the question. A fraction of a turn on a wheel, miles away, and we, too, would keep eternal watch with these other unburied ones.

The post was merely a waterlogged depression, little security against fragments. It was useless to attempt better cover by digging, as any work would fall in. And so we were left, knee-deep in water, to the cold, the shells, and our thoughts.

Few words were spoken, but one could sense the swirling thoughts of the others. In those long minutes of the endless nights were many bitter things thought of the higher command. Dugouts, they said, were bad for the morale of troops. Over the way, Fritz lived warm and comfortable in deep dugouts, secure from fire and cold. We had to endure this—for the sake of our morale! But illogically enough, any captured dugouts were always promptly occupied.

War of attrition! To us it was the last word in ineptitude.

The higher command seemed to say, 'We will give you three dead British for two dead Germans.' Many a long and bitter day was to dawn before the genius of Monash would light the way to victory.

The enemy warned of our attacks; troops thrown defenceless on to waiting machine guns; attacks launched against the strongest points.

Blundering always, and the price was our lives. 'Another division come to France, let us make another attack.' Just as subtle as that, it appeared to us. A few yards of pulverised earth, bought with thousands of lives, acclaimed as a victory!

So our thoughts of the war were not good company, though none of us doubted eventual victory, or ever lost his feeling of personal superiority over the enemy. But the human mind, that unexplored and wonderful thing, is full of resource.

When actuality becomes too depressing, it creates for itself a pleasant and romantic dream world. And so, in those nights, when time seemed to have halted, bogged too, in this deadly mud, my mind ranged over all the beautiful things I had seen or heard.

Hours would I search for the lilt of a song I had loved, the words of a stirring poem, or to recreate a remembered face. I am convinced that the front-line soldier developed an extraordinary power of appreciation of the beautiful in all its forms. Those naked hours of watching, enduring in the teeth of man-made horrors, rain, sleet and bitter cold, could leave no man unchanged.

Far and wide around us throughout this night shells and mortar bombs crashed, each showing an instant of red flame. But, to our great satisfaction, nothing burst closer than forty yards away. The lagging hours were sufficient tribulation. Our physical condition was bad. Just how bad it was is indicated by an entry in my diary, written at the time, and quite free from exaggeration: 'Every muscle in my body is a line of acute pain, every bone and joint an ache. Rest is impossible.'

Once in the night, word came that a post had been blown up, and all the five occupants killed. They were men well known to us. From out of the flare-lit fog, patrols came at intervals; a word or two, and were gone. A novice would have been hopelessly lost at once in that terrain, where the only signposts were the sprawling dead.

After an age the dawn came, a slight diffusion of light. We left the post for our allotted dugout, only to find it occupied. Cursing, we were sent back to the gun-pit dugouts. These, too, were crowded, so back down the Folly we went again, shielded by the fog. We were separated and put into any dugout that could hold another man. A generous nip of rum, scalding and suffocating, but bringing, for a time, a feeling of wellbeing. Breakfast of fried cheese, and then the drowsing march of daylight. From outside came the thud of shells that marked the hours and told where death stamped with feet of fire.

The grey light that filtered through the entrance became faint, and it was night again. We troglodytes emerged from the reeking dugout into the gripping cold of the night, and silently clambered out of the sunken road into our post.

Some days and some nights leave searing memories, but worst of all was this night of 22 February. Barely did we stand in our places than the night awoke to the snarling of shells. Trees of flame arose and were gone, continuously, all about us. The air vibrated with the organ notes of hard-driven metal. A mad fury seemed to have possessed the enemy. But what we did not know was that this was merely the disposal of surplus ammunition, and a cover for his first move back towards the Hindenburg Line.

One big howitzer opened on us every twenty minutes, firing five shells each time. First would come the faint, far-distant tap of the gun firing. The whispering of the shell would come, growing fainter and fainter as it climbed high into outer space, until it merged into silence. A long ten seconds would elapse before the whisper, now full of menace, would be heard again.

Slowly, deliberately, the sound would multiply into a screaming roar, a hissing as of driven flame, triumphant, devilish shrieks, a last mad rush, and the first shell would land forty yards in front. A fan of flame would stand sudden against the night. Then all consciousness would concentrate on the wail of hard-driven metal, as we crouched, remembering how frail is flesh and bone against white-hot hissing steel.

Far and wide would come the pattering of falling debris, now twenty yards away, now in the water by our sides. Then would come a little silence, during which we would disregard the uproar of the lesser ordnance, but would wait tautly for what must follow.

Tap. 'There she goes,' someone would say, in flat, hopeless tones. Now the bolt would strike thirty yards in front. The ground would leap beneath the blow, and the fury of the concussion would jar us through and through. Overhead, above our tense and quivering carcasses, would sweep a yelling swarm of destruction. The choking smoke would roll sullenly over the post. Now did we wait on the edge of hell and peer with staring eyes into the dread world of slime, where shattered things keep eternal watch.

Tap. In foreboding silence we would wait, every nerve screaming in protest against the measureless fury that we must await, passive and unmoving. The shell would trail into silence on its upward climb, then again whisper of things unspeakable—louder—louder—chaos of sound, of flame, violence beyond all possibility of telling. This third shell would land just in front of the post. Under these blows I felt a weak desire to weep quietly. When the uproar would cease, came a feeling of pleasure that we were still alive.

Again the gun would fire. The fourth shell would land just behind us. If the gunner's hand trembled ever so slightly in the setting for the last two shots, our post would be a shambles of smashed bodies. If the driving charge varied ever so slightly, then would our earthly watch be done. If the weight of the shell was but a fraction untrue, this tale would never have been told. And we knew these things as we stood at our posts. The fifth shell would land safely, forty yards in rear of us. We would then sigh with relief, knowing that at least another twenty minutes of life was ahead of us.

All things are relative, and the relief of dawn was infinitely distant, as seen through the vista of this fire. Twice did he send six shells instead of the usual five, and someone snarled, 'you louse-bound ——!'

Once, in the uproar, I heard the flopping sound that metal makes when it strikes flesh. 'Who is hit?' I asked, despairingly. But no one answered. No mate was sinking limply into the mud. We were still unscathed, though we felt, that should we live, the scars of this night would ever be on us. In the minutes between the shellings the cold bit farther into our bones. A patrol brought us word of an intended raid. More strafing for us. We heard the raiders struggling through the night, and there was a little space of silence.

The Stokes guns opened with a hail of shells. Bombs tapped swiftly, showing little jets of flame. Rifles pecked. A machine gun opened, jammed, fired and jammed again. Then stillness closed once more on the drama of sound. With the hours, life seemed to ebb from us. Wonderment that I did not die possessed me, but man is hard to kill.

Before the dawn came a mad half-hour of whizz-bangs. The air was torn by their screaming. We crouched and waited the inevitable. The sky lightened. Incredible, the night finished, and all of us alive. A perverse desire possessed me to stay a few more minutes on post, to jeer at Fate.

A double rum awaited us. 'Cripes,' said Olsen, 'give me another like that, and two bombs, and I'll get to Berlin.'

Four of us sat in the little dugout. Nine inches of liquid mud constituted the floor. My equipment comprised my seat, but the rising mud necessitated adding my goat-skin vest to the pile. Mud will dry out and crack off a web equipment, but picture for yourself the four-inch hair of a goat-skin after immersion in the Somme mud. If some peasant located it in after days, he need fear no claim of mine. A Tommy cooker, set on a water tin, oozed a lazy blue flame. Over this I fried cheese, while the livening effect of the rum was still on me.

Again we sat drowsing through the short daylight hours, the dread of the coming night sitting close beside us. The stamp of heavy shells outside recalled how the sword hung ever above us. The hair of Fate might even now be fraying. One shell near this sodden funk-hole and the whole thing would leap in on us, and we would be forced down to choke in this mud. Grey mud within, mud and grey skies without, the hidden sun plunged downward to the eclipse that would send us shelterless to face the hours of flame, steel and cold. Fear mounted with the failing light, fear that grips the heart with clammy fingers, and saps will and strength.

Ears were attuned to catch the slightest move outside, for the call to what we regarded as practically certain death. No glory, no compensation in such a fate as this. No action to take one's mind from the sordid death in the stinking mud. We would not die shouting in mid stride, shooting or lunging, but like a starving, bogged cow beneath the axe.

Splashing, sucking, and gurgling footsteps approached our dugout, halted. 'Get on post.' That doorway is the unreturning way to eternity. Without comment, we hauled our equipments from the mud and buckled them on. The mud from them oozed and ran down. Without a word, we filed, bent low, through the entrance. We fought with the mud as we climbed the bank, slipping, stumbling and falling. Fears fell away as we opposed stern reality.

We splashed into the gloomy, empty hole that was our post, and fitted once more into the night of watching. Tensely we waited the recommencement of last night's howitzer fire, and as minutes passed without it, our spirits rose, till we were almost jovial. Fire there was, in plenty. Shells plunged in flame and thunder all along the ridges, and in the hollows. But it was scattered, and caused us no concern.

Visiting patrols and ration parties brought us the news that only concerned ourselves. Leave and death, patrol actions, when we would be relieved. With great gusto was told the tale of one of our gunners. He saw movement several nights ago. Two hundred yards across No Man's Land moved a half-dozen men. None of our patrols was reported out. So he opened up with his Lewis gun in a single burst. He hit every one of the party. But they were our men. Fortunately, the wounds were slight, in every case. He was ordered to appear before The Bull. He went in fear and trembling.

'I wanted to have a look,' said The Bull, 'at the gunner who is such a marvellous shot. I also want to tell you that you are in no way to blame for what happened.'

Report came also of last night's raids. Our battalion party was held up by uncut wire. The enemy threw bombs and fled, our men unable to clamber over the wire to pursue. One of ours had been lightly wounded. A 45th party on the right had been completely successful. Good mob, the 45th, we agreed.

The world of flares, of thunder, of cold, and mud, went on, as though it were the normal, and would last for ever. Released from the fear of close-plunging shells, the cold seemed worse on this night. But orders came that each man could spend two hours of the night, in his turn, down in a dugout. I departed joyfully. My two hours being up, I again climbed the bank with renewed strength. Johnny Paakola, the Finn, was crouched over the gun. I barged into his near shoulder.

'Get below, Johnny, your turn for the spell.'

'No, Mitchy,' he said, 'I stop. Zere is a raid on tonight, and I tink I get a shot at zese baskets.' He would not budge, insisting that I take his turn below.

Now, I could just as conveniently spray an aggressive party as any warlock Finn. As well try to move a bogged gun as shift Johnny. The piercing wind clinched his words, and I went below again, wonderingly. Again the two hours fled in the comparative warmth of the dugout, and once more I faced the night. Johnny still stood like a rock behind the gun. My pleas that I was entitled to a share of any fun that might be going were futile against his impassive purpose.

Great was my surprise recently, on reading a book, *The Charles Men* that told of a forgotten war hundreds of years ago. The Russians were driving the Swedes and their Finn allies out of the Ukraine. Finns would stand in the snow beyond the campfires, on watch. They would refuse to come in at their appointed times for food and warmth, saying, 'No, I stay on watch.' A strange race, but what mates to have.

A line of red flares arose all along the enemy line. We tensed in expectation of a storm. But nothing happened. We knew later that it was probably the moment of his evacuation of the front line in his move back to the Hindenburg Line. So cold were the remaining hours of our watch that the lice did not move or bite.

At last another dawn showed in the faint flushing of the east. Seizing gun and panniers, we made our way into the Folly. Other teams drifted in as we awaited our rum. One corporal reported ammunition and post blown up, but no one hurt. One man solemnly thanked God that he still lived.

Again settled in our dugout for rest in the daylight hours. But an increased tension was on everyone, as our relief battalion was due this night.

The tide of mud had risen. Never did the lousy rat-hole look worse or more liable to fall in suddenly. Pigs, kept in a place like this, would sicken and die. Wild animals would desert it. We humans have a lot to learn. Aches and pains, cramps, 'coal boxes' and aerial torpedoes kept us awake. Miss us for just a little longer, we would think, and we get our rest.

The prospect of sleeping stretched out on a dry floor, secure from enemy fire, seemed as an elusive heaven to us. But it had happened to us before, so why not again, provided one of these blasted five-point-nines did not write 'finish' to our little chapter.

When it still wanted an hour to darkness, we packed up ready for departure. With darkness we again went on post, and listened breathlessly to every shell burst. In ones and twos the relief battalion arrived. They were in extremity, and each man collapsed for a space until strength returned. When they had recovered enough to take an interest, we pointed out all things that they should know.

At seven o'clock we were due to depart, and even by that time two of the five could not stand on their feet. Our feelings were torn between relief at the finish of our watch, and an intense pity for those on whom it had fallen.

The Folly tried for the last time to hold us, and did indeed bog us all for a while. But we struggled on with our backs to the flares, and at last our feet met the boards. No more than our usual quota of falls and we reached the debris piles that had been Flers. We discovered then, to our dismay, that we had to go back to Mametz, an all-night march. I knew that I could not do it, and told the skipper so, asking permission to sneak into a deserted dugout to rest until daylight. I was peremptorily ordered to stay with the column. But at that I became stubborn, and claimed my right to be paraded before a medical officer.

A corporal took me to an aid-post. A weary MO glanced at me, 'What's the trouble, lad?'

'Relieved from front line tonight, due to march back to Mametz. I am too done-up to do the march, and I want permission to camp till daylight.'

'That's all right,' he said, in a kindly tone. In the blurred night shadows I found a dugout with only one occupant. He grunted as I lay beside him. Piercing pains lulled me into a sound sleep.

Cold, hungry and cheerful, I was up at daylight. Someone had pinched my rifle, but I found a tin of pork and beans. That evened matters.

A muddy scarecrow trod the boards to Delville. At a brigade cook-house I invited myself to a feed, and picked a rifle off the dump.

Delville Wood was the same tale of graveyard mists, but I was going the right way. The Comforts Fund joint at the entrance came to light again.

Dinner was being dished out when I rejoined the mob. They raised a cheer for their senior wangler, and then told me of the frightful trip I had missed. They had been arriving in ones and twos since 4 a.m., absolute physical wrecks.

6
Rustle of spring

With the morass of Flers no longer waiting to engulf our sorely-tried carcasses, our spirits rose high. A diary entry may give an indication of the change:

As the sun rose high the fog was blown away, and her rays lit a world that was not torn by shells, on trees that were not splintered wrecks, and shone too, on the delicate green of young grass. A thrush sang, calling its mate. The mate answered. These trifling things towered all-important to us, for Spring and Life are taking over from Winter and Death.

The diary entry of 1 March described how we came to Henencourt, a delightfully remembered oasis in the stormy years:

We packed up and assembled our equipments in fighting order. After breakfast we moved off in blessed sunlight. After passing over a hill we

103

saw Albert and the surrounding country from a new angle. Green valleys reached in three directions, dotted with little spire-topped villages. It seemed we were entering a brave new world.

Beyond Albert, ploughed fields flanked the road. We said farewell to the war where two enormous shell holes showed to left and right. Jokes passed down the ranks as we marched between them, someone saying, 'Rabbits must be bad about here.'

Through the winding streets of pretty, peaceful Henencourt we went past the gates of the big château. Half a mile beyond we turned to the right and followed a track through a tall forest. On the clear hilltop we came to a hutted camp, and there all the gunners were put together in one hut.

After tea I went to Warloy for a feed. It was a pleasant walk home. Every star shone like a diamond. Around the full moon was a great halo, and a soft wind stirred the forest.

Far down the road came a party of our chaps singing 'A Long, Long Trail A-winding'. A peaceful, restful night, seemingly far removed from wars and rumours of war.

To a stunned and disbelieving mob was announced that henceforth early morning parades were to be cut out. The morning parade would be from 9 a.m. to 12.30 p.m., and afternoons would be devoted to sports.

So the 'heads' were human, after all! On the man with the foresight and intelligence to initiate this regime, may all the blessings rest. Sick, worn-out men became strong and active once more. The amount of food we could absorb during our recuperation was astounding. Walter and I would stroll into Henencourt each midday to the home of the pleasant Yvonne. There would we feast on 'erfs' and 'murfs'.

Our first feed was a generous one. Four eggs each with fried potatoes, bread and butter and coffee. Yvonne opened her eyes wide at the order. The lot cleaned up we sent her off for four more each, with the necessary spud and coffee accessories. Then we sent for four more. Beyond words, Yvonne brought them in. With much gusto, I ordered another four, making a total of sixteen each.

Yvonne murmured '*Mon Dieu*' faintly, as she went out to cook up the last order. I was all for sending for another plate, but Walter demurred, 'She might think we are gluttons.' But nature knows her business, and wasted tissue has to be replaced. A few Malagas put me at peace with the world.

On 5 March came a heavy snowfall. We regarded the beautiful mantle with complacent approval. During the afternoon sports a number of officers, The Bull among them, were on top of a steep bank. They were snowballing another group of officers. I shepherded a few men to a spot where a shot would catch us sooner or later. It did. So we returned the fire, after which they opened on us. Just what I wanted, give them a lesson in tactics.

I sounded the rally on my whistle, and a number of Diggers galloped up. Lined them up, detached flanking parties, and moved in line of skirmishers against the officers. They tried to stop us, but we were three to one, and with the first rush swept them off the ridge. All except The Bull. As leader, he was left to me. At three feet we slammed snow at each other, and I got better than I gave. But I gave plenty. So I blew my whistle and called the dogs off, leaving The Bull to his moral victory.

We waged a heavy fight against chats, and with the aid of hot baths and clean changes, managed to get them down. A diary entry of 8 March gives an idea of how our spare time was occupied:

After tea I slipped in to Henencourt, had a good feed, and other forms of cheer, such as hot spiced wine. Then, in brilliant moonlight, in a cutting wind, we walked home.

I was in a beatific mood, but the others would persist in talking of war. They told of Pozières, of men blown to pieces before their eyes, of a landscape decorated by heads, arms and legs of the freshly killed, of men smothered to death, dying of gas. Of fearfully wounded men making their way to the dressing-station with a joke on their lips, and passing out in their tracks. I tried to head them off on to any standard topic, but they would not be turned.

In the living present the moon swung high overhead. The keen wind from the icebound north played on the harps of the forest. The tall swaying trees reached great arms to the sky. Glistening frosted ivy clung to the branches. A fire and good fellowship awaited me at home.

'God's in his heaven—
All's right with the world !'

Our hut was a place of comedies and comedians. One night, after lights out, came a party, chock-full of Malaga. Big McMahon was carrying his mate on his shoulder. A fight had started between machine-gunners and bombers. When it was all over and every one had collected black eyes and skinned noses, no one knew who had fought whom, and why. Marvellous spectacles they were, when all were safely gathered in.

Johnny Paakola's hangover lasted throughout the next day. At dawn he was dashing round, throwing bottles and Finnish imprecations at low-flying planes. The orderly officer tried to place him under arrest, but Johnny said, 'No compre arrest', grinning widely. The OO relented, and Johnny went to bed to sleep it off.

Day followed day—sunlight, rain or snow. We worked hard at our gunnery. An NCO class was held, and at the examination, I rose to the dizzy rank of lance corporal.

I remember, while I sewed the stripe on, dissertating to the mob as to how they must in future treat me with the greatest respect, never use words starting with 'B', in my presence, and have my boots cleaned ready for parade. I got to the point where I was telling them that I would not insist on their standing to attention before me, and they need not call me 'Sir'. But I got no further, for they threw me out the door into the mud, stripe and all.

Everything contrived to raise our spirits. Bapaume had been taken, and the enemy still retired. Baghdad had fallen to our arms.

One day the battalion marched through Henencourt. As I looked back along the ranks pride rose high. Never before, or since, have I seen such a splendid sight as that evenly-stepping, powerful body of men. The Bull's eyes reflected his feelings as we marched by. Efficiency, fitness and high spirits were writ large on that display.

But, there was none to tell us that in a few short days nine of every ten would fall among the wire in the shambles of Bullecourt.

7

Moving up

The short and cheerful days were ending, for on 22 March we received orders to prepare to move forward.

Never do birds sing so sweetly, never is the sweep of forest-strewn country so beautiful as when we are under orders to move up. There is so little certainty left of life that we greedily try to make the most of it. In the gatherings at night a stranger might wonder at the high spirits of the old hands; the songs they sang; the tales they told. But these were the men who had endured the winter, and come from out of the blast of Pozières. They knew that their lives were spent; that there was little chance of their survival. This they had weighed and accepted, but sought to wring from the fleeting minutes all pleasure there might be.

In contrast, the newcomers were silent and thoughtful. They had much to wonder about, as to how they would react to the storm. Then they also would have become veterans, as these others—men for whom there was no future, only the careless present.

With 'Cork' Daley as offsider, I paid a last visit to Warloy. There, by divers tortuous methods, we became possessed of a case of whisky. We rambled home through the forest beneath a glorious starry sky. The entire personnel of the hut awaited our return with a flattering certainty of our success. Homeric tales there were, and laughter that rang strangely.

'If Fritzy stonkers Mitch in the next stunt,' said Matthews, 'I'll go crook a treat.'

'They'll get him, all right,' someone assured him, 'now he's a mug gunner.'

But there were other opinions, freely voiced. 'He's too bloody silly to get cracked. You notice that it's these stoopid ——s that come out every time. He's been going since the Landing. Time he was dead, anyway.'

Songs were sung, and listened to in absolute silence. Men who scorned any display of sentiment were these, who listened as if afraid to miss a note. Far away their thoughts were carried to places and memories made trebly dear by time, distance and the shadow of death.

At the conclusion of each song, banter would break forth anew, as though to sever sharply thoughts on which it were not wise to dwell too long. These were the original Digger meetings, of which post-war reunions are the palest of shadows.

At long last the night was given over to silence, broken only by the forest noises, and occasionally a distant rumble that spoke to wakeful ones of our rendezvous. The morning of 23 March brought the thought-destroying cheerful bustle of departure. Limbers packed, companies assembling, and the battalion in swinging column of route, breaking into roaring song at the 'March at ease'.

Tramping rhythm that led beyond the newly greened forest, the singing of birds. Albert of the leaning Virgin; streams of traffic, like unceasing rivers.

The air seemed to become chilly and more still in the brooding zone beyond Albert. But nature, with her promise to make all things new, was already at work. It was strange to see the delicate green of young grass among the foul wreckage of war.

That night we camped at Pozières, near the great waterlogged mine-craters, and rested until 28 March, storing our strength against the demands of the near future. Forward again to Martinpuich, where we billeted in dugouts, and on to more dugouts by the Butte de Warlencourt.

All through this country were unburied British dead, left from the attacks of last year. Here and there solitary men kept their abandoned watch. In places where the wire was thick they clustered densely. Tales were there to be seen by those who looked, where khaki and grey-clad forms intermixed with crossed bayonets, even in death. What untold heroisms were enacted here! One wondered of the last thoughts of these ragged, mummified heaps, as their world darkened about them.

Some of our men devoted their days to reverend burial of these men. To those who knew that a bed and certain rest comes with night, that would be a little thing. But these men knew not what demands would be made on their strength. A soldier in the forward area rests and sleeps every possible moment. Thus was the action of these voluntary working parties the more splendid. As many as possible were removed from the too revealing sunlight, to merge again with Mother Earth, the kind green grass overhead.

My tale of the winter draws to a close. I will now quote from my diary under 30 March 1917:

Good and early we were out of bed, and off on fatigue. I was in charge of an isolated party on the Bapaume Road. After dinner I went for a walk across the battlefield. The sights were ghastly. For diversion I started throwing stick-bombs, and they made lovely soul-satisfying explosions.

I passed beyond our old front-line trench and our wire. Our dead ended at the German wire, and from then on the grey-clad dead clustered in ragged putrefying heaps. Beside one was a shorthand diary in which such names as Bapaume and Thilloy cropped up. In this region the shell holes made by our guns are enormous, and all waterlogged. In my walk I did not set foot on an inch of unturned earth, but here it was unbelievably pounded. A light train was halted nearby. The open trucks were crowded with wounded—Scots and Australian. Stoic and uncomplaining, they lay in their bloodstained bandages and torn uniforms. They had no cover from the bleak piercing wind. A feeling of complete unworthiness possessed me, and I felt ashamed of my healthy self, certain that were I smashed I could not measure up to this standard.

A tin of lollies was soon divided among the occupants of a truck. One silent Scot, stiff lips blue with cold, seemed almost started on the unreturning way. Him I wrapped carefully in my greatcoat, and felt much better for so doing. 'Thanks, Aussie. Good luck to you,' he said, so quietly that I could barely hear.

'Good trip to Blighty, boys,' I said, and left, unable to look longer on the suffering that I could do nothing to alleviate.

Climbed the Butte de Warlencourt, a prehistoric mound, about seventy feet high. The keen cold wet wind made vision difficult. The brown tormented earth stretched back to the horizon, an utterly desolate vista. The smashed villages showed as little mounds. Here and there the fragments of a tree pointed skeleton fingers to the sky. A few rays from the setting sun gleamed on the busy wet road.

Below ran a sunken road, crowded its whole length with partially submerged bodies, and protruding arms and legs. Then I turned full round. There, like the promise of Paradise lay the good green land and unspoiled trees of our latest conquest. The red roofs of Bapaume gleamed invitingly amid the trees. But it was too cold to linger there and I made my way to the dugout, to be greeted by the welcome reek of a coal fire, and 'Hop into this stew you ———. Thought you had managed to blow yourself up.' And me a lance corporal and all!

8
Bullecourt

The winter is ended. This was the burden of my thoughts, as I stood on the Butte de Warlencourt and looked around. Grey mist was all about. Behind was the utter desolation that reached to Albert—the vast cemetery of the nations. Below was the sunken road, thickly strewn along its whole length with bodies, and parts of bodies. That was the recent No Man's Land. The enemy had retired to the security of his great Hindenburg Line, laying waste the country between. Red roofs of Bapaume gleamed warmly inviting. The fields between were greening and but barely marked by shellfire. Brown bands of futile wire divided the countryside in swerving lines.

The boys were in great nick. The battalion was up to its full strength and pride, trained to the minute. The hardships of the winter were history, and the big, fit men were laughing and joking as they marched. The road led through a gap in the wire. 'To keep the rabbits out of Bapaume.' Bapaume, with its shattered walls, but to us still a desirable place. Only the Town Hall stood intact.

'Decent of Fritzy to leave that,' was a comment. But the Town Hall was a heap of rubble from a delayed-action mine next time we were there.

Achiet-le-Petit. Dugouts reeking of the strange leathery German smell. 'Don't touch any souvenirs. Don't move any dead uns. Don't tread on loose boards. Look out for man-traps and mines.' A man flies up the stairs in the still night watches. 'Look out, I can hear something ticking.'

'Aw, dry up, blast yer—too cold up there.'

Three balloons flaming to earth, a small black-crossed plane rocking and spinning in a sleet of bullets.

'Game cow. Deserves to get away.'

A lonely cross by the wayside inscribed in ornamental German lettering:

HIER RUHT
AUSTRALIER TIM LAWLER
3 COY., 17 BATT., 5th. BGE.
FEB., 1917.

Midnight. Our backs hunched to the drifting snow. Two limbers with Lewis-gun equipment at the side of the road. The snow-whitened horses' heads hang dejectedly. Lieutenant Imlay flashes his torch on a snow-crusted signpost, 'Vaulx, 3 kilometres'.

'Gone five kilos out of our way. Gunners, unload guns and ammunition from the limbers and carry them. Where is that bloody guide?'

'—— the war! —— the Kaiser!'

Eighteen-pounders baying across snowy fields.

Noreuil. A line of dead 50th battalion men. Many old mates of the original 10th among them.

'How long, oh Lord, how long?'

On the afternoon of 9 April 1917 we sat in our dugouts in the sunken road before Bullecourt.[1] A man gets into actual conflict by a series of mental elevations from plane to plane. And each change of plane is accompanied by a varying feeling of fear at the moment of transition. In the last and highest plane of all, in desperate and hopeless conflict, a man stands very near to the gods, in a strength that may have its source in the utter absence of hope. But when Sergeant Don Latchford blew in with a casual air and said, 'We fly the bags in the morning. See to your gun and ammunition,' I felt a twinge of fear as I rose to the plane of preparedness.

The evening was spent in packing up and collecting the requirements of battle. Icy winds swept across a snow-covered world, as we waited ready in the sunken road at midnight. I checked over my team for spare-parts bag, bombs, sandbags and ammunition—all business-like and unemotional. 'Stick to me like a brother,' were my final instructions. At 3 a.m. we filed out beneath the glory of a moon which shone on a world of snow.

By the edge of a ploughed field we lay in our rows, dark blots in the snow. My gun rested on its bipod, snout raised as if snuffing the battle. The moon went out under a snow-cloud, and the falling flakes made into white heaps the line of prone forms. Cold in the snow-laden wind, we lay, hoping for the order to advance.

Away on the left, artillery pounded heavily, but ahead and behind us might have been dead polar regions for all the sign of life that we could see or hear. A light rocketed up, perilously close. Rockets shot grape-like bunches of coloured lights, which hung in the air for seconds. Four Maxims commenced to jabber fiercely, and strings of bullets hissed overhead. We tensed in preparation. With numb fingers, I thrust a rustling magazine on the post and rotated it a segment. With the cold, weakened fingers of both hands, I managed to get the cocking handle back.

Lady Death was ready to take the stage. A heavy barrage fell on the far left. In the awful penetrating cold we lay until the blackness of cloud-wrapped night gave place to grey dawn. Over the hill in mobs, as if from a football match, came the crowds of our advance waves. We rose with them, and went back, unconcernedly, without care or order. Not a shell or a bullet came towards us from the plainly visible wire-fronted Hindenburg Line.

The attack had been called off till the following day, owing to the non-arrival of tanks, which were to smash a way through those acres of rusty, long-spiked wire.

That evening the post corporal brought me seven letters. Always throughout the war I noticed that a large mail seemed a prelude to hot action. Throughout the evening I read those letters. Outside big shells crashed into and fouled the virginal snow, and gusty, shrieking shrapnel swept the terrain. Those letters told of Christmas down-under, of warm seas and crowded beaches, of a summer camp high in the hills, amid the yellow glory of wattle and the riot of singing birds; of laden fruit-trees and other beautiful things. All steeled up for battle as I was,

I regretted having received the letters at that time. A man needed to fasten his mind to the grim job in hand.

Out in the sunken road was the black bulk of a tank. From its interior came the sound of a machine-gunner tuning up. Bill Davies, my No. 2, sat with me through the long hours. We talked little, but thought much.

At 2.30 a.m. on 11 April we again lined up in the still-falling snow, and moved in muffled silence across the fields to a shallow hop-off trench, dug more for alignment than cover.

'Prepare to advance,' came the order after a few minutes. Caught napping, I slapped a magazine on, and had to run to catch up with them. The lines of waves were halted. We were in the fourth wave, and about three hundred yards from the German line. Things were normal. Machine guns sent bullets smacking through our line. Occasional flares shot up. Whizz-bangs came over in slow, deliberate salvos, making red flames amid the white fields. As another stream of lead whistled just overhead, I quoted to the imperturbable Sergeant Major McDowall lying beside me:

> Oh to be in England,
> Now that April's there!

'Well,' he said, unexpectedly (in Bairnsfather's phrase), 'if you know of a better 'ole—go to it!'

The faint muttering of tanks came to us. This was to be a silent attack, without artillery. We saw the tanks over on the right—big black blurs outlined sharply against the snow. They lined up and moved forward, slowly. They would stop, move on, then stop again. Their exhausts flared red in the night. Their droning noise aroused the German lines. Big shells smashed among us. Our platoon commander, Caldwell, got it first. Others staggered back looking like snow men, save where blood showed black.

A suddenly revealed moon lit a fierce panorama. On the right flank a gas wave was billowing over the German lines. Showers of sparks rose out of the gas cloud as enemy countering shells fell. Pieces of metal thudded about us. Machine-gun bullets smacked around, and occasionally men jerked at the impact.

A long, cold half-hour dragged past in which we lay silent, unmoving and vicious. Probably the most effective way in which men can go into action. 'Prepare to advance.' My gun was slung in a hip sling, and could be fired while I stood. 'Advance!' Ranks rose swiftly. Many men rigid with cold could not move.

Down a steep bank I slid. The gun broke the sling, and plunged its nose into the dirt. Precious seconds were wasted while I slung it on shoulder. My team ahead called on me to hurry.

A tornado of thunder and flame fell upon us, beyond anything I had known or imagined. Close as trees in an orchard were the trees of flame. The blast of one shell would send me reeling forward, while another would halt me with a wave of driven air. A headless man fell at my feet, and as I rolled over him a sheet of flame fanned over with blinding light. A score of men just in front melted in bloody fragments as a big-calibre shell landed. The air was dense with crackling bullets, and thick with the blood-chilling stink of explosives. The plain was carpeted with bodies, mostly lying still, but some crawling laggingly for cover. A man cannoned into me and fell, leaving a bloody patch on my shoulder.

But there was no sound of human voice in all the storm.

'These can't hurt you,' I yelled in the direction of my team. I had lagged behind under the weight of the gun. 'Can't they, though,' I said, as a draughthorse seemed to kick my right arm, and I went sprawling. 'A Blighty,' I next thought; then, 'They'll want the gun, even if you can't use it.'

Carefully I picked my way through the wire and the limp forms that dangled over it. Sometimes I was hooked up. The deep front line was manned by 46th men. I walked alongside a sap toward the second line. On top of the sap lay a man on his back, who was swinging both arms to and fro in a strange, restless action. Caution whispered into my ear to get into the sap ere I shared his fate in the bullet-lashed zone.

I walked circumspectly forward up the deserted sap holding the gun ready to send a blast of bullets at any enemy who might appear. It was a strange and exciting world. Little heaps of hastily shed German equipment littered the way.

There, in the farther trench, were the survivors of our company, with McDowall in charge. My team grouped about, two men short. We gazed up at the parapet, feet above our heads. My team was set to work digging a fire-step; as soon as it was complete I stepped up, heaving my gun into position.

The landscape lay sparkling in the snow, untouched by the hand of war. Two villages were set among the snow-powdered trees, and in one was a splendid château. It was the perfect Christmas card in reality. Horsed transports trotted serenely along a road a thousand yards away, and odd groups of the enemy moved about in confusion in the middle distance.

'Did ever a bloody man see such targets?' I crowed with delight, and poured magazine after magazine into the now galloping transport. That'll make 'em breezy, so early in the morning, I thought. Then I turned my attention to the parties. After this there was a lull.

Somewhere across the gap to the right the 4th Brigade had secured a lodgment. Our left also was hopelessly in air, and unsupported. The commander of another Lewis gun called to me, 'Keep your gun up, Mitch, while we strip and clean our gun.' So I kept my gun up, sending playful bursts of bullets into any stray parties of enemy who showed up.

'Right-oh, Corp,' called the other. 'Do your gun now.' I passed the gun down to Davies's capable hands and took his rifle. In seconds the gun was in its component parts on a groundsheet.

Three men ran towards the road at about nine hundred. I slid the sight up to the notch, marked nine, and pecked at them. They dropped prone, outlined clear in the snow. I continued firing, letting go a shot at each in turn. Two rose and ran, but the other lay still.

'Got one,' I reported delightedly to the boys below. A blast of fire from the sap-head forty feet half-right, called me up short. A group of long-backed helmets and levelled rifles had appeared. A sergeant to the right of me raised his rifle and fell dead across the parapet. Another man fell backward off the fire-step spouting blood. I swung my rifle at one enemy, the last to remain up. Big, fair and handsome he looked as I pressed trigger. But my rifle was sighted at nine hundred, and the bullet went high. He saw my rifle puff, and waved a cheery greeting before he got down. I was spitting with fury. 'Pass up that blasted gun. I'll fix him.'

The gun came, and I passed the rifle down. I settled the bipod firmly, shuffled my elbows solidly into the soil, and waited. For twenty long minutes as the gathering storm mounted, I stayed still. No Fritzy was going to grin at me while I shot at him and get away with it. What were we playing, anyway, war or hide and seek? He stood up again to get the purchase to throw a bomb. In a squall of bullets his face disappeared, his helmet flung high in the air.

A rifle snout appeared gently above the parapet, ready for a swift move. With a grin, I swung my gun to bear on the exact spot. What a soda! A dark face appeared beneath a porkpie cap. For a long fraction of a second we looked at each other's muzzles. My gun jerked, the magazine spun a quarter turn, and he was gone. Other heads appeared, also to be sprayed with lead.

Trench-mortar bombs began to burst along our trench. Men laughed at little things, or told a tale of enemy brought low. Once, a man feeding my gun leaned heavily against my shoulder as I bore on the sap shooting at head or arm as it appeared to throw bombs. Blood poured over gun and me as he bore heavily on my trigger hand. 'Lift him down, Bill,' I said, not daring to take my eyes off the sap-head. Bill Davies lifted him down, becoming drenched in blood as he did so.

Another man then stood by, clapping on filled magazines as the gun emptied them. Soon he, too, slumped over the parapet and fell slowly back into the trench. 'Pass the magazines to me,' I said to Bill. 'It is too expensive keeping two men up.' I felt a great certainty that none of these bullets could reach me. I had forgotten my damaged arm.

During a little lull, food was brought out, and the men began to eat. Bill was still busy with an improvised crew, stripping dead and wounded of ammunition and feeding the rounds, clicking into the empty drums.

Down on us came a sudden squall of shells. We realised that they were from our own guns. Leaning against the back parapet we cursed our gunners, who had not opened until now. One man in each bay held watch at tremendous risk. None of the fabled ancients ever held a more perilous watch, as the screaming, thudding pellets and fragments swept the ground like a hailstorm. I was well down with the others, convinced that a gun commander was too precious to stand up in that.

Three officers, of whom N.G. Imlay was one, survived in the battalion. They sped up and down, busy as blue-tailed flies, endeavouring to cope with each fresh danger. Not one of our company officers was left; McDowall kept calm wardship of us. Grim disaster could be felt tightening round us. But our shells pinned friend and foe alike inactive.

Sudden hollow detonations of bombs came from the rear. I had heard bombs too often at Anzac to be mistaken. I turned to McDowall. 'Better mount guard on the back parapet. It sounds as if the old front line is being bombed out.'

'Impossible,' he said.

On the heels of our words a man raced in from the sap gasping and reeling against the trench wall with his message of despair.

'Stand to arms. The other battalions are being bombed out. You are surrounded.' He was a 47th Battalion man, H.L. Dunnet, who had turned his back on a chance of safety, to warn the members of a sister battalion and to share their fate. This was gallantry of the very highest order. We, the survivors, owe him a debt that we can never hope to repay.

Swift orders followed. Men leaped to the back parapet. Heads and shoulders of the enemy showed in hundreds. Saps full of them. They had attacked in flank, with organised daring, by way of sunken saps. We had seen nothing of the preparations.

Lines of bombs burst down the trench in rear of our position. A dozen steel hats flew spinning in air, bullet-pierced at one time. Little parties of the 46th and 47th Battalions were being blown to pieces as they ran. It was a terrible and incredible sight. Our guns could not be fired over the back parapet, recessed as they were for heavy German machine guns. Big Bill Carr lay under his gun to raise it. Other guns were taken forward to fire. Our Lewis guns and rifles opened in a blast. A dancing crest of German steel helmets flew in the air.

Remembering our exposed backs, I remounted the front parapet and kept solitary guard. The last survivors of our sister battalions died in flame as they fought or ran. The enemy, with one accord, now faced our way, and a sleet of bullets beat about us. Half our force went face down in a few seconds. Evil, snaky German rockets hissed and spun all round us in a constricted circle, bringing to us startling knowledge of the proximity of the enemy on all sides. I wondered when the natural feelings of fear would come. Men actually laughed and asked, 'Hell, what do you think will happen now?' None could answer. But we did not think. That would come later.

'Bombers, to me,' called an officer. He led his little grim-faced band down the sap to battle for our existence. We saw none of them in life again.

The shrill din of Mills mingled with the heavier crash of German bombs in the sap behind. This sap was our only avenue of escape, and our bombers were striving to clear the road for us.

'Hand over all bombs,' called another officer. The gleaming segmented ovals appeared from pockets. A fresh bombing party was formed, and he swiftly led it out. These men caught the

Germans in the moment of their victory by the annihilation of our regular bombers, and drove desperately into their teeth with steel, bullet and bomb, forcing them back to the old front line. Our men then divided and cleared a space.

'Back to the old front line,' called Imlay, as a bloodied messenger raced in. I glanced round the trench as I swung my gun on shoulder. Bright mess tins lay about. There was half a loaf of bread with an open tin of jam beside it, and bloodstained equipment lying everywhere. The dead sergeant still lay massive on the parapet. Other dead lay limp on the trench floor. Wounded sprawled or sat with backs to the parapet, watching us with anxious eyes.

'You are not going to leave us?' asked one of me. I could not answer him, or meet his eyes as I joined the party moving down the sap. For some reason I felt that the guilt of deserting them was mine alone.

Here was a tangle of dismembered limbs and dead men. The air was heavy with the reek of explosives. One man, with his foot blown off, leaned wearily back. He had a Mills in his hand with the pin out. He would not be taken alive.

Our party—about sixty strong, with our two remaining officers—spread along the German front line, men with ready bombs and bayonets on the flanks. No other Australian force was left in the Hindenburg Line.

Our shells still screamed about the parapet. When this fire died down the might of the German Army would fall again on our outflanked few. Between us and our line stretched masses of brown wire, and fifteen hundred yards of bullet- and shell-swept level land, over which for a long time no messenger had lived in attempting to get across. Wounded men stood or sat silent on the upper steps of deep dugouts. I leaned on my gun, pondering the utter hopelessness of the position. A Fritz machine gun sat askew on the parapet. I was forming a project to bring it into action.

Word came from the left flank, punctuated by bomb bursts, 'Enemy bombing back. We have run out of bombs.' All stores of German bombs had been used up by our men. An officer's voice called clear, 'Dump everything and get back.' Discard my beautiful gun? They mightn't give me another!

Our few unwounded climbed the parapet. Heavily I started to climb the steep trench wall where a shell had partly blown it in. I looked up to see Bill Davies standing on the top amid the bullets, with hand extended to help me up. A vast indifference settled on me, as I stood on the parapet. Three yards out a man lying over a strand of wire called, 'Help me, mate.' I put down my gun and tried to heave him into a shell hole. He screamed with pain as I heaved, so I stopped. 'I can't do anything for you, old chap,' I said, and hoping that I would be forgiven the lie, 'I will send the bearers back.' 'Thank you,' he said. I picked up my gun and walked on. A shrapnel from the enemy flank churned the ground just in front, as I picked my way through the wire. A piece of shell fragment cut my puttee tape, and dropped the folds round my boot.

In complete indifference I trudged over the field, making the concession of holding the gun flat so as not to be too prominent. A man reaches a blasé stage after too much excitement. Once I thought of settling down and blazing defiance at the enemy with my last solitary magazine. But the thought of our wounded in the track of the bullets made me refrain.

Five-point-nines burst black on either hand, and futile bullets zipped about. They could do nothing to me. Silly cows to try.

Someone ought to tell them. I sheered across to have a look at a burned-out tank, around which shells burst regularly. It was still smoking hot.

The sunken road containing battalion headquarters was not far off. A little tremor ran through me. What would The Bull say at one of his Lewis gunners retiring armed from the enemy? What a blast of terrific wrath would be levelled at me. As I neared the road our company Lewis gun corporal (Davis) rushed out: 'You stuck to your gun?'

'Course I bloody well did.'

'The Bull wants you. Come with me.'

'Now for it,' I said resignedly. I stood to attention waiting the storm.

'Good man,' said The Bull. 'Take his name,' he said to the adjutant.

I wandered off in a daze. Men crowded about in congratulation as I mounted my gun and put Bill Davies in charge. Corporal Jack Fennel came to me. 'Let's go out for some of these wounded.'[2]

We laboured at the stretchers till darkness fell. The cold of the night would claim the rest. One man we found wandering in circles, blind from the shock of a bullet that had creased his head. He walked beside me with his hand on my shoulder, trustful as a little child, while we struggled along with another man on the stretcher.

Night brought a piercing cold. I collapsed from lack of strength to carry on. A sleet-laden wind soaked us. I had no coat. Shells fell heavily. At ten that night our relief battalion arrived, fit and strong. We moved out in a weary file in the teeth of wind and sleet. With cold fingers I took off the magazine and tried to unload the cartridge which lay ready beneath the guides. My numb hand slipped off the cocking handle, and the shot raced towards the grey sky.

At every step I lagged farther back from the others. Davies came down the line searching for me. Secure in his greater and more phlegmatic strength, he took the gun from my weakened hands and put it on his broad shoulder. It was death to collapse coatless out in this cold, wet night. Once I fell into deep mud. Shell holes and dead horses lined the way. 'Bill,' I said, 'I'm well goosed. We must find shelter and make a fire.'

The battalion had long disappeared into the night. At length we came to a factory by Vaulx. Through glassless windows we could see a number of men round little fires. On going in, we found that they were survivors of other battalions in the attack. We pulled out windowframes and made a fire. I went out and filled our dixies with snow, broached our iron rations, and made tea. Then we collected bags and German greatcoats, and made a bed.

Fierce and completely terrible were the tales those men told in matter-of-fact sentences. A listener could have gathered material for a hundred books, each more terrible than any yet written. Cold dawn winds were hissing through the place when we slept, dreamless, and unmoving. My gun lay close beside me. Someone might try to pinch it as a replacement!

The following afternoon we drifted in to the battalion. Two officers out of twenty-one and about forty men out of six hundred in the actual attack were still on their feet.

A pitifully weak company was all that remained of the proud, strong unit that had marched that way a few days before. Major Ben Leane and Captain Allan Leane, outstanding men, were 'gone west'.

The other battalions of the brigade cheered us as we marched. We looked our surprise.

That night in Bapaume we sat through a picture-show. It was strange and unreal to watch slapstick comedies with minds not yet detuned from battle. A few days later we stood on parade while 'Birdy' delivered some of his 'usual'. Then he spoke of our losses. 'These have not been in vain,' he said. Officers—hard-faced, hard-swearing men broke down. From the silent other ranks came a deep feeling of warmth and sympathy, a feeling that endured as long as the flame-racked years, and beyond.

I stood near a party of 16th Battalion officers, who were discussing the 48th's retirement. One said, 'They stepped up on the parapet, looked round, slung their rifles, lit a fag, and walked home.'

The war was only beginning!

9

Lull in the storm

The winter, and now Bullecourt, were just behind us, memories fresh, vivid and terrible. The future was flame-racked gloom, not good to contemplate. It was a strange, calm time of utter peace. Never is the day so restful as when the cyclone has passed. Never do the birds sing so sweetly as amid the wreckage of the trees.

And so it was with us. The more terrible the storm of battle the more complete and restful the following period in billets. Only one in each ten who went over on that April morning was here unscathed. Our trials and tribulations were over. Why live for tomorrow if today be sweet?

But we thought much, and said very little, of those faces that were gone, of those voices that were first in banter and song and that we would hear no more. Perhaps we grieved the less because we had such an excellent prospect of going west on the path that they had taken, and so were not very far from them.

Most religious orders have a ritual which claims to make man clean of sin. But the soldier who survives a desperate battle has no need of any ceremony. For he feels that, as steel is purged of all flaws by fire, so has he been cleansed by that other fire, and he can face the future without stain or weakness. Calm, tried and tested, he is haunted by no memory, save of the faces and voices of comrades left behind. Three days after the battle we were in huts at Fricourt. Barely the faintest rumble of battle reached us. No shells would crash through the roofs; no cold winds penetrate. Albert of the leaning Virgin was close, and beyond Albert was firm ground.

The few officers who had not been in the hop-over were very gentle with us, and seemed reluctant to issue the mildest order. Rather, it appeared that we were being petted. The officers were dashing round all day, like blue-tailed flies, attending various and mysterious conferences. Sergeant Major Max McDowall called me up on 15 April and asked, 'Lance Corporal Mitchell, would you like to take a guard tonight?' The shock of being asked, instead of being ordered, made me let myself in by saying, 'Right-oh, Serg-Maj,' when I should really have gone coy and pleaded my youth, inexperience and general unworthiness to do the duty of a sergeant.

Knowing the shortage of officers, and the unlikelihood of being visited, I carried on in the best old soldier tradition, by allotting the reliefs, and ordering the boys not to waken me throughout the night for any one less than the colonel. So, when the guard was relieved next night at five o'clock, and I received an order to report to the adjutant, my conscience was not quite clear. I stood more rigidly to attention before him, and looked more innocent, than was strictly necessary.

But from his few words, it appeared that by some magic I had lost my post as the right marker of the bad boys, and was henceforward to be regarded as a full and worthy member of the battalion. He even shook hands with me, and then led me before Colonel Leane.

As the colonel sat there talking to me I watched his face. A new and wonderful world rose about me. Here was the beau-ideal of his men—admired so greatly that men forgot to fear him. A clean-cut face, so strong that no one feature could betray weakness. A giant frame that was all bone and sinew. This was the man who had buried his most beloved brother four days before, and had carried on without a tremor. Here was the man who had led his company against impregnable Gaba Tepe and had achieved the impossible by getting them away again from the muzzles of the Turk machine guns.

None of our men, but had a special tale to tell of him. Now it was of Pozières, amid the worst of that hell of shellfire, where he went unflinching from post to post, and rather than come out empty-handed, carried a wounded man on his shoulder, easily as if the casualty were a babe. A man so great that he could not understand weakness in another. A man of mighty anger, yet one who would console a bereaved Digger in gentle and sincere language. He was the complete and classic warrior leader, and we could most easily visualise him armoured and with short sword at the head of a Roman Legion. His strength of purpose, undeviating character and pride permeated the whole battalion, even when battle was most deadly, at those times when panic can so easily sweep the ranks. We rather pitied other battalions, who, in their darkness, had not The Bull to look up to.

And this man behind the blanket-covered, candle-lit table, was saying things to me that made the weariness and desolation of the winter as nothing, and the hazards of Bullecourt well worth encountering a dozen times. My tongue refused duty. I listened in a wondering amazement. 'I will see,' he concluded, 'that you get a commission. I will not be able to send you to England for a course. You will carry straight on.'

He did not ask me, as a lesser man might, if I would like a commission; if I would accept one. He assumed that I would be honoured to take up the responsibilities and added risks involved. And he was right. He shook hands with me again and I blundered out with the adjutant. At battalion orderly room I affixed an uncertain signature to my commission papers.

I sneaked back to my hut to have a look at my old Lewis gun, standing in the corner, sleek and grey. I patted it, the good old gun that had led me through the maze of fear, doubt and danger to this. A score of questions were shot at me as to why I had been called up, but I could not have answered then.

Outside in the utter blackness a sweeping wind raged down from arctic wastes. It did little to cool me, and though I could hear my iron heels ringing on the road, my body seemed to have no weight. A little hard-bitten Tommy sat by a fire in a shelter at the crossroads. In greatcoat, and sheepskin gloves, he stayed close to the warmth. His face reflected the stolid outlook that probes neither past nor future. I can still see his calm profile beneath the peaked cap as the firelight flickered upon it. He told me scraps of epics of those 1914 days when they were swept like chaff by the storm of the great advance. I found myself telling him my story. He congratulated me in words strangely well chosen and apt.

For miles I walked those deserted windswept roads, and did not notice the rain that came lashing down. When, awaking from my daze, I found myself at my hut door, all was quiet-breathing sleep within.

'Back to Henencourt,' ran the rumour next morning and we joyously buckled our full marching order together. The rain that pelted in our faces did not damp our joy as we headed for that clean, green field on the hilltop beyond the forest. Our packs sat comfortably and firmly on our backs and we were almost grateful for the weight.

Albert was now out of field-gun range and was coming to life. It was strange to see civilians amid the all-pervading khaki. Solid-tyred, canopied service trucks rumbled in endless procession through the streets from which the debris of wrecked houses had been cleared. Beflagged staff cars slid impatiently through the traffic. Over all leaned the Virgin and Child. Green untouched fields once more, and down the long avenue of the paved road.

Henencourt again. The comfortable, whitewashed houses, straw-roofed, that stood flush against the road. White walls that were brown-splashed here and there by swift-moving cars. As our familiar blue and white shoulder patches showed in the village, women, girls and old men turned out to see again the faces of their friends. As each short company went by, they looked more and more anxiously as the numbers lessened, hoping against hope that they would still see the familiar faces and forms. We would be besieged by questions when we returned this night.

As we sat in the comfortable chairs by the big tables, well within the range of the warmth of the large stove, the catechism would commence.

'Where is Monsieur Zhack?'

'*Mort.*'

'*Ah Mon Dieu! Le pauvre garçon. Quel malheur! C'est la guerre terrible! Et Monsieur Blue?*'

Questions and answers while the wonderful eggs were eaten, the glorious coffee disposed of. 'But you are safe. You have the good luck.'

'Yes, they are saving me for the next battle.'

Perhaps it was that we imagined that the eggs were bigger and more carefully cooked than usual, that the potatoes were piled higher, that Yvonne fussed around us a little more intently than usual. *'C'est la guerre,'* was their watchword, through the battle zone; their hopeless reply to all, their losses, fears and tribulations.

But life was very good and very sweet to us. The poet who wrote 'A kiss snatched on the edge of hell is tenfold bliss,' knew the soldier.

The windy hutted field was a happy sight, and equipments thudded on the wooden floors with homely sound; the pounding rifle butts, as they were slung from shoulders, spoke of rest and peace. But for five days only did we stay there. Each dawn the naked forest showed a brighter tinge of green as fat leaf buds swelled. Each day there was a stronger suggestion of warmth in the winds that blew. For over there, winter is a time of bleak death, and each spring is life and joy new risen, while summer is glory.

And we had tasted the full bitterness of the coldest winter in forty years. And we had endured it among the indescribable horror of the waterlogged sea of mud that was the Somme battlefield. And then, in the snow, we had gone into Bullecourt. Each bud, each green blade of grass, every bird that sang, woke an answering chord of joy within us. On 22 April we packed up and moved to Millencourt. Not so nice, it was a bit closer to the war, and we thought we were due for a long rest.

But we settled down in the big windy barn comfortably enough. Walter Webb was my mate, and no man ever had a better one! We took it in turns to go to the cookers for our joint grub. When I suggested that he get breakfast each morning, while I drew dinner, he did it cheerfully. All I had to do was to sit up in bed each morning and eat what he brought in. He would even go back for the buckshee issue for both of us. But, of course, I would get the dinner. I did not have to get out of bed for that.

Anzac Day, and in fighting order the battalion marched to join the rest of the brigade at the sports held at Henencourt Wood. Throughout the long cold windy day, we watched the sports.

There was plenty of time to think over the fact that there were twelve men now with the battalion who had been present at the Landing. Even now the power of the nations was being gathered for another offensive, to be fiercer than anything that had gone before. How many of that twelve would be carrying their equipments next Anzac Day? But Walter and I ate none the less heartily that night in the cosy little home, when the bright and pretty Yvonne placed eggs and chips before us.

Three days later Walter brought my breakfast in as usual. As I was granted leave to Amiens, I did not get up at once. But Sergeant Major McDowall soon put a stop to my rest. 'Come on. We have to parade before the OC.'

Nine prim young NCOs lined up before The Bull, McDowall by reason of his senior rank being right marker. I, as a junior lance corporal, was on the extreme left.

'I am pleased to be able to tell you that your commissions have been granted, and that you are now second lieutenants. I congratulate you, and am pleased to have you as my officers. Put your stars up and carry on right away.'

'Party,' ordered McDowall, preparatory to marching us away, 'attention.'

'Second Lieutenant McDowall,' said the adjutant severely, 'that is a party of officers. You don't march officers away like defaulters. Salute, taking your time from the right, then break off.'

Rather dazed, but very rigidly we did so. The Bull was watching us intently. Each man of us was being appraised as to his value in the days to be.

Mac and I meandered together, orienting our minds to the new order, making no effort to secure stars. It rather seemed that we were reluctant to rip off our stripes. A last moment value seemed to have been set upon them. Yes, Norm Imlay might be able to rob a tunic to supply us. Must see him when he came in off parade.

'We will see Blighty again after all,' I told Mac. He agreed with a faraway look in his eye. He must have been thinking of a girl over there. And so an aimless hour went by until the adjutant found us.

'Still with your stripes up,' he proclaimed fiercely. 'You are disrated.' With that, he produced a little pocket-knife and ripped them off in the street. Onlookers gaped in amazement at such summary demotion. 'Now come with me and get some stars. You're regimentally naked.'

The stars were placed on our service tunics and we emerged as temporary gentlemen.

The parade was breaking off when I arrived again at the billet. Walter was straightening his gear.

'Wally,' I said, 'you will have to draw your own dinner.'

He looked up, puzzled as to my meaning. 'How is that. Aren't you hungry?'

'Yes, but I have to feed down the road.'

Then he saw the star, jumped up and congratulated me. The others crowded round, each in turn claiming his right to congratulate me. Those handshakes and words from mates with whom I had shared shelter, shell holes, food and danger, were very precious, and will be a treasured memory when most other things are forgotten.

NCOs came up for their say. These men might easily have felt some resentment at the most junior lance-jack shooting over their heads, but their words and tones were as the others. And when Corporal Jack Fennel—a man I had always admired—came up in his usual direct way and said 'I'm damn pleased. You deserve it thoroughly,' I could not escape the feeling that he was talking of someone else.

'Don't desert us altogether, now that you are an officer,' they said, as the mess-call rang through the village, 'and you will have to wet that star!'

It was strange filing into the mess, to sit down at tables after nearly three years of lining up with mess tins. It was a gala occasion when the new-fledged nine entered the mess in a body. The older officers, before whom we had had to stand at attention and say 'Sir', now came forward with congratulation, chaff and badinage, calling us by our nicknames. It took quite a little getting used to.

The Bull sat back with a fatherly, possessive look in his twinkling eyes. This mass promotion of officers from NCO rank was the outcome of his aversion to receiving any officers save those he had picked himself. He recognised the great value of peacetime training, but regarded reaction to fire as the supreme test of an officer.

Other armies, other ways. Some pinned their faith to social position as the qualification for commission. But the plunging five-point-nine does not ask to what school the man beneath belonged. And men do not ask more of their officer than that he can endure equally with them, keep his head, think well and fast.

Our relations with the ranks were the happiest. For my own part, to the very end of the war, I was never given cause to crime any man. Our promotion was proof to them that officers were not a class apart, but that commissioned rank was open to all.

Extraordinary good fortune attended our party. None was killed, though all save myself were wounded on many occasions. All were decorated one or more times. All types were represented among them. The imperturbable McDowall was offset by Bob Rafferty, of boisterous ways, Harry Downs, quiet, likeable and efficient, was a perfect foil for that big cheery Englishman, Wally Pritchard, who always had the most cheerful grin on his chipped dial. Wounded or well, that infectious grin was always there. In every battle, he contrived to get a face wound, until the legend became general that five-point-nines always bounced off his face.

It was heard afterwards that The Bull boasted, 'I have a bunch of young officers in my battalion who go into every action, and never get killed.'

That day we were all allotted to our different jobs. To my delight I was given the congenial job of being Lewis-gun officer. With a sergeant like Shepherdson, and a corporal like Jack Fennel it was the sweetest job in the battalion.

Beautiful warm spring days followed, full of the joy of life, while we laboured with the new material to shape it to the standard of the old. Funny incidents were in plenty before we had time to procure our officer's rigouts. One day, in the lazy sunlight, I was leaning against the billet doorway chatting with a group of old D Company.

An acquaintance, a brigade signaller, joined us. He noticed the mark of the departed stripe. 'Hullo,' he said, 'they have reduced you to the ranks again.' Then he noticed the stars and his eyes stuck out. 'What you got them on for?'

The boys assured him that they belonged to me. 'Hell,' he said, 'I thought you were one of these blokes who masquerade as an officer.'

Maybe he was right.

Military medals came out in orders for most of the new Loots, and it was now my turn to congratulate them. A few days later, the adjutant glared at me. 'The CO wants you.' With an uneasy mind I made my way to battalion headquarters, and stood before The Bull.

'Ah,' he said, 'your DCM has come out in orders. I want to be the first to congratulate you.'[1]

This was a bolt from the blue. I tried hard to think of anything I had done to warrant a decoration, but failed. Bill Carr, who had made a human tripod of himself, received the other DCM given to the battalion for Bullecourt.

The adjutant was waiting outside for me and led me round the battalion until he found a DCM holder who had spare ribbon. I was a little vague as to the value of a DCM as compared with the MM. But when Twining assured me that it carried a grant of twenty pounds, I regarded it most favourably.

Next day, the adjutant said to me casually, 'The Air Force has sent for you.' I jumped with eagerness. Life could hold nothing more. Fancy rocketing round the skies in a beautiful shiny plane.

'When do I go?' I demanded.

He was non-committal. 'You had better see the CO.'

No tide flows for ever. Always there is the high-tide mark from which is only retreat. I did not realise that as I hurried to headquarters with visions of packing that day, with Blighty and the delightful stink and roar of engines in the background.

'The Air Force has sent for me. When can I go, sir?'

But today was not yesterday.

The Bull fixed me with a look. 'Do you think I had you commissioned just to lose you? Go back to your job!'

To the adjutant I just said 'Gutzed,' and he grinned a knowing but unsympathetic grin. Seeking to extract some crumb of comfort from disaster I said to him, 'I was due for leave as a Digger. How soon do I go?'

'You are the junior officer of the battalion. You are right at the bottom of the list of officers. And you are picked to go into the next stunt. You won't get leave till after that.'

The world isn't fair. Things are dead crook. Reinforcement officers, who had never even been in the line, to go on leave before me. I looked on the dismantled gun with a bilious eye. The tale of how the gas impinged on the cupped head of the piston left me unmoved.

There is an historic field by the Albert–Amiens road shielded by a high bank. Ten months later our brigade stemmed a great attack at that spot.

On 12 May, the 4th Division formed a hollow square. General Birdwood arrived and spoke. He distributed decorations, and famous men stepped forward to receive them. Major Murray, VC, and Captain Jacka, VC, were the first to go.

The unusual sound of unchecked applause was heard as different recipients stepped forward. Many young NCOs received special tribute from the ranks, and we were left to wonder what was the untold tale of these men. We clapped loudly for Bill Carr. A man who will lay himself down in a sleet of bullets, so that the Lewis gun resting on him can be raised high enough to be effective, is indeed a man among men.

10
Back to Flanders

'Off to Belgium,' ran the rumour.

And reading the signs of the imminent move, we knew that the long lazy days were ending, and that soon we should again be under the flail of the guns.

Grey battle gear was being packed and stacked. Great rolls of grey blankets were placed on wagons. Grey machine guns were bedded carefully into grey limbers, there in the heavy shadow of the vivid forest. The hoofs of our sturdy transport horses stamped deep into the moist fertile soil. The grey wheels of war cut long swathes in the scented grass.

Hot sunlight and clear blue sky sped us from Henencourt. The battalion swung in perfect rhythm on its way, a thousand men moving as one. The thoughts of a thousand men quested out on their individual ways, some to probe the future in hope or fear, while most agreed to meet the demands of each day with stoic acceptance.

We were not to look again on that green countryside till the shadow of disaster rested on the world. Men who marched with us that day were doomed to die on our very bivouac field, a year later.

Grey painted trucks, bearing the familiar legend that eight horses or forty men were of equal value, awaited us. Soon there was the leisurely progress of the troop trains. Such a journey would be boresome to civilians. But we were soldiers. What need was there for hurry—to the welcoming guns? We would get there soon enough.

Civilians hurry to the comfort of their homes, the welcome of wife, family or sweetheart, or the urgent needs of a thousand little things. But we had none of these, so time with its fretting problems was allowed to slip by unheeded. Our attitude in those days was more than tinged with the fatalism of the East.

The spires of Amiens greeted us in passing. Little steeple-dominated villages were spread across the plains amid the crops and forests.

Small menless towns bestrode the rail. From the near fields, women and old men paused a moment from their labours to wave at our going. Others plodded on at their toil with a bovine indifference to the world outside themselves matched only by the beasts that cropped the grass about them.

Each truck door was lined with Diggers watching the changing panorama with keen and interested faces. All down the trains came the singing that made a bridge from the present to the best things of other days. We know today, in our reunions, how those same songs transport us back to the days of wonderful mateships that the reaper cut asunder.

Dark Etaples came leisurely to us, out of time and distance, then faster the train sped north.

The last time I came this way, the skies and the land were grey and bleak and drab. Now, all was blue above, with bright green of forest and meadow below, save where the fields were marked with a Milky Way of daisies.

Our rail journey ended out on the lowlands by Steenwerk. Stiffened muscles limbered up and iron heels clattered on the paved roads as we marched out to our appointed village billets.

'Erfs and murfs pour cat,' we demanded largely in our bedroom French. Madame of the farm protested volubly, 'Compris erf but no compris murf, messieurs.'

Pottsy, who prided himself on his schoolgirl French, explained: *'Pomme de terre, madame.'*

'Ah! Je comprends, je comprends. Tout de suite!' and she bustled away.

Three days we lazed there, drilling sparingly in the grassy fields, drowsing and smoking on flowered banks. From up in front came the rumble of guns. Strange, that when we halted, or stopped to talk, we always seemed to face towards that low thunder.

The machine of war turned another cog. On Sunday, 20 May, came the order, 'Prepare to move forward.'

Fully equipped men took their places, the companies merged together and the old battalion was on its way once more. The captive balloons swayed at their cables ahead, growing larger as we marched. The cobbles jarred feet used to mud, and the later carpet of grass. We sweated under the weight of equipment.

The sight of a bunch of Enzedders literally made our tongues hang out. They sat at a table placed on the grass beneath the leafy awning of a spreading tree. Lazily, and at ease, they sipped from their long glasses of cool beer.

Only the unwritten law that enjoined politeness towards our New Zealand cousins, prevented an outburst of thirst-evoked satire.

But, no inhibitions were there when we encountered the outliers of the 3rd Division with their oval colour patches. The fortune of war had kept the 3rd Division at hard training for months in England. While the other divisions had endured Pozières, the winter on the Somme and Bullecourt, the Third had only occupied comfortable trenches in a quiet sector.

Edged badinage flew fast at each group of onlookers. One chap in my platoon was the most virulent of all.

'You eggs-a-cook ———s have been malingering down here while we have been doing all the fighting. Wait till we get going, we'll show you what war is! Write home and tell your mothers you have seen some soldiers, you lead-swinging ———s.'

I turned to look at the speaker. He had joined us fresh from Australia, two weeks before.

'You,' I said pointedly, 'had better shut up. If any chipping is to be done, Kirk, here, should do it.'

Kirk, lean and silent veteran of Mexican rebellions, South Africa and Gallipoli, smiled dryly, 'I'd sooner have a beer.'

The observation balloons were overhead when we marched along a road. The signpost on the left said 'Belgium', on the right 'France'. The same grasses and trees grew on each side of the road. The beasts of the fields, the birds of the air, all looked the same on both sides. It is only the lusts of man that make the boundaries of nations into graveyards.

The balloons were behind us, the low ridges of Kemmel and Hill 63 close ahead, when we debouched into a field. There, working against the coming darkness, we erected small tents.

Three thousand yards ahead, rum-jars crashed, and flares made waves of hard light. The thin tapping of machine guns drifted back to us. Roads and rails surged with the traffic of war, working up to the pitch of an offensive. Hidden in copses and folds, all across the country, guns stabbed the sky with lances of brief light. Their thunder had the vibrating noise of great storm waves dashing against a rocky headland. Overhead, in the marching night hours, came the pulsing music of bombers. Flaming onions climbed in questing strings to bar their paths.

The stars lit the peace of our bivouac, and we slept well. We should find out all about tomorrow when it came.

Under my diary entry of 22 May 1917, I find:

It is marvellous. This is not war! The smiling countryside stretches round. Scarcely a shell hole to be seen. The observation balloons are behind; the guns all round.

Fritz bombards points close round in a lazy, desultory style. We sit and watch the spectacular effect of five-point-nines biting brown lumps out of waving fields of green wheat. Now a tree is skittled, now a new gap appears in a hedge.

Birds and beasts; the bees amid the flowers—all things are beautiful. Daisies and buttercups nod across the fields. The deep green of the tall trees all about is infinitely lovely.

I was thinking of these things in the peace of the evening. Overhead, our planes were as homing pigeons. Far up, gauzy, transparent and tiny was a German plane. *Crump*! A window-smashing detonation, a giant column of smoke rose from a point a mile away. High and higher it rose, greasy, black and dense. Surging as though constantly renewed from within, it climbed to the height of a tall mountain. The air was filled with the hum and zipp of falling metal. It was only one of our ammunition dumps blown up.

Fritz commenced to shell the place of the explosion. We turned out with glasses to watch the scene. All very spectacular, all very unimportant.

The calm, long days unroll, our time runs on happily. But, behind the drowsy restfulness of all things, forces are being gathered for another blow.

We who revelled in those sights of the beauty of nature, the warmth of the sun at noon, could not remember back beyond the mud-bound hell of Flers, had no other gauge to measure the changed conditions.

The battalion mess was a bright place, where alert young men crossed rapiers of polished, or not so polished, wit.

Our irrepressible Barney Allen had just acquired his second star, and would go out of his way to condole with our bunch of one-pippers. 'You poor coots,' he would say, 'don't you know what you are in for? One star—one stunt. I will get a line to myself in the casualty list now, but you poor cows only get put in the column— "Second lieutenants, unless otherwise mentioned".'

Barney seemed to derive great satisfaction from the prospect of a full line to himself in *The Times*, as against the undignified lumping of the 'unless otherwise mentioned'.

I have deliberately lit the third cigarette from a match before an attack, and found myself the only survivor of the three. I have conscientiously run counter to the accepted superstitions of wartime on many occasions. But there seemed to be something in this 'one star—one stunt' theory.

I shall always feel, that if there be a power or fate that guards some so carefully while dooming others so relentlessly, that power left me quite unshielded in the battle of Messines.

It may be a fantastic theory that death is other than a matter of mere chance. But I have seen so many men who foresaw with certainty their approaching end, that I would be the last to scoff. I have known with equal certainty, many times, that I would be unharmed.

After darkness closed another day of peace, I led a large and casual fatigue party to a farm that was a Garden of Eden sort of place. Like giant toads sat the nine-point-two battery in the concealment of a row of leafy trees and a tall hawthorn hedge. Ancient and serene was the tree-shielded farmhouse.

Two trains of ammunition were we to unload.

The first came at 9 p.m., with its burden of great shells. We gathered round the trucks, and regarded the shells in puzzlement. They were too heavy for two men to carry, but there was no room for more men to take hold.

While we held a wordless conference, one man acted. He pushed a shell over the side, to thud down on the grass. He dropped on his knees behind it and rolled it along the sward. Without spoken word, all along the train men dropped doors and pushed shells over. Soon a hundred men were rolling shells to the ditch, where they klocked to rest among tens of thousands of their kind. A refinement of technique developed when some stood up to roll the heavy shells with their feet.

'Great Scott,' said a regular gunner officer to me, 'those chappies of yours are juggling the shells like coppers. Would you care to come and have a spot?' I followed him to the hospitality of their underground mess.

A British regular's mess makes a deep impression on a

newcomer used to the boisterous routine of our messes. The correctness, the extreme courtesy, the absolute changelessness of age-old things, causes the less-polished Digger to toy furtively with the idea of making a good, healthy *faux pas*.

One gained the impression somehow, that the war was an intrusion into the social order; a thing to be tacitly ignored. The conversation floated airily round unimportant things. In our messes officers would be discussing problems of fighting with single-mindedness known only to cruder beings. Yet, one glance at the clean-cut faces of these regulars showed that they were indeed soldiers and men. The beautifully appointed table was laid. Trained waiters were bringing the first course. A glass of whisky awaited my disposal.

There was a heavy crash close by; the scream of a shell— another crash. The officers grabbed gas masks and climbed the stairs. I drank my whisky and followed them. I was too old a soldier to take the risk of leaving that unconsumed.

I looked interestedly into a shell hole that was right against a gun. The blast had stripped away the camouflage. The edge of the crater was within a foot of the mass of shells that filled the ditch for a hundred yards. A trail of bloodspots showed black on the grass.

As I followed them, they led to a group of trees. There, I found my party, sitting and smoking in the velvety night. One of my men had had his cheek gashed. Four Tommies had been hit. Gunners and Diggers working swiftly together had got them away at once.

No more shells came out of the night, so I strolled back to the mess.

'Where have you been?' they demanded as I re-entered the mess.

I was a little puzzled. 'Up to the guns,' I said.

'Why on earth did you go up there? We went back to the deep dugout.'

'Why, to see to the wounded,' I replied.

The battery major looked at me as one who reproves in sorrow.

'But surely that is work for your NCOs?'

The gap between our viewpoints struck me then. But of course they had no steely-eyed Bull to ask nasty questions in edged tones, such as, 'Why were you under cover and your men exposed?'

I took refuge in the Englishman's sure retort by explaining that in the AIF such separation of men and officers under fire was 'not done'.

My lame reply produced a thoughtful silence, which was broken only by the first course.

We were a long way apart from our English brothers. In our army, the man was nearer to the officer, the officer nearer to the man. I would not have it any other way. We were not hounded by the fear that our men would not respect us if we associated too closely with them. If they did not respect us, well—blast 'em!

Journey's End, with its five company officers sitting together in a front-line dugout, could never have been written of an Australian company. Rather would you have seen each platoon officer glumly feeding from his mess tin among his men, the company commander sitting in solitary glory. I have often had my rum issue swiped by some dissolute private when my back was turned. And cigarettes—blazes! While I had one left, the platoon considered they had an option on it.

I completely enjoyed myself throughout the cheerful, but cathedral calm of that dinner. Nothing was missing, not even the nuts and cigars. Gently and obliquely they probed for information as to the ways of Australians. The clipped, concise English was a delight to hear. But, even in my enjoyment, I had a sneaking feeling that my hair was fuzzy, my loin-cloth somewhat frayed.

From dinner I went to shift the men back, the first train having been unloaded, to a point beyond the immediate danger of the blast, should the stacked shells be exploded. At every move there was a subaltern or captain waiting to lead me back to the mess. My glass of 'White Horse' stood filled and to hand.

Lit up and talkative, I dropped that hardy annual, supposed to be the Englishman's opinion of the Australians. 'Stout fellas, stout fellas, but socially—impossible.' A shocked hush followed. That one should tread so callously on sacred ground, that any Englishman should so forget the laws of hospitality to make such a statement.

'No one but a cad would say such a thing about your people,' they assured me earnestly.

I was tickled to pieces over it. My worries about the social aspect! I more than suspected that some hairy Digger had formulated the slander out of the depths of his own foul mind.

With an inner glee that may have been the whisky, or even the happy recollection of their horror, I went to where the firefly glow of cigarettes placed my men.

'Come on home, you lazy ——s,' I said.

I was vaguely trying to gauge what would have been the result of my using such an expression in their mess. Bateman alone could have done justice to that idea.

The fatigue party followed me placidly in that scented hour before the dawn, along hawthorn hedgerows, past tiny canals, over the flower-strewn meadows, until we were home. Lights climbed and fell beyond Kemmel. Toc Emmas crashed in Ploegsteert. Guns about us anticipated the cockcrow of dawn.

We should worry. We had filled a night with honest toil, and would have this day off duty.

Here is a typical day taken from my diary dated 26 May 1917.

The authorities have decreed that there shall be one bath per man, per day, per haps. So Pottsy and I took our families into Nieppe where there is an almost luxurious bathing establishment. We sat and sizzled up to our necks in hot water.

But I had seen and liked Nieppe, and evening found me back there again. Not yet satisfied with my explorations, I turned my steps to where the spires of Armentières showed, two kilometres distant, through the long shaft of the Flemish avenue.

Green fields flanked the road. The stream that wandered so lazily through the countryside repictured the scarlet glow of sunset. The white walls, red roofs, spires and towers of Armentières, set in emerald, stood beauty etched in the last level light of day.

I talked with Mademoiselle of Armentières. A charming brunette is she, of great poise, a Parisian taste in frocks.

But it is a silent town, where few civilians live in fear of the hammers of doom. The arrogant khaki of the alien dominates the place, with swaggering indifference.

At ten o'clock I was dining in the officers' café, fortifying myself adequately against the walk home. Contentedly I strolled through the arch of the interlaced trees.

Three thousand yards away, Very lights rose and fell in graceful curves. Bunches of coloured lights spouted and spread. A line of parachute flares hung and burned with their fierce arc-light glare. Rockets shouldered high up their spark-traced ways. Occasionally from the trenches came the crunching explosion of rum-jars, the distant tapping of Maxims.

Big guns, near and unseen, would leap to life, each lighting the world for one harsh, brilliant second. The thunder voice would shatter the night, till one would think that never again could there be the partial silence of nature. But as the last echo died, only the climbing white smoke cloud would tell from whence a gun had fired, the muted night noises would be heard again. Then, with a spear of intolerable light, another gun would rip the night. Coveys of big shells whistled, grumbled, or sighed as they passed high overhead. Just routine stuff.

All is peace, perfect peace.

A favourite pastime during the unoccupied hours of day was to watch the flying shells of the nine-point-two howitzers. The eye had to be trained to look above the gun. Detonation, flames and turmoil would mark the firing of the gun, and the quarter ton shell was on its way—a small black object, moving so fast as almost to beat vision. Then it would be easier to watch as it climbed on its journey into the stratosphere. Smaller and smaller it would become, till at last the keenest eye could no longer see it.

Occasionally eighteen-pounder shells could be seen in travel, but only when one was standing well behind the gun.

I have seen rifle bullets in travel like a streak of silver. One so seen killed a man. I have also caught glimpses of enemy shells falling. But the possibilities are governed by light, angle, range, and many other things.

We had occasional reminders that there was a war on. It happened so one night. The camp was wrapped in deepest slumber, only the gas sentries awake.

In my dreams I was in Blighty by the sea. A dream girl was beside me. We were watching the wreck of a steamer, fast on the rocks. A yelling demon crew swarmed up on deck. With sledgehammers they commenced to stave in the plates of the ship. There was a din beyond comparison.

I woke. Gas gongs were ringing all down the line. Eighteen-pounder cartridge cases, lengths of railway iron, were being hammered.

'Gas! Gas! Gas!' men were calling.

Within the tent was darkness, men were stirring. Outside, running feet, men called sharply of the danger that was on us. Sharp from sleeping to urgent danger, the moment of waking was utterly beastly. Even within the tent, sharp, biting, pungent was the first reek of gas. Panic, unreasoning and wild possessed me. It was the sort of panic that squeezes the heart with cold fingers, maddens the victim to scream and run.

My mask! Where was it? I could not remember. My frantic fingers met everything but the gas mask! After what seemed long minutes, my fingers touched it, and I remembered then where I had left it.

There was a swift straightening of rubber bands that would get crossed—the mask was on.

One officer was struggling with his mask. 'I can't get it on, I can't . . . Put your mask on, skipper. Put . . .'

Gurgling horribly he collapsed writhing at my feet. Still fear-ridden, I felt at his mask. It was turned inside out or some way, but in the darkness I could not straighten out the tangle.

The sound of a friend strangling to death did nothing to soothe me. I felt completely helpless. Unclothed, I could not locate matches. In desperation I thrust the mouthpiece into his mouth, clamped his jaws shut and pinched his nostrils tightly. After much fumbling, the elastic at last clipped into place. Many times I felt round it to see that it was still in position.

I walked outside, and strolled along to see if the company were all masked. Across the countryside, waist-high, was a misty cloud, rolling slowly along in the light breeze.

Men spoke sleepily and rolled over to snore, slobbering into their gas masks. Awful fuss to make about a little thing! The clamour of the night gave way to silence once more. But God help our poor civilians if they ever encounter poison gas, unprepared.

'How'd you like the gas alarm last night, Mitch?' Pottsy asked.

'Gave me an 'ell of a fright,' I replied.

Pottsy laughed.

Not all awakenings were like that, however. Two mornings later I woke to find that practically all the young officers in the battalion were either sitting on me or trying to displace others so that they might so sit. When they observed that this treatment had really wakened me, they started a round of congratulations.

'What the hell?'

'You're going to Hyde Park to get your DCM from the King.'

'Don't believe it,' I said, and did not for one moment dream that I should.

But the information had come from brigade headquarters, and all day long various ones came up to envy my good fortune. 'When I'm on the boat,' I told them, 'I'll believe it.'

The adjutant came to me in the evening, with the air of one granting a great favour: 'Oh, Mitch—it has been decided not to send you to the investiture. You will go into the next stunt as Lewis-gun officer instead.'

That was all right. It stopped the mucking about, and uncertainty.

I oriented my mind to the battle, and went regularly with those who gazed for hours, memorising that great relief map of Messines.[1]

It was an amazing and ambitious piece of work. In the open, carefully fenced, constructed in miniature, were the forests, the farms, the rivers, the villages, all the details of the Messines area.

So big was it that hundreds could gaze at one time. Tens of thousands came to look and walked on to play their parts in the drama of life and death.

On 30 May officers took parties of NCOs to the trenches before Messines. Warm through the wheatfields we strolled. Forest-clad Hill 63 rose from the plains.

'Ploegsteert,' 'Red Château,' and 'Kemmel' said noticeboards.

We wandered through the great labyrinth of trenches. Before us was Messines on an island ridge. The village looked like an old Roman ruin. Our massed guns were shelling slowly and persistently. Red and black dust-clouds arose as shells burst. Twelve-inch howitzers were emplaced in front of eighteen-pounders!

We stood on the parapets to see better, and to show our contempt for the enemy cowering before British might. Only once, a piece of whizz-bang that smacked into a U frame, alongside my face, caused me to think hard.

Homeward we walked, in the heat of the afternoon. Well pleased were we as we trudged amid the leafy beauty of the road at the foot of Hill 63. Dust swirled beneath the grinding limber wheels as they swept past us. Pleased were we at the massed guns that bayed so confidently from every cover. And pleased were we at sight of the well-trained 3rd Division. They were out to show us that at their first blooding they would be at least the equal of the older divisions.

'Eggs-a-cook divvy,' as a term of reproach, died with the taking of Messines.

Pleased too were we at sight of the stalwart figures of our trusty New Zealand cobbers. Only one complaint had I against them.

As we walked in the hot sunlight my tin helmet was slung for comfort at my waistbelt. An Enzedder picked me from amongst various passing officers for the honour of a very regimental salute. He probably chose me on account of the 'A' on my colour patches. One cannot return a salute bareheaded. I halted in front of him, after much fumbling detached the tin hat, put it on, and regimentally returned the salute. Then I replaced the helmet at belt, and duty done walked on. I did not say anything, but gave him such a look.

A truck dropped us at Pont Nieppe. We dined, and returned to camp at 11 p.m. The mob was carousing in a nearby *estaminet* on champagne and eggs. We joined in the uproar, and so to bed.

In the small hours, a big shell howled to earth beyond the camp. Another crashed in the midst of the camp. Bingley told me to get up. But the familiar shells roused none of the grisly horror of a night gas-attack, or else my mind was again tuned to battle.

'C'est la guerre,' I answered drowsily and turned over. Like giant footsteps each succeeding shell stamped farther beyond the camp, and all was rest again.

Vivid days were these. Enemy planes would swoop, greatly daring, from dizzy heights on to observation balloons. Observers would float from spreading parachutes, gently down to their fourteen days' leave. Fierce flame would wrap the balloon, charred fragments drift smoking to earth. A lead-spitting countryside would speed the wildly twisting plane on its way. Another iron cross.

The tempo of preparation was speeding up. Mars was buckling his armour. My diary entry under date of Sunday, 3 June, tells of another routine visit to the front line.

The moment of inspiration has left me and I am cold, prosaic and sleepy. How am I to describe our visit to the trenches? Our barrage that made an impenetrable hard-ruled line of flame-split smoke. The mighty spouts of earth that made of Messines a hell. The black of high-explosive smoke, the white shrapnel smoke, the red clouds of brick-dust, the white and mounting spray that told where shells struck water, the man flung a hundred feet in air. How can I describe the wall of multi-coloured dust and smoke rising from the enemy lines to merge with the blue of the heavens, up and up from its flame-torn base?

The mad, terrific drumming of our guns pulsating to furious heights till we are stunned by a primeval frenzy of joy to leap full up on the parapet, there to yell our puny defiance. These are our good British guns that roar with ten thousand voices. Now it is the turn of the arrogant enemy to taste the full bitterness of death and disaster.

Victory is in the air!

A plane falls like a broken-winged bird from the very gates of paradise.

How can I describe the little drama of the enemy plane that dived out of space spitting fire at a balloon as it hung placidly in mid air? How the little demon failed and fled, twisting in wild flight.

And how shall the genius come to me that I may describe the glowing night that glides over the brilliant glory of day? Words are too feeble a medium to paint such a canvas.

This day is ended—GAS!

But that day was not ended. I sat there in the tent, tired mates asleep, and struggled in the candlelight to find words to describe the fury, the beauty and the magnificence of the happenings of the day.

My eyes had smarted for some little time, then I realised what it was as the gongs leaped to strident life. I wrote 'GAS', clapped my diary away, woke those still sleeping and went out into the moonlight. Misty, white and low, the cloud came rolling across the plain. The out-thrust streamers were even now among us. The sting and smart of gas became more acute. I put on my mask. In their tents our men had drowsily put on masks, and were dozing again.

Again and again throughout the night came the rolling gas waves heralded by the clangour of gongs. At about 3 a.m. the last wave came. I heard someone grumble as he put on his mask, 'Gawd help the first Fritz I catch.'

At dawn we packed and moved forward to where there was a siding to the left rear of Hill 63. The railway led past the tin huts that we occupied. Tall trees in full leaf were all about. With zero two dawns hence, all across the plains thundered our heavy guns. The great unrest of battle was on man, beast and machine. The battalion had gone forward to close support. Headquarters and a nucleus remained.

Laden parties toiled in the sunlight towards the line.

A massive twelve-inch railway gun beside our camp loosed off by day and night in stunning double detonations. Smoke-rings would climb high and far at each shot.

Our band, to justify its peaceful existence gave us a concert as the sinking sun made long shadows of the trees. The bandsmen waited the command with instruments poised. Overhead by a threadlike cable hung an observation balloon. Long-eared mules all about us in the open field ceased their cropping a moment to look on boredly.

Four things happened together. Up came the baton, the instruments blared, the mules bolted noisily, a big tired-sounding shrapnel burst with an organ note near the balloon, the two observers leaped out and floated to earth beneath the spreading snowy shapes of their parachutes. It all seemed so beautifully timed to the conductor's baton, that the music was drowned by an instant roar of laughter.

That night we went to bed early. A crackling noise from an adjoining hut woke us. We turned out to see two of our officers in gay pyjamas looking disconsolately at their blazing hut and worldly possessions going up in smoke. Ammunition spluttered like crackers. We made a tarpaulin muster of blankets and clothes, warmed ourselves at the blaze, and turned in again.

Another alarm came. Long-range shells whined down to explode about us. We ran for the cover of a near ditch. A stone caught me between the shoulder-blades so that I gasped with pain. A little higher, and my diaries would have finished then. Back we went to bed when the hail had ceased, taking care to have our tin hats close handy.

Another hot day came, the last still thoughtful day before attack. Throughout the hours of light and darkness the unending thunder of the guns continued. Dump after dump went up in oily smoke, and night came down again. We went to bed in pensive mood. Far into dreamland was I, when someone said, 'Get up, it's after three!'

Oh, yes, of course, there is a war on. The railway gun deluged the night with sound. In yapping chorus from all over the countryside, the guns were baying, neither faster nor slower than usual. Flares rose and fell beyond Kemmel, Hill 63, and Ploegsteert, in just the usual volume.

The night wind blew through our pyjamas as we waited the zero moment of 3.10 a.m. The long drawn-out agony of the enemy would be ended soon. We knew that tens of thousands of men were waiting to leap forward, thousands of waiting guns with mountains of shells to hurl, and scores of tanks ready to grind forward.

'A minute to go,' said someone solemnly. Many men would die in the next hundred seconds.

The breeze stirred the tall trees overhead, light-clad, we shivered a little. The ground leaped beneath us, again and again. Nineteen great mines, thousands of tons of explosives gone up. Rockets flared and spread.[2]

The belly of a low-hung cloud reddened to a dull glare. Such a glow do you sometimes see when bushfires, gale driven, devour a dense forest. The glare brightened, faded, and was gone. We knew it to be the funeral pyre of complete battalions.

All together the guns opened, stunning comprehension. The greatest artillery fire of all time. Swelling and roaring it climbed up and up to climax beyond incredible climax. Waves of sound beat about us in a madness of vibration, a debauchery of sound.

All past standards of measurement were useless. We rather took pride in the fact that we could stand calm and upright in the bedlam, that we were prepared to move forward into that storm with stoic indifference. We watched a while. The flame-spears leaped undiminished from the ground, earth and sky still shuddered before the blasts of sound.

We went back to bed and slept.

11

Messines

Daylight was flooding in through the door, but the thunders of the night continued unabated.

No haste was laid upon us. Our few headquarters men had to rejoin the battalion about midday.

Leisurely I got up, checked over my battle kit, field glasses, maps, compass, ammunition, flare pistol, service pistol, food and so on.

Then came the packing away of all other gear in the valise. This had to be done with the thought that these things might be finished with, that alien hands would unpack them seeking those personal articles that could be forwarded to next of kin in memory of another who would not return. I never saw any carelessness in this little ceremony among my friends. Letters were scanned, and burned or kept. Nothing was retained that might not be shown to the world.

And so the valise would be strapped up and sent down to the transport lines, with a last idle glance of wonder as to whether we should see it again.

At 10 a.m. I started out, accompanied by my dependable Sergeant Shepherdson, tall, cheerful and taciturn. A veteran of Gallipoli and Pozières was he, good company in bad times.

We sweated under our equipments as we headed towards the left shoulder of Hill 63. Deep shell holes thickened on our pathway. Dead horses were swelling in the sun.

We gravitated towards the wreck of one of our planes, intent on thieving the machine guns. A Tommy guard eyed us suspiciously. Odd shells made trees about us, and the stink of donnerite, acid and biting, was familiar and hateful.

We were now among the field guns with their tireless, unending yapping. We followed the roadway round Hill 63, a camouflage hedge hiding us from enemy eyes. By the roadside was dust-coated wreckage of battle, and we were pleased to drop into the deep trench beyond.

In virgin bush, you have seen the ant hills with radiating paths worn deep in the ground. You have watched the busy insect parties laden and unladen, hurrying impersonally on their multitudinous errands. Just such a place was this. Men slugged forward under the weight of plum-pudding bombs, Stoke bombs, and the various other munitions. Men laboured back with uncomplaining burdens on stretchers. Walking wounded came proudly along displaying that elated confidence so general in a successful offensive.

We found the battalion in the support trench, high up the rise of Hill 63. They were in the stalls watching a drama. We, too, became engrossed, our glasses levelled.

The second phase of the battle was being enacted before us. Messines, on the ridge in front, was smothered in shell bursts from end to end. But now these were enemy shells. Beyond Messines could be seen the oblique avenue of Huns' Walk. Sloping to the right front the terrain ran downward to the bed of the Douve River.

Our gun thunder was at another hysterical climax. The farther landscape was bounded by trees of smoke, renewed and re-renewed. All beyond was smoky eclipse.

Like sword-strokes, the white puffs of eighteen-pounder shrapnel slashed at roads, trenches and paths. Ripped and limbless trees, outlined against the sombre background, sombre even in the full glare of the midday sun.

In the near foreground a fleet of tanks was grinding forward. Like prehistoric monsters they seemed as they rolled and plunged. Now their snouts would be raised to the skies, now they would plunge from sight into a mighty shell hole. Dust and smoke would rise in clouds as they fought to free themselves. Slowly they rolled and lurched past the right flank of Messines, cheered on by our watchers whose voices would not carry three feet in the din.

As the tanks ground their way ahead there moved with them a storm of big high velocity shells churning the country, constantly hiding the monsters in smoke and dust. Time and again we exclaimed as a tank seemed to have been obliterated. Each time the tank thrust an ugly nose clear of the murk and waddled on.

This storm of shellfire that sought to smash the tanks seemed to convey an impression of devilish and unbridled fury. The sound of the snarling explosions of these shells carried to us even above the mad thunder of our own barrage. Eyes glued to glasses, we watched.

'Oh! What a pretty little thing!' exclaimed Lieutenant Charlie Stoerkel.

'Eh?' we grunted. Pretty was no expression to cope with that hell of flame and smoke in front.

'That dear little bird.'

Forty feet ahead, on the wire sat a little robin. We levelled our glasses. Perky and bright-eyed it sat, scarlet and brown. All the thunders of war were nothing to it. We watched and admired a long time. When we looked at the battle again, the tanks were well ahead, still un-hit.

The lines of our infantry moved forward in their ranks behind the tanks, looking from our distance as though they had nothing more urgent in hand than sightseeing. Two tanks reached Huns' Walk, and diverged in opposite directions. They were obviously in action. Their machine guns continuously jetted needles of flame, and their small guns belched smoke from time to time.

Peer as we would, we could sight no enemy through our glasses.

Our infantry went to earth at their objectives, the tanks belatedly returned.

The hedge of our shell smoke moved farther into enemy territory; the tempo of the guns slowed a little.

The wreckage of battle, the limping assisted and unassisted wounded, the stretcher parties, commenced to drift back.

Like a tide, the carrying parties commenced to flow forward with all the needs of an embattled front line.

'Prepare to move,' the word came down the trench. And so

we prepared, but it was near midnight before we were ordered to go forward.

On the tail end of the battalion moved Guthrie and I with our headquarters parties. Not a shell all the afternoon had landed in the old front-line area. But, on the old enemy front line, the shelling had been intense.

We emerged into the No Man's Land of yesterday. Up we moved towards the right shoulder of Messines. There was a hesitation in front, and Lieutenant Guthrie and I made our way up to investigate. Our leading man had lost touch. We took the lead and searched.

A nightmare storm of fire broke over us. Great shells landed to left and right, fierce flame towers in the dark. The concussion jostled and shook us. Homeless and shelterless we wandered, weary and fearful. Bars of stinking smoke hid our way. Shells right in our path changed our direction.

Seeking shelter in deep shell holes, we would be moved on again by a fresh shell shower that threatened to entomb us. The night was filled with the roaring and feral fury of the shells.

An hour before dawn, by sheer accident, we came on battalion headquarters. We placed our men in a sap. The fury of the bombardment continued. I put my groundsheet over me and lay, waiting the flame that meant finish. Instead, I slept.

With the dawn, we found that enemy gunfire had ceased. It was like a great weight lifted from us.

The first sight that greeted me as I climbed up on the parapet was a Fritz. He wandered, stick in hand, with vague incomprehension, as though the only thing left of life to him was the power of halting movement. His idiocy was not to be wondered at, if he had survived our barrage. A New Zealander carelessly directed him back towards Hill 63.

All about were linked up enormous shell craters. Here and there were concrete block-houses, mostly unharmed. Some of them had been uprooted and stood on edge, concealing the entrances and the living or dead within. Near the entrance to each pillbox was a carefully piled stack of dead defenders. They had been mostly placed there by their comrades, a few by our men. They were black-faced from the manner of their deaths, swollen and already putrefying. Amid the shattered German trenches were dismembered bodies of the fore-doomed garrison.

My instructions were to await orders at battalion headquarters. Colonel Imlay had charge of both 47th and 48th Battalions in the first half of the attack. Colonel Leane had been retained at brigade headquarters.

The idea of loafing round battalion headquarters, out of the fun, and right in the heaviest of the shellfire, did not appeal to me in the slightest. So Shepherdson and I set off across country, heading for our battalion front.

Bushes survived among the scattered shell holes, grass was green beneath our feet. We passed over the ripped *pavé* of Huns' Walk, the tank tracks of yesterday showing clear beside the scarred tree trunks. A few bullets pinged about. A whizz-bang raced overhead to burst beside the road. We trudged on in fatalistic indifference.

The first company we dropped in on was consolidating a newly captured section of trench. The men were digging furiously. Several of our dead and wounded were lying about. Charlie Stoerkel had just been carried away badly wounded.

We showed only our eyebrows over the top. But, full out in the open was Walter Webb with his party on the corners of a stretcher. They trudged at a slow walk, with sublime fatalism. Throughout the days, they endured their tenfold perils, never sparing themselves in the service of their stricken mates. No braver men trod the battlefields than these who never fired a shot.

Heavy sniping fire was coming from a pillbox and hedgerow. The left flank rested on a pillbox. Beyond was in the air, a gap of unguessed width. We collected all Lewis guns and German guns, and set them up in a circular strong-post of twenty-one machine guns. Any enemy trying to get into that gap would have all his birthdays at once.

There were cartloads of Fritz ammunition to play with.

While I was setting the guns, Kirkpatrick, our old veteran of sundry wars, became annoyed at three snipers. Men who saw it told me that with his usual calm, pipe in mouth, he put his head over the parapet. Bullets smacked all about him and sizzled past his ears as he picked the snipers off, one after another in three deliberately aimed shots.

Like a half-tide wreck in the near front was a large artillery pillbox, the snouts of two 'seventy-seven' guns protruding.

Shep and I wandered out, and rolled a bomb in for safety. We found the usual stack of blue-black dead beside. Inside were tiers of bunks, weapons against the wall, pictures from *La Vie*, and a thousand interesting things. A small wash leather bag caught my eye. It was crammed full of maps with battery positions marked in. Also there was the photo of a beautiful woman.

We returned to our lines to study the maps with the nearest company commander. He suggested that they be taken back to battalion headquarters at once. So I left Shepherdson to keep a watchful eye on our firing-line interests while I went back to my rightful place at battalion headquarters.

Fritz sped me in his usual genial manner, rifle shots, machine-gun bursts and an odd whizz-bang.

One message entrusted me was to direct Corporal Strugnell's party up to the line. I had met them on the way up, and sheered across to intersect the right spot. But Strug was not there, though his party sat about.

'He stopped a brick with his napper,' said one.

Now, Strugnell was a cheery soul, an interstate footballer with his full share of beef and brawn and bone.

I inquired if he had been badly knocked.

'No,' snorted my informant, 'but he damaged the brick something terrible.'

All about the pillbox that sheltered battalion headquarters, great shells thundered. Dead and wounded were more numerous than when I last passed this way. Ginger Clarke, our RSM, was outside, quietly directing his men. I admired his detachment as I slid through the low thick-walled doorway out of the ravening day.

Across the pillbox were the various functions of headquarters in operation. Men wrote at tables, signallers sat at their instruments. Some officers and men slept. Candles lit the windowless place with wavering light. Shadows danced on the concrete walls. Men could not stand upright. The unventilated place was a reek of foul air and tobacco. Every few minutes it would leap and ring to the impact of shells. The boom of explosion would come in to us muffled.

Colonel Imlay questioned me as to the position on the front, then he looked at the maps.

'These may be very important,' he said, 'you will take them back to brigade headquarters right away. I will send another officer with you. If one is hit, the survivor will get the maps through.'

He ordered one of his 47th Loots to go with me. It seemed to my untrained mind that he was rather prodigal in using officers as runners, but mine not to reason why, mine but to do a guy. Neither of us would be hit, and it would be pleasant to get away from that blasted place.

Afresh into the day, we found that it was hailing metal. High-velocity shells earthed with fearful rushes, to burst twenty feet away, smoke column towering over us. Instinctively we separated so that the one shell would not reap both. I remember thinking, 'It is very noisy, and very terrifying, but not really dangerous. Still, I will be glad to get out of it.'

Overhead, like the cracks of doom, great black shrapnels burst. The ground whipped in sprays of dust from the driven fragments. Something clanged off my tin hat. The 47th officer swayed on the edge of a shell hole, great surprise on his face. Then he fell forward.

My job was not to tend him, but to get back with the maps, so I trotted out of the storm centre. When I was in the depression that had been the old No Man's Land, the storm was behind me.

This party was like a busy city street. Parties were going forward with the high-carried Yukon packs; stretcher parties were moving back. All across the valley was the constant going and coming of men. Engineers were driving in level pegs and other specialists were engaged on their various jobs. From overhead came the tinny shriek of gas shells. One after another they landed about us with flopping thuds. Lazily the gas curled and flowed.

Every man stopped. In the space of five seconds each had quietly placed his mask on and continued. The patients on the stretchers had been attended to. Goggle-eyed the bearers were moving away. In my admiration I almost forgot to put on my own mask.

At our old front lines, as by magic, the fire ended. I wandered up to brigade headquarters and handed the maps to the brigade major.

The Bull questioned me about the position. Then he asked what sort of place battalion headquarters was. I described it mostly in adjectives. I told him that the farther I could keep from battalion headquarters, the better I would be pleased.

'I don't mind going out on patrol,' I said, 'but I'd hate to spend an hour round that HQ.'

'You know,' he said, 'I keep writing my wife that as battalion commander, my life is safe. But I don't think she altogether believes me.'

If his wife had been able to see the maelstrom round his future home, she might most reasonably disbelieve.

I lay on a haystack by the old front line. For two hours the storm around headquarters beat with such fury that I felt to try to make the trip would be plain suicide.

At last the fire eased, and I ran the gauntlet. All 48th headquarters men had been sent back to the trenches on Hill 63, and I had to join them. Salvos of shells sped me, my tin hat flew off, my nostrils were filled with smoke and dust. When I won clear, I was in a great silence, broken only by the little pinging noises of deafness. It was a close call.

I soon found the men, a waxy-pale horror-stricken crew. My batman had been buried and dug out three times. There is no more convincing way to taste the dread and bitterness of death,

than to be buried by a shell. But three times in succession—
Hell!

Although the forward slopes of Hill 63 overlooked Messines,
not a shell had landed on them all day.

The Bull called me up. For reasons best known to himself he
said, 'You and Lieutenant Pritchard get a good night's sleep over
the hill.'

That sounded well. On the back slopes of Hill 63, among the
dense trees, were numbers of comfortable huts. Congratulating
ourselves, Pritchard and I lay down to slumber.

Sleep comes easily in the stress of battle.

Pritchard was shaking me, 'Gas shells coming over!'

In hurrying succession they came, whistling high and shrill.
Some landed so close that the hut rocked. The bite of gas became
marked. Then five-point-nine high explosives started to burst
round and, forest-confined, the noise was terrific.

Masked, we stumbled outside to find our way to somewhere
beyond the gassed and shelled area. Our eyepieces misted, we
slobbered over the mouthpieces, we hated the gas, the night,
the shells, the Hun, even ourselves. Like bodiless spirits we
were hounded through that night. Everywhere we went, the gas
shells fell round us in thickening showers. Once we found a gas-
proof Nissen hut built half into the hillside. Joyfully we took off
masks and went in. At first sniff we fell out backwards. A gas
shell had burst in there, and it was a chamber of concentrated
gas.

We finished the night sitting in a shell hole by the edge of
the open country, dismally putting on our masks every time the
gas drifted our way.

The joke was on us. Our men on the forward slope had

slept undisturbed by gas or shell. But by the time Pritch and I had shaved, washed and breakfasted, we had forgotten the strafe of the night. So much so that we lined up to The Bull and asked permission to go on a reconnoitring trip to the front line. Permission was granted, and we moved off.

When, in passing Messines, black shrapnel thumped overhead, and high-velocity shells shrieked to earth close by, we repented somewhat of our rashness.

We reached the front line to the greeting of bullet squalls. We moved along the line to a pillbox, and went inside to shelter and rest a while.

It was time to be moving. Without a word we went to the entrance to resume our exploration. A blast thrust us backward, half stunning and deafening us. A whimper thrice repeated from outside, each time weaker. We went out. Where seven men had stood when we went in, now seven shattered corpses lay, chopped and distorted. Amid the hot reek of blood and the sour smell of new death, mingled that hated acid stink of high explosive.

I walked down the trench with expressionless face, expressionless to hide the fear and repulsion that raged within. For a little time I thought of each shell, assessing its power to mangle and mutilate.

Nothing ever lasts, horror or joy. Soon Pritchard and I were laughing at dangers past and to come. We came through the smoke of Messines unharmed.

The battalion was withdrawn to our old support line. They brought with them terrific battle-weariness. Why the stress of battle bites so deep I cannot tell. Nerve strain must have a place in it. Messines battle was child's play to any other battle we had ever encountered, the troops had been engaged only forty-eight hours, yet never before or since have I seen men carrying such a burden of exhaustion. It came to me, too, later.

We were again in our box seats, and could judge the rising fury of the enemy shellfire. Most of the fire came from the flank of the attack, making the Australian front probably the hottest part of the line. Almost hourly it seemed that new guns, heavy and of high velocity, were joining the fray from towards Lille. The peculiar snarling note of their shells seemed to dominate the land.

We lolled, secure, under the shade of the little hedges, watching the fury throughout the daylight hours. Shellfire is always fascinating to watch. At dark, the battalion prepared to move up, still dog-tired.

Captain Imlay and I set off together at midnight. I had a nasty, windy reluctant feeling that did not vanish until we started moving. The sky was overcast, the night dark. Unconcerned we picked our way towards the front line. Death was abroad among the noisy ruins. Dead lay beside our path. Flame trees rose and were gone. The stench of gas-tinged shell smoke and rotting flesh lay in zones on our way. The trees of Huns' Walk loomed ghostly above our heads, the cobbles hard beneath our feet. Bullets hissed and spanged off trees and road. That did not concern us. They were feeble things after the big shells that had been thumping to earth so close.

We came to the front line, where shadowy men stood beside the stubby butted Lewis guns, the sightless guards of our vanguard. There I sat on a fire-step and promptly fell asleep, my mind released to wander back in dream paths through the ages. Battle evokes many dim memories of the yesterdays of time. Nothing is new, only changed.

In my dreams I knew that there was always the period weapon with which the sons of England opposed the enemy nations at the battle outposts. Today it is the Lewis gun, fat-barrelled and grey. Its stammering voice seemed to tell of mad and futile haste. But our enemies knew how it could stammer through the longest day, deadly to the very end.

In a dream yesterday I marched, banded and musket-armed, over these very fields. Our smoke of discharge making a curtain before us. Time again contracted. Still we were in these familiar fields. The strings of our long bows were twanging taut. Soon we would prove that the cloth-yard shaft was master of armoured horse, mail-clad rider, and those little cross-bows. An arrogant self-satisfied crew we waited the order to go forward.

'Come on, Mitch.' It was Norm Imlay, waking me to go with him to search for a mislaid gun crew.

It was not so nice coming over six centuries from leisurely and heroic times, to night in a front trench. There was the thud of shells and guns behind us. Machine guns raked the terrain perfunctorily.

Norm was saying, 'Just as I went in, a shell landed outside the pillbox, killing four. We're going to the same pillbox now. Don't hang round outside it.'

'I won't,' I said. 'I've had some of that already.'

We stepped on to Huns' Walk, from a sap-head that was littered with bloodstained equipments and broken stretchers. On the far side of the road, thirty yards towards Germany was the pillbox, looking, in the darkness, like some low dingy hut. We went in without any delay. These pillboxes were ranged to an inch, and shelled at odd times.

The smell of iodine hit us. Wounded and dead lay all across the floor. Candles gave out dim light. A thing that struck me most was that among all these wounded, some of whom were dying, there was not a voice raised in complaint.

Dawn was making things take form when I got back. First the trees showed, hedges changed from black to grey. Then the Lewis guns roared, sharp and short as stray unsheltered enemy were revealed. A rifle cracked sharply away in front, the bullet thudded into the parapet, a dirt spray fell round us. Far ahead a German machine gun opened in lagging bursts. The bullets whistled overhead. Birds sang in the trees, and it was day again.

Sergeants Shepherdson and O'Brien found me with news of a deep shell hole just in front. Guns were all well planted and supplied. We climbed out, and dropped into the hole. We ate our fill and followed up with a long drink of rum. In the warmth of the summer sun, we slept like tired dogs.

At noon we stirred and rose like giants refreshed. No sooner does trouble cease looking for men, than they go hunting for trouble. There is keen interest in searching for enemy positions. The call of field glasses and pistols has led many a man to his end. We prowled forward, pistol armed, and searched pillboxes and trenches. A few bullets schooled us to caution. We returned laden with souvenirs, helmets, daggers, and so on.

Diggers filled in the parts of the battle that I had not seen. This mighty attack had so demoralised the enemy that his disorganised counter-attacks had been wiped out without trouble.

'They came at us at daylight,' one told me as he tested his gun. 'We waited for them to get close. The skipper got ready to put up the SOS. We said 'Don't call the artillery. Let's have a fair go at 'em. We can fix 'em without help.' 'No,' he said, 'we will get more this way!' Then we opened and the artillery opened. Poor cows didn't have the chance of a dew-drop in hell.'

A reinforcement officer, first time in the line, said to me, 'Mitch, there is a machine gun about four hundred yards out. You've got a decoration. How about you going out and capturing it?'

I thought hard for a bit, then replied, 'How about you going out and capturing it? Then you'll have a decoration too.' But neither of us went.

A sudden raging of big shells called our attention to the near edge of Messines. Amid the trees of shell bursts galloped horsemen. Groups were drowned out in flames. Riderless horses sprayed outward, and the show was over.

I did not think that that incident concerned me personally, but it did.

12

Daylight patrol

An hour later, Captain Joe Mayersbeth came to me. 'Mitch, will you volunteer to take out a fighting patrol?'

'Where?' I asked.

He picked out a point on the map. We located it through the trees, by some racecourse buildings, two miles away.

'If I take a patrol there,' I said, 'I won't get back again.'

'The cavalry reports it unoccupied,' said Joe.

'You know that the cavalry hasn't come within a mile of us, much less gone out in front,' I said.

'I know that,' replied the skipper, 'but my orders are to send out a patrol to that point. Will you volunteer to lead it?'

Thinking that I might avert a useless slaughter, by discouraging him, I said, 'I won't volunteer. If you order me to go, I will go.'

He said no more, but walked off.

I noticed a bustle up the trench. NCOs and men were grouping, so I went up, to find that Joe had appointed Pavy, an officer first time in the line, to take out the patrol.

I had an idea that our men's lives were more precious even than material. Some of these men detailed for the patrol were cobbers who had come out of Bullecourt.

The swift certainty came to me that Pavy in his inexperience would lead his men straight on to the objective. The enemy screen would let him in, but the return journey would be barred by machine guns. A shrewd and vengeful enemy would not let one man get back.

Not from any heroic motives, but to prevent unnecessary loss just to prove that some inefficient cavalry officer was wrong in his report, I went up to Captain Mayersbeth.

'I'll take the patrol. Leave Pavy out. He's too new to the game.'

But Joe was stubborn. I think he was a bit peeved at my not volunteering at first. The only thing he would permit was for me to accompany Pavy, and share responsibility.

I took that compromise, knowing that Pavy would fall in with any reasonable plan. My plans were simple, merely to buy a fight with the nearest enemy party in front, not go so far that we would be outflanked, and to send back word that we were held up by fire. In that way we could expect a loss of not more than two or three men, and the cavalry report would be proven wrong.

On the other hand, it would be comparatively easy to charge bull-headed through the outpost line. Many a burglar has heard a door slam behind him.

The march of the afternoon was half done as we stood, a small party each, ready to go. Hedges and tree rows divided the land. The sun blazed in full strength. Much too beautiful for the business of death.

The accoutred men waited, wondering the manner of the storm into which they were to be thrust. Odd bullets smacked to earth, shells chased droning overhead.

No point in hanging about. We clambered out and were above ground. Spread wide we ran forward, boots pounding the sun-dried earth and grass, equipment rustling and rattling. Every nerve was alert for the expected squall of metal. Machine guns sprang into chorus, but I found myself grinning happily, and with good reason.

The enemy guns were firing right enough. Every Fritz gunner who saw us advance hurriedly pressed those double buttons. But not one of the guns was pointing in our direction.

Judging by the *claquement,* some of them were dropping their bullets a thousand yards away. Odd rifle bullets spat into the ground in the spaces between the running men. Just enough to remind us that there was a war on. Half-screened by a shell-gapped hedge, was the concrete top of a pillbox. Our men fanned out against the menace of expected close-range machine-gun fire. No fire came. We closed in quickly. A Mills bomb spun hissing into the gloom that lay beyond the small square entrance. Smoke gushed from doorway and firing slits. We crowded in, now that the place had been fumigated, pleased to get below bullet level.

As distinctive as the scent of a fox is the smell of any enclosed place that has been occupied by German troops. It seems to be, in part, the reek of tanned leather. But additional to this was the smell of high explosive and another more subtle and intriguing odour. For a moment we did not recognise it. The floor was wet. Then we knew. That bomb had smashed a case of beer.

The sun was hot outside. Battle is thirsty work. We could have sung a hymn of hate with ease. It would have gone hard with any Fritz who had fallen into our hands just then.

As our eyes became accustomed to the gloom, we saw the interior as the mirror of the happenings of the attack morning. Blankets were flung aside as the occupants had sprung up at the warning of the mine explosions. Eagle-crested helmets hung on nails. Rifles leaned against the walls. Leather equipment tangled our feet. Letters and maps cluttered a table. A pack of playing cards had dribbled half on the floor.

I stood a while before a picture tacked on to the wall, '*Stiller Tag am Ammersee*'. The pictured calm attracted me greatly in contrast to the storms that we must face. A girl stood by a stile beneath a spreading willow. Below was the gleam of blue water.

War does not wait on art. I tore the picture from its retaining tacks and folded it carefully into my tunic pocket, that I might appreciate it in less crowded times.

My plan for a bloodless skirmish was proceeding beautifully. We left the bulk of our men in the pillbox and placed a small party in a deep adjoining shell hole to guard against surprise. We had only brought sixteen men with us. Sixteen more awaited our orders in the front line. Pavy stayed to take charge of the post, I went back to bring up the rest.

Close by a long hedge I trotted, jumping fast across the shell gaps. Odd bullets spanged and howled away. The sixteen men stood gloomy in silent anticipation of a brainless rush that would mean their annihilation. I might have relieved their minds, but did not think it politic to do so at that stage.

Food had just come up. Bags of lumps of boiled beef, bags of boiled potatoes, petrol-cans of tea. I suddenly knew that I was hungry, and settled down to a gigantic feed, eating enough for six men.

The waiting party watched me without a word. Years after one told me: 'That feed you had did me the world of good. I knew it couldn't be too bad out there if you could eat like that.'

We climbed out into the open and ran forward. Bullets whipped through the spaces between us, but no one was hit. This bunch was added to the collection in the pillbox. Now to buy a fight.

Taking four men, unreeling a field telephone as we went, Pavy and I advanced in short rushes from shell hole to shell hole. We were advancing along slightly higher ground. A very shallow valley on our left was in plain view. Soon the fun commenced. Three hundred yards to left a Fritz was peering cautiously round the rear corner of a pillbox. Now and again he raised his rifle to fire. 'He's mine,' I said. 'Gimme your rifle.'

'No, he's mine,' said Pavy. 'It is my rifle.'

We tossed and he won. I took the glasses and watched while he fired. His bullet must have spattered on the concrete, for Fritz fell over backward, picked himself up and ran for his life, arms and legs and equipment flapping. As he ran others joined him. They would drop for cover in the grass, now knowing that they were in full view, and side on to us. They thought that the fire was coming from our lines.

I had grabbed a rifle from a signaller, and for five minutes we fired and laughed at their comic antics until the last target disappeared. We were still laughing, when bullets started to spit round us. They came from the left of our line.

The signaller passed me the receiver and soon the skipper was on the phone.

'Will you ask those ——s on the left as a special favour to stop shooting at us?'

'They're not shooting at you, are they?'

'Too eyes right they are. Tell them if they don't stop we will take some pots at them.'

After a few minutes this fire ceased, and we commenced to think about a farther advance. A hundred yards ahead was a row of poplars.

The air was suddenly filled with clamour, six gay-painted, chequered planes of Richthofen's circus thrust their noses in line over the trees, up to which they must have raced close to the ground. Noses tilted down, streams of tracer bullets spat towards us. Thirty feet above us, goggled and grim, showed the pilots' heads behind their chattering guns.

The ground vibrated under the drum of their engines. A surprised snapshot as they came, another at their backs, and they were gone, while we cursed with rage. The clamour died away as swiftly as it arose.

A ditch nearby led direct into the German lines. Armed only with my pistol, I decided to do a lone patrol of it. It was quite interesting as I went farther and farther, expecting each moment to run into a scouting enemy, and picturing the surprise on his face. The ditch became shallower and shallower. At last I was seen and bullets commenced to smack about me. It was high time to do something. So I ran to one side and dropped into a deep shell hole.

The bullets that pecked away could do me no harm, so long as I kept low. So I settled down to wait for darkness, but popped my head up to watch from time to time.

Unfortunately for my peace of mind I saw that enemy parties

were making short rushes to close in behind and cut off my retreat, and I had no rifle to discourage them. So I must get moving, and chance the bullets. These whistled about me as I dived from shell hole to shell hole.

As I prepared to race out of one, I saw a German lying in a bunch of thistles in my line of retreat, grimly watching me about thirty feet away. Behind him showed patches of the field-grey of others.

Instinctively I emptied my pistol at him. For the first shot, the slim tall foresight rested on the space between the watching eyes, the muzzle jerked up slightly in recoil. The next was sighted lower, the third aimed at the ground just in front, so that the bullet would do its work on the rebound. The rest were hurried snapshots, then the hammer clicked on an empty chamber. He treated its spitting with complete contempt, not flinching or moving.

Below the rim of the shell hole I reloaded, confidence in my marksmanship sadly shaken. Never did the cartridges slip into the cylinder so slowly. Each second I watched to see the shape of attackers above me with levelled rifles. Each second I held myself prepared to slam shut the part-filled pistol to fight on. There appeared no chance of getting past those better armed, waiting men; this seemed to be the end of the section for me. But it was not a bad place to end up in. There was no fouling mud, no crashing shellfire, the sun clear above, and the enemy clear in front. It would be shot for shot. One chance alone appealed to me. Bounce out of this shell hole, right into them, and give them shock action.

Words a VC once used came back to me: 'If you hop right into 'em, you've got 'em paralysed for a second or two.'

Now to try that advice. The pistol full loaded and cocked, balanced nicely in my hand. I climbed nearly to the back rim of the ten-foot shell hole to get up maximum speed and to cut down the time of reaching them.

As a man dives into ice-cold water I launched myself. A score of men lay there among the thistles, their rifles beside them. The face of the watcher was set in a sardonic grin as I raced up. They did not move. They would never move again. These were enemy who had been mown down by our people as they had counterattacked.

Sharp in memory was etched the sight of them as I hurdled their bodies, the twin buttons on their coat-tails, the steel-shod jackboots at unnatural angles, the filled cartridge pouches that pressed against the earth, the helmets that had rolled clear, those that pillowed their owners. The first dark onrush of putrefaction showed on outflung clutching hands, and necks bare to the sunlight.

I found myself laughing as I continued my rush, laughing at the joke against me.

Bullets were flicking around as I reached the advanced post, dived in, rolled and sat up, still laughing.

'All right for you,' said a Digger in an aggrieved tone. 'You enjoy this sort of thing.'

I did not explain to him that I had had the wind put up me by a dead man.

The drowsy afternoon came to sunset, with a few bursts of rifle and machine-gun fire, and odd shells making fleeting trees across the country.

13
Relieved

With darkness came our relief. Captain Jacka, VC, coldly efficient, came up with a bunch of men and took over from us.

We moved back to the front line. Slowly the line started to move along the trench. A five-point-nine howled down tearing the night with its mounting roar. The trench walls leaped as it burst ten feet to our left. After a short interval, the rain of debris spattered all about us. Again came the roar of a shell, and we crouched under its menace. It burst with terrific impact, ten feet on our right. We were bracketed, and waited in fear for the next.

Lieutenant Potts was just in front. This was his first turn in the line. Such an opportunity for a chipping was too good to let pass, so I called: 'How do you like your eggs cooked, Pottsy?'

Pat and prompt he came back with: 'Hard shelled, you———.'

Pottsy had become a full member of the fraternity of Diggers with all rights and privileges. He finished the war with MC and Bar, but now the poor cow, he is teaching kids away out where the crows fly backward in Western Australia. I hope he never uses such language to them as he did to me.

In one of those pauses that occur in the shelling, we reached the forward edge of Messines. In front of us was the rubble heap of the village. The men were placed in odd trenches, and fell asleep in whatever position they struck the trench floor.

Battle-weariness is a strange thing. It does not seem to be governed by the amount of physical exercise involved, or loss of sleep, but rather by the mental strain of watching death play round one. It is at its maximum in forty-eight hours. After that it seems, paradoxically, to diminish until a soldier in a long-drawn battle carries on automatically beyond the reach of exhaustion, pain, fear and it often seems—death.

I searched in the darkness, among the ripped dry earth, and soon found a pillbox with its usual stack of dead outside. Flickering match-light showed a double row of empty bunks. A shaving-filled mattress rustled as I climbed up. Sleep came with the dying of the match.

The world jarred about me, and the instant full waking of the soldier was mine. Daylight was streaming in the low square entrance that faced the German lines. The bunks were now all filled with sleeping men. On the floor, among the littering debris, lay other men in the deathlike sleep of exhaustion, physical and mental.

Beyond the gloom of this pillbox was the snarl and thud of shell bursts. The concrete vibrated in a strange way at each new burst. Wide awake, but resting, I waited as the noisy minutes dragged by. Tongues of driven smoke would invade our retreat, and the air became sharp with the acid tang of it.

There came a mad minute of shell bursts, each so close on the heels of the other that never a full second passed between explosions. The pillbox rang and rocked, then leaped as a shell took it full on. A man blocked the light of the entrance, blundered in:

'I'm hit!' It was the skipper.[1]

I slid from my bunk. Something in his voice filled me with a dragging, cold dread.

As he rocked on his knees I lowered him back, pushing aside an enemy equipment to give him room to rest. His hand was clenched tight below his left collar-bone. Undoing his belt, I unbuttoned his tunic, pulled his shirt clear and forced his hand away. From a tiny pin-point wound came a jet of dark arterial blood that spurted clear across the pillbox. Three times, at each heart-beat it sprayed, while I knelt by his side helpless and horrified. From some recess of memory returned the words:

> Not so deep as a well
> Nor as wide as a church door,

then I jammed my thumb hard on the wound.

'Bandage it, bandage it!' called a Digger urgently. No bandage could stop the force of heart-pumped blood.

'Go and find the medical officer,' I told him.

He went out through the entrance, but did not return. 'I'm done. I'm done,' said the skipper.

My war-bought knowledge of the ways of death told me that it was true, though I faintly hoped that the doctor might have some marvellous instrument that would stop arterial bleeding where there were no pressure points.

I could find no words of hope for him. One cannot tell cheering lies in the face of death. Weak tears of grief were falling as I pressed hard and stopped the outward flow. I dared not ease the pressure long enough to lay him on a bunk. But while I pressed I could hear the gurgle of blood flowing into the chest cavity from within.

'Say good-bye to the boys. Tell my wife ———.' Then he recited a prayer. There was a choking sound. He relaxed. There was no blood-pressure against my thumb.

Instantly the pillbox was permeated by the astringent smell of new death. The air seemed to have grown very cold. I stood up and looked a moment, with blurred sight at the now waxen face of the man who had been my friend, then climbed back into the bunk.

Into a strange half-world I slid, somewhere between sleeping and waking, between life and death.

A high-velocity gun was firing at the pillbox. Shells fell short by feet, others struck on each side of the entrance, rocking the place. It was a matter of time before one would come in the entrance and destroy all within that confined space.

Vivid and clear formed the picture of what some wanderer would find when the storm died. I could see all of us as charred and ripped corpses. Even could I see the broken bunks, the smouldering bedding, the smoke-blackened walls.

It seemed useless to go out into the storm. That way would be to meet death the quicker.

Hope, fear and love of life all faded into stark resignation. Like some strange and familiar cinema film, my life, from earliest childhood, unrolled, incident by incident. Forgotten places came back clear and distinct, forgotten happenings returned with startling vividness.

'This is death,' I said to myself.

The skipper lay on the floor, the others as still as he on the bunks. Within was soundless and unmoving as a morgue. Outside the storm continued. The pillbox jumped beneath the hammer-strokes of the shells. Smoke curled through the entrance.

Still my mental pictures ran on and on towards the final scene.

A voice woke me. The light in the entrance was the faint grey of dusk. Men were buckling their equipments to move out. The cannonade was now on more distant places. Someone asked me to take charge of four men to bury the skipper and another who had been killed during the day. The speaker told me that the skipper had left his pillbox during the height of the barrage, to order some of his men who were moving about to keep under cover, and so he had died.

The company filed away into the gloom on their long march round the flank of Messines. It was too dark to see the face of the skipper, or of him who lay beside.

Shells chased overhead, burst red among the fallen masonry. A fragment struck the helmet of a Digger. I searched memory hard for a form of prayer. Staccato Maxim bursts seemed a fitting requiem. Lights rose, wavered, and fell behind my back. Flame and thunder leaped in wrecked Messines.

The Diggers stood at attention a moment, the long-handled German shovels beside. Fragments pattered over the country like the first drops of summer rain.

The Diggers covered them. Two less to bear the weight of the days.

We marked the grave, saluted and turned away.

The others had gone through a long and much-shelled trench that wound beyond the flank of Messines. It would be a weary, dangerous march of three hours for them. By plunging straight through Messines, we could do the distance in twenty minutes. Owing to the terrific fire on Messines, the shorter route was not used. We would either get through untouched or be wiped out. But I decided that I could time it to get through between the barrages.

With orders to make speed, we strode out. The main street was a depression between piles of masonry. Not a living man did we see there.

All the way we were stepping over German corpses. One beautifully uniformed officer lay with highly polished field-boots. In a less dangerous place, those field-boots would have gone.

Up the rise to the centre of the village we hurried, listening intently for the sound of death racing up behind.

Down the slope the rubble heaps ended, we were clear of the village. Late shells thundered at our heels.

We passed a water barrel. Still in the danger space we were moving fast. One man was missing. Cursing I went back. He was drinking at the barrel. I stopped him in the middle of his drink and started him on. A great flame shell burst over the top of us. Bone-searing phosphorus sprayed all about. Five-point-nines crashed on each side. I was still expressing my opinion of this man when we rejoined our party.

Soon we were out on the flat and grassy lands beyond the slopes. The thunders of battle were at our backs.

We weaved across the roads in utter weariness. I knew that I would never again be a young man, strong with the joy of life. If battle did not claim me, I would go through my few short years spent and decrepit.

The hidden sun made plain the world. The beauty of the new day made no appeal to our weary souls. For us the world had ended.

Men led us to our billets. I fell on a bed. That was at 4 a.m. At 9 a.m. Bingley and I were dressed in our most posh uniforms, asking permission to visit Bailleul.

The wine was good, the food was good. Everything was fair in a pleasant world.

14

Joyous interlude

Returns of casualties and equipment replacements had barely been sent in, when I was ordered to attend an infantry school, just out of Hazebrouck.

There, in the lines of Nissen huts, foregathered the new generation of Australian and New Zealand Infantry officers. Young, wild and hard-bitten were they. Life was to them, between stunts, a thing from which all available joy must be seized as a duty. I found it hard, at first, to keep pace with their nightly raids and various stunts.

The camp adjutant incurred their disapproval. He was young and pompous, without any front-line service. As well put a Pekinese in a den of lions.

One night stunt I remember. The adjutant's hut was in darkness. Duckboards were leaned against the door. The hut was ringed with concertina wire. The fabric windows were pushed out and lighted ground flares thrown in. Fire-buckets followed, water and all. The adjutant must have had a busy five minutes, but he never slept in that hut again.

The parades ended at midday on Saturday, and we were free until the first parade on Monday morning.

With a New Zealander, I wandered to the railway station. Over four sets of rails stood the leave train, jammed full with its happy freight. It started. Without a word we leaped to the rails, sprinted and caught it. There were fresh fields to explore.

As it rattled on its way, we clambered along to the guard's van, and found the conductor, a little Tommy engineer.

In slow, broad English, he told us that the destination was Boulogne, but that no one could get off the platform there without a pass. But the train would pull up at Wimereux, a hospital centre a few miles out. There we could disembark in safety and lorry hop into Boulogne.

Wimereux sounded well to us. It was well known that that place was inhabited by the most beauteous of WAACs.

We were comfortable throughout the long afternoon as the train thrust the miles behind. But when Wimereux raced up, the train did not even slow its pace.

Visions of court martial stared us in the face. In the hollow showed the towers of Boulogne. The train steadied for the station and we jumped off. Innocently we walked away, and up to the town.

As an anti-climax rain came pouring down. We stood under a veranda. Over the road, two charming damsels were arranging their shop window.

'I'm going to have a talk with them,' I said.

'No chance,' said New Zealand, but he followed.

We chatted with them. All the time I could sense the bar that middle-class French girls keep to guard their reputation against foreign soldiery.

All the time I sought to get past it.

An opening came. 'Would you like a cognac?' they asked.

We would. One went out to get it, to bring it into the shop. But I discovered my dignity, just in time, and explained in flowery language that it would be a terrible thing for two British officers to be seen drinking in an open shop.

That impasse lasted a quarter of an hour, with the unwillingness of the girls to admit us to the intimacy of their private rooms.

My eloquence mounted to glorious heights. New Zealand listened in approving wonder. At last, with a great show of reluctance, the girls ushered us into a back room.

That was a different world altogether. It was a long time before we remembered to drink our cognac. We were to go out to dinner, and return after the shop had shut.

Louise clung to me as we were about to go, demanding my stick and gloves as hostage to ensure our return. I left those things willingly.

We dined largely and well. All the meaning glances of dark-eyed professional charmers left us cold. We talked and drank with scarred, bemedalled, and· thoughtful-looking French officers.

With carefully selected bottles of wine, we made our way to the welcome rendezvous.

Next morning, as we set out to the railway station, the only shadow on our lives was the thought of the trouble that would ensue if we did not turn up at the first parade on Monday morning.

So we inquired at the RTO's office about trains for Hazebrouck. We were told that we must take train to Etaples, and there be drafted to our units, which would take about four days. To travel on a French train would require a special pass. If we could get to Calais we might get a through train.

Beaten, we studied a map, to see how we could get to Calais. In an equilateral triangle showed Boulogne, Calais and St Omer. But St Omer was only thirty kilometres from Hazebrouck. I advocated trying to get a direct motor lift to St Omer, ninety kilometres away.

So we strayed along the road and hailed anything on wheels. A civilian in a car, and a Tommy ambulance raced past without stopping. Then a fast Vauxhall shot over the rise. Brakes squealed. Could we get a lift to St Omer? Certainly. A pleasure. Get in. Labelled luggage showed our benefactor to be Philip Gibbs, war correspondent.[1]

The wind howled past, the beauty of the country unrolled map-wise to our appreciative view. All too soon, square towers rose from a hollow, and we were in ancient St Omer.

Two Australian nurses smiled at our salute in sisterly style. We dined with them and talked of our far off homeland.

Despising trains, we again waited on the open road. A Frenchman picked us up. His shrill engine unwound the kilometres. The mess gong was ringing as we climbed out.

New Zealand and I walked in and split a bottle of wine in mutual congratulation at the finish of a successful adventure.

During the month that the school lasted, each weekend found us at Boulogne. Never again did we take a train. Sometimes we waylaid generals in their beflagged cars. They seemed tickled at our company.

At the last parting, I said, 'Back to the war, Louise!' She wept a while, but there was no hostage that I could leave to ensure my return.

But not all men at this school were the same. From my battalion was Lieutenant Maynard. He was a thoughtful, dependable chap, who spent his nights studying textbooks, while I went out to see what the world had to offer a soldier. Death chooses in strange ways. Maynard did his duty to the bitter end and went west, leading his men.

The school ended, and we were again among our noisy battalion friends. They were preparing to go up the line.

A big batch of mail awaited me, and orders to go to another school.

As the battalion marched out for the line, I moved off to the school at Mont des Cats to imbibe scouting, observation and sniping. It was a strange sensation to see the boys marching towards the line without me.

This school was on the heights, beside the old monastery. All Flanders, in her summer green, lay below us.

The school was run by English regulars of 1914. Their calm hospitality further heightened the calm and peace of the place.

The windows of my little cottage would brighten at night from the explosions around Ypres, prelude to a new and terrific offensive. The windows would rattle softly in their frames.

By day, on the far rim of the plains was the line of our observation balloons. Waspish little black-crossed planes would swoop on them. One set six alight in turn. The observers floated to safety under their snowy parachutes.

One friend, made there, I shall always remember. He was a guardsman of 1914, probably sent to attend this course for a rest.

It is hard to describe him in words that usage has not distorted. To me, he represented all that was the best of the old English army and aristocracy. He was about thirty, tall, straight, and good to look at. Generations of privilege and domination had gone to produce this man. But there was no self-conceit about him, and one knew instinctively that he could never say a word, or perform an act that was not completely right and just.

Many easy hours we sat on the hillsides and talked. His mind weighed and considered all things, and so the tragedy of war and the loss of his friends bore heavily upon him.

It was almost impossible to persuade him to speak of the dark days of 1914, but one could vaguely guess at all that those losses meant to him.

He had a consuming curiosity regarding the Australian forces, and always probed for information as to the sources from which arose our energy and spirit.

Once, after a long pause, he said: 'Your chaps are splendid,' and I have always felt very proud of that praise.

Relations with our English cousins were not always of the happiest. We were often arrogant, some of their officers were pompous and self-sufficient, sure that colonials were of inferior clay. Sparks often flew. But, so long as England breeds men of the type of that Imperial captain, she will stand secure.

I lost sight of him in the fog of war, but I like to think that no little uniform cross yet bears his name.

Return to the battalion took the form of another rowdy reunion.

'You're for leave, you tinny blighter,' they said.

'About time,' I replied.

It is impossible to describe just what leave means to the soldier. For a similar depth of happiness, one must go back to childhood days.

The leave pass with its printed and written lines is a passport to ten days of heaven. There is delight, even in filling the pack with all the simple needs of ten days. The train is a golden chariot. Songs of joy ring in one's ears. My only difficulty was the stowing of various souvenirs.

Our carriage was packed with men of Canada, England, Scotland and far-flung islands and colonies.

Our leave boat soon brought the white cliffs in sight. The train raced through Kent. The Englishmen became silent as their family reunions came nearer.

The dim vast space of Victoria Station housed us. There were cries of joy as waiting women claimed their menfolk. They clung to them as though they had returned from the dead.

I stalked through the throng, hat tilted, vastly pleased with myself. Ten days of absolute freedom. Not one tie, not one relation, not one friend in the whole of the land of England who cared whether I came or went, lived or died. Not even a dog to wag its tail at my passing. At our headquarters I filled my pocket with crisp new Bradburys. Such is freedom.

We Diggers were a race apart. Long separation from Australia had seemed to cut us completely away from the land of our birth. The longer a man served, the fewer letters he got, the more he was forgotten. Our only home was our unit, and that was constantly being decimated by battle, and rebuilt by strangers.

Pride in ourselves, in face of a world of friends and enemies, was our sustaining force. For a parallel, one would need to go back to some Roman Legion, serving many years in a foreign country, cut off from Rome, alien to the new land and the old, sure only of themselves.

My last letter, from a girl in Australia, received months before, had stated, 'Send me something for me to remember you by when you are killed.'

So, beneath the old felt hat I swaggered down the Strand with an air that inferred, 'Make way for an Aussie on leave.'

I had my share of approving side glances. Plenty of time to pick and choose. Largely, I swung into a restaurant. Two pretty girls sat nibbling toast nearby. They looked across coyly.

I called them over. They came most willingly. They may have been eating toast at their own table, but now, they developed a most amazing appetite.

They decided that they would like to see a movie show. I was easy. The show was only two blocks away, but the girls hailed a taxi. They decided that only the most expensive seats could be occupied. I was still easy, and did not mind paying for the privilege of hearing soft English speech from pretty lips.

Plenty of Bradburys in my pocket, and the paymaster had any amount more.

The chocolate boy came round with his tray of boxes. It seemed that they must have chocolates to sustain them. They called the boy, and each selected the most expensive boxes. I paid.

They were planning further methods of spending money when the picture ended.

I had heard of their type. They were a development of war. Nowadays we would call them gold-diggers.

The boys had a toast to describe them:

> Here's to the girl in high-heeled shoes,
> Who eats your food and drinks your booze,
> And then goes home to sleep with mother,
> Stingy ——

Outside, they were on their toes, trying to catch the eye of an elusive taxi-driver.

By this time I decided that it was time I had some say in the spending of my battle-earned cash.

'Where are we going?' one asked.

'Wherever you are going,' I said, 'I am going the other way.'

Off they went to find some other colonial, trying by the spending of money to crowd into hours the years of his forespent life.

There was a quiet joy in moving about among the crowds, watching the vivid dramas of war days. The trench-stained Tommy with his fear-ridden wife and idolising children. The battle-haggard English officer, sitting in the café with his wife or fiancée, their reserve in the face of elemental things. Swaggering Scots, striding with swaying kilt and conscious pride. The soft American brogue of Canadians. Hours spent in bars with them. High wild laughter, tall tale on tale.

Precious hours in the open, along the upper Thames. The quiet English folk who look as though they would give much to break their generations of reserve, to meet the man from far away, come to fight in their wars.

Those beautiful girls with whom we came face to face, girls whom we could worship, but shut off from us by convention.

To fill our need for companionship, hordes of harpies competed. But those whose friendship we should have valued, we could seldom meet.

One day I thought me of Scotland, where any Australian is completely at home. The Flying Scotsman sped me north to Edinburgh.

A friend who occupied a hospital bed beside me in Egypt was there to greet me. His girl kissed me impartially. They led me home to sit before the fire.

A bright-eyed lassie sat on each arm of the chair. I was fussed over and petted. It was a queer new sensation.

This book would not suffice to tell of our wanderings through that town of beauty, the strange fisher-folk, the closes, the castle and that bridge of sighs.

Relentlessly the days slipped by; too soon was the parting.

The roar of London seemed to have taken on something of the roar of Flanders. There was a little cold feeling within my chest. Then that last night of leave.

In time-honoured fashion I went to a theatre. Beside me was a Canadian Loot, with his two lovely sisters. He was half-drunk. He was to go to France for the first time to-morrow. The sisters burst into tears at odd intervals. I did my best to console them. When I saw that he was an Army Service Corps man, I grieved for those wasted tears. Either or both of them could have wept on my shoulder without hindrance.

The boat train. To how many hundreds of thousands had that been the way to the grave.

With a feeling of content I settled back in a corner with a large cigar. I had cheated death for a lot of fun.

The time of departure drew near. With contempt-tinged pity, I watched the partings. Women clung to their men, tears making doubly hard the parting. It seemed, that by the strength of their love they would try to hold their men back from the great graveyard of France. That last long terrible kiss, that last reluctant release of gripping hands.

Others were quieter, but the tenseness of their glances showed that the strain was none the less for being subdued.

The whistle sounded, calls of parting from tear-dimmed voices, a forest of urgent waving hands, the wheels moved, we were in the grip of the iron-hard times again.

I sat back and puffed at my cigar contentedly. Thanks be to the gods, there was no one to make a fuss over me.

Someone produced whisky. Soon most of us were singing. Others sat with faraway looks in their eyes.

The cross-channeller lunged into the seas. The coasts of France came familiar out of the murk.

'Thought you'd declared a separate peace,' said the boys. 'Fritz is laying for you this time.'[2]

15

Backs to the wall

The blood-bath of Passchendaele had drained our battalion. New faces replaced those of men tried and known. Men died but the battalion lived on.

The whole British army had been shaken to its foundations by the blind fury and futility of the third Ypres offensive.

The year 1917 had been one of disaster for our arms in all save the Messines attack.

The Russians had caved in. The French were at a standstill. It would be many months before American troops could arrive in sufficient force to be of any importance.

Throughout the long winter nights came the rumours of the coming enemy offensive, with new divisions loosed from Russia.

It seemed that the creation of an atmosphere of fear was the aim of the foe. We were rather amused at the idea of Fritz launching a big offensive. Our Lewis gunners promised themselves good shooting.

But there was a hint of uneasiness at the prospect of new gases, and new fast tanks.

The cold winter dragged by. Early in the new year we took over a section at White Château, our left flank resting on the Ypres–Comines canal.

I lived on what had been a church. Near my possie were two airmen, covered with bricks, only their boot-toes protruding. Above them, fit memorial, was the charred wreckage of their machine.

There were many bad five minutes from whizz-bangs. One gutted my adjoining post. A very gallant sergeant, Tom Loxton, had his leg blown off. He asked quietly for a cigarette as he lay on the stretcher. He bid me goodbye in a conversational tone of voice and shook hands as the bearers took him up. To our great delight, he recovered.

The tour of duty was uneventful. I was secretly very pleased that we did not have to bear the artillery concentration of a frontal attack. We handed over to the relieving battalion on 20 February 1918.

Sleet and snow followed us back to our stamping-ground around Meteren, where the friendly peasantry might have been our own kin.

Glorious weeks of training and sports went smoothly; the sun shining more brightly every day. The Estaminet au bon Fermier rang nightly to our celebrations. We insisted, at the conclusion of each beano that cheery, comfortable *maman, papa*—a grizzled, silent veteran of the Franco-Prussian war—the married daughter (whose hubby was a *poilu*) and her son, each walk a chalk line.

They returned the compliment, but drew the line up the wall.

All the time the black clouds of the projected enemy offensive were piling higher. Information kept coming through of the great resources available for use against us.

The general opinion was that he would waste his strength and leave himself weak to our counter blow. True, it eventuated, but—.

At nights—before retiring to our warm-sheeted beds in a snug room in the café—we would stand at the back door, looking towards the line. Gleaming, unfamiliar constellations of the northern skies overhead, a cold wind from frozen worlds, and the ceaseless flicker, flicker, flicker of guns from left to right as far as we could see. And each night the intensity was greater.

As we shut the door carefully the rumble of guns would bid us good night. 'Your turn soon!' they seemed to say.

But we should worry! Daily the Lewis gunners, with furious bursts of speed, clipped seconds off their assembling times. Cracking of rifles came from many miniature ranges. Bombers slinging their grenades, gained inches in distance over their previous best. Rifle grenadiers, with thoughtful expressions, lobbed grenades dead on the mark. Signallers wagged uncomplimentary messages to each other across greening fields.

I was attached, with Second Lieutenant Clarke, to Lieutenant Charlie Stoerkel, and we trained a bunch of dare-devils into a raiding party which we hoped would become the pride of the division.

Nightly, we raced across fields and made sudden charges with the bayonet, combining speed, certainty and silence. There was not a care in the whole battalion, unless someone with an unrestrained imagination let his thoughts wander too far ahead.

On a mass parade one day, 'Birdie' said, 'Wherever the Hun attacks, there he will meet you.'

'Too bloody right he will,' was the consensus of opinion.

Daily, the battalion was being hammered into a higher state of efficiency, reaching a pinnacle of perfection, such as that attained early in 1917, before Bullecourt.[1]

Came 21 March. To our amazement, far-flung shells were bursting over square-towered Meteren. Fifteen miles behind the lines! Planes squabbled and fought above. A heavy rumble from the front line. We were mildly surprised. But the next day came rumours of the enemy success, which we did not believe.

On the 24th came orders to stand by to move off in motor lorries—or 'Tommy route march,' as our mob called it.

Sat idly by a stone wall catching all the sunlight there was. An old grizzled peasant, with a bowl of grain moving slowly up and down, broadcasting wheat. As was done in the time of Abraham—and was ancient then.

'Whatsoever a man soweth that shall he also reap,' sayeth the Scriptures, but little wotted the sower that his reaping would be done by the guns ere the crop was ripe.

In solemn, almost incredible groups, we discussed the breakthrough. How could it possibly have happened. New tanks, and gases?

But we had a last woolly night in the *estaminet*.

On the 25th we marched to the lorries. A cold, clear day. The wind blew up clouds of dust.

Maman of the *estaminet* had wept, embraced and kissed Gelston and me, who had been billeted with her. 'The Boche will come now,' she said. She gave us each a lucky five-franc Napoleon. *'Pour bon chance.'* Filled our water bottles with the best wine, and had packed cakes in our haversacks, with another bottle of wine. Her last words as we tramped out were, *'Je vais prier pour vous.'* Strangely enough, the enemy line later reached the Estaminet au bon Fermier, and Gelston and I came through the rest of the war unscathed.

Into the lorries. Long hours in the cold wind. We stopped in Lillers. Many pretty girls about. One girl—half hysterical—was telling Captain Carter, with a wealth of gesture, that Paris was being shelled. 'Impossible,' we said, 'im-bloody-possible.'

But as we progressed, cold and hungry, new shell holes appeared alongside the road . . . Darkness. Colder and colder.

Arras ahead. An occasional flare unpleasantly close. An odd gun-flash, but no roar of battle. No rush of traffic. Queer. I loaded my pistol. Flashes right ahead, but no sound above the drone of the Leyland.

At 11.30 p.m. the fleet of lorries stopped. We marched. 'Berles au Bois,' said the skipper, as we came to a half-ruined little village. The men billeted in the best barn, the officers in the house. To our surprise, there were civilians here. I put an armful of straw under the kitchen table, and slept well.

Had just finished breakfast when the call for company commanders sounded, followed immediately by the 'at the double' call. As Lionel Carter shot through the door we looked at each other blankly. Were the skies falling, that stately company commanders had to go at the double?[2]

Carter was back as suddenly as he had gone, calling over his shoulder to the company to turn out. Jerking a map on to the table, he stabbed a spot with his finger:

'German armoured cars through to here—four kilos away. Get the men out in fighting order.'

As we were turning the company out the 47th moved up the road at the double. Colonel Imlay commandeered a motor lorry and had it smashed up along the road.

We manned suitable walls and waited. Lewis gunners scrambled hastily for armour-piercing bullets. But nothing happened. Then came the news that the armoured cars were only French farm implements being dragged away ahead of the advancing enemy.

A stray English artillery officer drifted in, starving and weary. We shared our frugal dinner with him. Yes, he had lost his guns and men. No, he had not eaten since yesterday morning. Oh, yes, the Boche should be here any time now.

But what he did do to the bread and cheese! And drank tea as if he liked it.

Orders that we were to move at midnight for Albert. So we lolled about in fighting order, tensely waiting through the long day. A deep and sinister silence was over the countryside. The solitary crash of an exploding dump only emphasised the stillness. It was weird. We would have welcomed the stutter of machine guns to give us something to cope with.

The Bull (now General R.L. Leane, CB, CMG, DSO, MC, VD, C. de G.), called the officers up.

'Gentlemen,' he said, 'there is no front line between us and the enemy. His position is not known. We start at midnight on a twenty-mile march toward Albert. We do not even know that the road is clear or whether we can beat him to Albert. We must protect our own flanks and be prepared for anything.'

Night again. I was dozing on the straw beneath the kitchen table. The bustle of impending departure commenced. I heard madame rush to the captain, *'C'est retraite encore?'*

'Non, Madame,' said the skipper grandly. *'Les soldats d'Australie ne faisent jamais retraite.'*

But madame became hysterical, in spite of Lionel's efforts to console her. Could hear her frantic repetition, *'C'est retraite encore, c'est retraite, c'est retraite.'* Then, 'We have lived here for thirty-six years, and through all the bombardments. Now you go, we must go.' Well, I thought, sooner the skipper had the job of pacifying them than me. But thank God Australia is twelve thousand miles away.

Wailing bitterly, she with her aged husband and little daughter dashed in futile haste from cupboard to cupboard sorting the most precious possessions of their lifetime.

As we lined up outside, in the cloudless dark night, they had a hand cart loaded. On top of the load was a crucifix. Sobbing, they moved off, calling blessings on our heads. From the dark outline of my assembled platoon came the voice of all our thoughts, 'Damned awful—that!'

Shuffling of boots on the cobblestones, the platoon merged into the company, the company into the battalion, the battalion into the division, and we were on our way. The old Fourth Divvy, the 'Stormy Petrels', were for it again.

From overhead came the rhythmic throbbing of a triple-engined bomber. The light of stars went out as the plane covered them. Fritz all right. 'If you hear bombs whistling,' I said softly to the platoon, 'into the ditch right and left of the road.'

Very quietly we walked, as if the sound might reach the Gotha a thousand feet up. A forbidden cigarette then would have made the road a slaughterhouse. But the Gotha passed on.

Marching all through the long night. Villages where people stood in silent groups in unlighted doorways. Fear—terror was in the air. Isolated guns moving back. Small parties of aimless, mostly unarmed, men getting back. Always back. Only the stolid old Ack I Foof in this world of chaos. The menace of the unseen, incalculable enemy was as of an avalanche. We felt like Lilliputian actors in some gigantic drama of the gods.

> Hark to the galloping horses,
> The crash of the rending gun;
> The stars are out of their courses,
> The hour of doom has begun.

The first grey light of dawn suddenly showed an extended line of men coming over the hill on our left. The skin of my tummy went suddenly tight. Got out a precautionary 'nine platoon', and had a plan of campaign arranged. These must be Fritzes. I will gallop 'nine platoon' into them and stab and shoot them back over the rise. Then extend on top of the ridge and keep them back until the old battalion has time to move off the road to a defensive position. But as I held my breath the lessening distance showed them to be our men.

The long hours of marching told on us. Platoons became groups supporting each other. Men fell as they walked, got up unaided, or were hoisted to their feet. At each hour halt every man dropped where he stood. At the end of the ten-minute interval the stronger shook or booted the weaker till they woke.

Found myself alongside our inimitable Lieutenant Potts. He started to stagger all over the road, called me 'Suzanne,' and used endearing terms. Abused and shook him, and discovered that he was asleep on his feet. Took his arm and led him for miles while he slept.

At 8 a.m. on 27 March we staggered into Senlis. Someone was still fighting. Guns were banging over the hill. Tank or tractor tracks ribbed the soil.

The inhabitants had fled. Into the most comfortable house we went. A fire was started. The batmen slaughtered some chooks. By 9.15 a.m. we had eaten them. I wandered upstairs. Found a cosy boudoir. The bedclothes were turned back as the owner had left them on hurrying out. The smell of scent was still noticeable. Climbed on to the bed with a sigh as a runner came in. 'Battalion will move for Henencourt at 10.15.'

A glorious hour of rest, and we were on our way. I had no need to husband my strength, as I was not to go into the stunt, but was to wait out until a raid was required. So (to my later disgust) I carried little Connaughton's Lewis gun and a couple of rifles.

A sunny day. We topped a rise, and Albert showed clear on our left. All the panorama of open warfare was ours for a turn of the head. Albert was grey with the smoke of many fires. The tower rose above the smoke, and the leaning Virgin glittered in the sunlight.

Shells were spouting black smoke among the green fields. Stabbing white flame where our scattered batteries fired from behind hedges. Limbers driven madly to the guns and away again. Strings of wounded dribbling wearily back.

Motor lorries tearing down the roads flat out. Red-cross cars conspicuous by their signs racing even faster. New and constantly renewed trees of black smoke all down the avenue of the Albert–

Amiens road. Dainty derelict planes like maimed dragonflies scattered on the plain.

Above, swarms of our planes chattered and squabbled like a mob of sparrows, diving, machine-gunning, and bomb-dropping, in a gallant attempt to hold the enemy. We owned the air anyway.

Civilians carrying odd bundles saw us. They let out yells of 'Soldats d'Australie'. Saying they were safe, they turned and followed. They had more confidence than we.

Into Henencourt we came and were shocked. Henencourt we regarded as our own special home village. Buildings newly shattered by shellfire everywhere. A medley of men, horses and guns. Brass-hatted young staff officers packed their goods into Vauxhalls, with haste as great as the civilians.

We reached the centre of the town and wheeled left on to the Albert road. What ho! Now for it! New shell holes beside the road. A dead Tommy face down against a tree. I nipped over and took his entrenching tool, head and helve. A little cover is better than a wooden cross in this open warfare!

We debouched into the valley behind Millencourt and rested. Eighteen-pounders were blazing on the rise. One gun took a shell all to itself. Shells were bursting everywhere.

One burst about five hundred yards away. A piece came sailing and singing through the air. Lionel Carter was standing in the open. It landed squarely on his tin lid. But he was wearing one of the new pattern with a rubber ring in the top and was only shaken.

The brigadier and The Bull were studying maps. Runners were dashing in all directions. Skipper Carter called the C Company officers together and said: 'Lieutenants McDowall,

Clarke, Gelston and Jones, stay out with the nucleus, and Potts, Whittle, Ferguson and Mitchell, take the company in with me. The enemy position is not known.' What a bump for little Georgie, after it had been arranged that I stay out till the raiding-party operated.

'Well, you bloody neutrals,' we said to the other four, 'you had better nick off while your boots are good. Don't hang round with us soldiers. You might get hurt. We are particular with whom we associate.'

'Muvver said I wasn't to go out with an Aussie,' said McDowall falsetto. 'Anyway, it is time you lead-swinging blighters found out what a war is like.'

'Any special kind of flowers?' followed us as we deployed the platoons into blob formation.

Through a hedge and up a long green slope. Dead ahead across our path four big black shrapnel burst. Hares started up by our formation were dashing madly in all directions. 'Poor little blighters,' we thought, 'hope they get through.' A riderless horse galloped madly across the field, its flanks covered in blood. Hmm. Things develop. Over the rise we came under observation. Shells now began to burst among us; but there are lots of spaces in blob formation. Some landed among sections, and our track was now littered by little khaki heaps. 'When we top the next rise,' I said to me, 'we will run into machine-gun and rifle fire. So then we will extend into skirmishing order.'

Near the top I pipped on my whistle and gave the signal to extend. Like clockwork the platoon extended. From Lionel came a prompt washout signal. So I whistled again and the platoon went back in its old formation.

But there was no small-arm fire when we topped the second

ridge. Down came the gunfire in earnest. Roar of the shells, the spout and crash of high explosive, and the howl of fragments.

But as I looked through the rifts of flame and smoke there moved the battalions, steady and unfaltering, their sections spread across the whole countryside. Sole survivors of sections kept their appointed places and speed. It was worth the price to be with such men.

Where a little bank stretched across our front, we halted and took cover. Along came The Bull and the adjutant. Stood to attention with my back to Albert. A funny little tickling sensation up and down my spine. They stopped and spoke for some time.

If only, I thought about The Bull, your blasted pride would let you take cover, I could get down, too. Not half so likely to get a nasty, jagged lump of metal in my back that way. Kept thinking, strangely enough, of the time I hit The Bull in the ear with a snowball in Henencourt. I was a full private then, and he had just turned down my application for a transfer to the motor transport. You can bet your pants buttons that I was looking innocent, and walking away with my hands in my pockets when the snowball lobbed. They passed on, and I promptly went down on to the moist-smelling earth. The squalls of metal passed comfortably overhead. A little farther along the adjutant collected a Blighty wound.

Advance again, now skirmishing order, towards where the avenue of the Albert–Amiens road cut obliquely across our path. The hail of shells was redoubled, and complete sections were blown up. Bodies spun in the air like sacks of straw.

Astride the road we halted. Too blasted hot! Found a drainage pit alongside the road and got in it thankfully. The growling, thundering chorus ripped the trees, howled off the cobblestones, and bit pieces out of the good green fields.

Looking down the line, saw a five-point-nine burst right at the heels of the middle of my platoon. They fanned out in a semicircle and got down. Was all set to tick them off for moving, when shell after shell landed in the same spot. Their instinct was better than my logic, so I shut up.

Crawled on my belly to Pottsy for a consultation. We decided to stay where we were, and send runners ahead to where the skipper was. The first man went out and met a shell burst. I sent a stretcher party over to him. As they moved off a shell burst alongside them. They all went down in a heap—two dead and two wounded. Sent four of my platoon to help get them out, but was not prepared to weaken my strength any further.

Then I sent Coe to get forward to the skipper. 'Run alongside the trees,' I told him, 'so that they are not so likely to get direct observation on you. Then shoot out fast across the open.' But he staggered back shortly after, dazed, and with a gashed face. He had been blown up by a dud shell.

Crawled over to Pottsy for another consultation. Told him that I did not intend to waste any more men. But as I knew best how to dodge shells, I would go. He agreed to look after both platoons.

At this time the 47th tried to get out of the fire by going forward. But an increasing hail of perfectly aimed fire went with them. They stopped. Gave this business time to settle, then cantered down the avenue till I reached the nearest point to the steep bank which was my objective.

Then out across the field. I was the only man in view. 'Whoosh,' a dirty big five-point-nine just ahead of me. 'All right, your square-headed cow,' I said, 'I'll trick you. That isn't a rifle you've got. A howitzer shell is in the air a long time.' So I trotted half right. As I expected, the next shell allowed for me to go straight ahead.

Now you stupid big blighter, I thought, you will deflect to my present line. So I will swing left to your old line. Sure enough he did so. But no shell was farther than forty feet away, and some blasted off very close to me. This game of tig went on till he had expended about ten rounds, and I had reached cover under the big bank. Here was calm, for all that the maelstrom raged beyond.

Found Lionel and Fergy, and we went out on a reconnaissance. Odd, disorganised groups of the retiring Fifth Army sat in apathy. Three were grouped round a Vickers gun that was without mounting or ammunition. Nearby was a hare, killed by a piece of shell. Soft fur all bloodied, and wide, frightened eyes glazed in death.

With darkness the shellfire died. We walked back to our platoons, by the light of a sickle moon. By sunken roadways and across fields we led them to the front line, the railway bank before Dernacourt.

There was a keen, hard bunch of Scotties, their tails right in the air. 'Who are you?' they asked. 'Forty-eighth Australians.' They rejoiced among themselves, saying that Jerry's little promenade was finished. That now he would get what was coming to him. And much more that was flattering to us.

A burly, harsh-voiced sergeant told me in clipped sentences, epics of their last six days. How they had been cut off five times through their flanks giving way, and how the lessening numbers had hacked their way out each time. 'These,' he said, pointing to the assembling kilted group, 'are all that is left of our brigade.'

Up on the bank in broad Scotch accent came the challenge, 'Halt, who goes there?'

'Shoot, ye silly ——,' roared the sergeant, 'and challenge after.'

The rifle spat, waking hollow echoes in the night.

The sergeant and I charged up the bank. I grabbed the sentry's rifle, and together we blazed at shadows that faded into the trees. Then we descended the bank again to get on with the serious business of handing over. The Scots departed amid mutual good wishes, satisfied that earth's foundations were again solid. Poor gallant blighters. When they left us for a supposed quiet sector they ran slap into the enemy offensive in Flanders.

Our exhausted men dropped into the ready-dug rifle possies against the rails. Officers and stronger NCOs patrolled up and down, straining eyes into the darkness, in this our most dangerous hour. Later, I woke some of my men to stand watch, and, kneeling in a slit with my head against the clay, slept. Every twenty minutes or so, without any apparent reason, I would climb to my feet, patrol the line, and awaken sleeping sentries. Doubt if I was really awake myself as I did it!

At the first lightening of dawn, came a sudden, alarming scattered volley of rifle-fire from our right—on the 47th front. Hidden by the darkness there, a Vickers gun rapped out a few shots. Several enemy bombs burst, and the Vickers went silent. 'Stand to arms.'

Our men rose to their feet, accoutred and alert from the wells of sleep. A clatter as the stocks of their rifles touched the rails, soft clicks as safety-catches slid forward. Loud grating clicks as the cocking handles of Lewis guns were drawn back.

I raced along the bank to Captain Carter at company headquarters. 'Skipper,' I said, 'something has gone wrong with the 47th. Fritz is right into them. Let me have a dozen men and go down.'

'No, Mitch,' he answered, 'this is our pigeon right here. Look after your own sector.'

'But we are as safe as a blasted house,' I protested, 'nothing could ever get through C Company.'

As we argued, the increasing light showed a considerable body of men moving back from the 47th position. 'I'm off to have a look at those birds,' I said, and, without waiting for permission, turned and bolted down the bank through a hawthorn hedge. Lionel's voice floated after me, 'They're our men, aren't they?' Out on the flat, lugging out my gun, I yelled over my shoulder, 'How'n hell do I know.' But that was only to put the wind up Lionel, so that I could get the party I wanted. They must be 47th, retiring before a sudden enemy push. I would grab them and take them back to plug the gap. But if only I had a dozen of my own mob I would be much happier.

Halfway there. They stopped and all looked at me—rifles at the ready. Something funny about this.

Gawd struth! Bloody Fritzies!

Bounded four feet in the air with rage and astonishment. Marching into our flaming lines as if they owned them!

Yelled 'Stop!' and tore across the remaining space. They stood still, looking nearly as surprised as I was.

Picked out the officer and jammed my pistol barrel into his Adam's apple. 'Surrender! You so and so unqualified, misbegotten so and so.' His men stood with their mouths open, fingering their weapons uncertainly.

'Never shot a man with a pistol before,' I thought, 'shall I blow his head off?'

'Don't be a dope,' said the good angel perched on my right shoulder, 'if you do—you won't last as long as a dewdrop in hell.'

The officer's hands were down by his holstered pistol, so gave him another jab in the throat. 'Stick 'em up, you crimson illegitimate!' His life insurance policy would have been a good investment then.

He raised his hands. His men were grouped as before. He gave some orders. Rifles rattled to the ground. Equipment followed with dull thuds. A number of our men arrived with a gorblimey rush. I extracted the officer's pistol. In broken French, he told me to take the holster too, as it contained a spare clip; also, there was beer in his bottle. A new pair of British field-boots showed from the pack. 'I'll take the lot,' I said.

Asking my permission, he extracted a razor from the haversack. Held it up, saying, *'Très bon,'* wishing to take it with him. Now, I always wanted a German razor, so I said, *'Ouì. Très bon pour moi,'* and put it in my pocket. Have always felt a bit lousy over that. The razor was a dud, anyway.

Sergeant Fennel, from headquarters gunners, commenced lining them up. Thirty-one of them. Two captured 47th were released. One under-sized Fritz with a shot through his arm sat on his kit, sobbing bitterly. Pottsy put a fatherly hand on his head, saying, 'You are all right now, my boy. No more war. You will be treated well.'

Pottsy then found one who spoke English, and asked, 'When next German attack?' Fritz answered solemnly, 'No more German attack till next English spring.' Down the line came 'bish—bang—crash—wallop' of a full-blooded attack.

'Listen to that, you stinking little liar,' yelled Pottsy, and fetched him a swift kick. We roared with laughter.

The dejected column moved back, and we trotted across to our commands. Gibes from all ranks greeted me. Heard a Digger say, 'Mitchy's going to fight all the nasty Germans with his little gun.' Word came from the 47th that this party had bombed its way through them. Sergeant McDougall received his VC for looking after those who followed.[3]

Then came the scrap. Lines of grey-clad men doubled out of the sunken roads toward us. Waist-high over the bank we met them with rapid fire. Our Lewis gunners, disdaining the frontal attack, hammered with staccato bursts to the right, where black masses moved on the 47th.

Weaker and weaker became the advancing lines before our flailing fire, till at eighty yards all movement ceased. Our Lewis guns still chopped away at the right, where the main attack was. I was blazing with a rifle, having a lovely time, sending a swear word with each bullet.

When we stepped down to clean rifle-bolts and refill pouches with ammunition, one of my lot came up to me with a reproachful air, 'Mr Mitchell, you was swearing something horrible then.' Considering the speaker generally used very bad language himself, I did not know just how to take that one!

Quiet for a period. Noticed the German officer's pack. My boots were ruined by the march. I would change. Went through the pack. Tins of beef; bars of soap; a tin of Capstans; a pair of new socks—all our canteen stuff! Put the socks on. Something in one. Got out a piece of paper with the words: 'To some brave soldier. I hope these socks are comfortable. If they are not rub soap in them. Ruth MacDonald, 7 Manse Place, Inverness, Scotland, NB.' Grinning, I showed the note to a Digger.

'What a sell for her,' he said, 'thinking some brave soldier would get them!' The boots were a splendid fit. We must be winning. Those packs out in the open meant loot. I was puzzling my brain how to get out to them.

An idea!

I went up to Lionel with a long face. 'Skipper,' I said, 'we have not a bomb to our name. If Fritz gets under the other side of the bank he will blow us to ribbons.'

'Well, Mitch, we can't do anything about that.'

'Oh, yes, we can,' I told him. 'I will go out and collect the bombs off those Fritz equipments.'

'No,' he said, 'that would be too dangerous. I don't want you knocked.'

'Well, just think how dangerous it will be if Fritz starts bombing us.'

He grudgingly gave me permission to go out provided I took no unnecessary risks.

Wriggled from kit to kit. Cigarettes, pistols, and field glasses I put in a pack. Then came in strung all round with potato-masher bombs. But I had only ratted half the kits. Dumped the bombs at points along the line, showing selected men how to pull the strings before throwing.

Started back again, but Lionel stopped me. 'But we want all the bombs,' I said, 'these will go nowhere.' So finished rifling the kits. Got fourteen pistols, twelve pairs of field glasses, daggers and *beaucoup* cigarettes.

Sat for a few minutes with Lionel and Whittle at company headquarters. A crescendo of rifle-fire told of another attack, so hopped up for my cut. Returned when it was stopped and the grey-green survivors went to earth. Lionel handed me a long, hot, jagged lump of metal with, 'Landed where you had been sitting a couple of seconds after you got up.'

'Born to be hanged,' said Whittle.[4]

Shells were ripping over our heads, and bursting in the fields behind. Enfilading machine guns were returning the compliment of our Lewis guns. Trench-mortar shells were bursting along the permanent way. There were two ginger-headed brothers, both Loots in the 47th, named Paterson. Only knew there were two, because I had seen them together. One was in charge of the left platoon of the 47th, where it joined my platoon.

A trench-mortar shell landed on the rail, six feet in front of him, with a terrific roar. It bit a three-foot section of rail out, and the end of his rifle.

The blast caught him, and he sagged slowly from the ankles up. Then he picked himself up with a pained expression, and went on with the war. I had to grin.

Did a tour down the 47th line. They were getting it in the neck, but were holding firmly enough.

On returning I found another rush in progress. Pottsy had a bloodstained bandage round his head. He was standing and shooting, breathing fire and fury and swearing at the top of his form.

'A quid for a camera, Pottsy,' I told him. I hate to say things behind any one's back, but the fact is—Pottsy was not a good cusser. He had to stop and think up the words, and that is fatal to the best linguistic style. Of course, he had not my advantage of an apprenticeship to a company of Broken Hill miners!

Messages came up from the 47th. 'Hard pressed. Enemy attacking heavily.' Yard by yard the 47th flank contracted as they replaced dead with living in the vital spots. Farther and farther

I spaced my platoon to occupy the vacated territory. Before long Potts's platoon was on my old position. But still the shrinkage went on. It was the most logical method for us to assist them.

During a lull I cruised up to the Captain Elliot's company on our left. He was having high jinks potting at enemy parties who were trying to close in. Joined him in his little strafe.

Suddenly, apparently from my platoon sector, came a terrific explosion and a tower of smoke as if a dump had gone up. 'Ta, ta, skipper,' I said, 'that looks like my concern.' I started to bolt back. But I walked when I saw that it was much farther away than my position.

As I commenced to walk Lieutenant Frankie ran past, white-faced, to Pavy. 'Captain Elliot has just been shot dead. You are in command of the company.' So I went on thoughtfully to our company headquarters.

'Skipper, Captain Elliot has just been killed.' He looked upset, and replied. 'Whittle has just gone off on a stretcher. He is done for, too.'

Down from the left came Lieutenant Holton, staggering as he walked. Went out to him. Left arm shot through. Lots of blood. Lovely Blighty.

'Mitch,' he said, 'I've got one. How do I get out?' He was wobbling on his feet and ready to faint. I abused him as I cut off the bandoliers he carried. 'How the hell do you get these Blighties? Nick off that way before I go crook.'

He disappeared into the shell smoke as I stood watching and thinking. Clean beds, sleep at night, no chats, pretty nurses, convalescent leave. Blighty! You tinny cow, Holton!

Then things got tough. Waist-high we blazed over the railway. Trench-mortar bombs landing under our noses. A barrage of shell and machine-gun fire behind us. Double enfilade of machine-gun fire. No cover for us as we fired. Even our backs exposed full length.

Whizz-bangs grazed the line. Our Lewis guns all smashed. Corporal Joe Pitt working swiftly and coolly assembling the undamaged portions. Smoke, flame, stink and death.

Bad news from the 47th. We could manage, but we had no margin.

Two Fritzes appeared over the bank. We shot them. How many more behind! They were up to the railway and bombing the 47th, who were lobbing stones back in reply. The ginger Loot had taken his platoon still farther down towards the rail crossing. Turned to the next man to tell him to go farther right. But the top of his head was gone. A bullet from the right grazed my nose. Turned to the left in time to see young McDonald pitch forward dead, with it through the brain.

Told Sergeant Unwin to go to the right and report how the 47th were getting on. Found him fatally wounded a little later. He thanked me quietly when I wrapped him in groundsheets of dead men, but shook his head definitely when I told him that I would send him back with the first stretcher-party. Then our heavies opened—slap into the 47th. Saw men crawl slowly away from the bursts. No stretcher-parties had been able to get through for some time. The wounded lay where they had fallen, in a biting cold wind. We had no time to attend them.

Our fire seemed now to demoralise the enemy. They seemed to lose all cohesion, bunch, and move about aimlessly as we took our toll. None too soon did it ease off.

'What time is it, Pottsy?'

'Eleven o'clock, and you get twenty-one bob for today.'

'Bloody well earned it already, I think.'

'Thought you Anzacs liked this sort of thing?'

'Like hell!'

Sergeant Ford went back for stretcher-bearers. He led them up to us shrewdly through the weakest part of the barrage. Behind them came a party with four Lewis guns for us, bunched like stretcher-bearers. They were not machine-gunned.

Then forty men to reinforce the 47th came up. Bars of spattering machine-gun bullets lay across their path. Shells hounded them all the way. Men fell at regular intervals.

Their mates would kneel to inspect the fallen, do something for them, or pass on with a strange revealing gesture of finality. Steadily they moved to their rendezvous with death. One in four was the price left in their tracks ere they gained the railway bank. Things were better then. The wounded were evacuated. We had more Lewis guns and could keep longer under cover owing to the slower and weaker attacks.

'Troops are entitled to a smoke, Pottsy,' I said. Down the line I distributed the looted fags to the whole company. A big handful per man. Counted the men as I handed out the cigarettes. Forty left. We had come in with ninety. Extravagant thanks from everyone. We had all shared out our last gasper long since. My platoon dag lifted his smoke-blackened face from the jarring Lewis-gun butt. Grinning from ear to ear, he said, 'We will get you an illuminated address for this.'

At two o'clock droves of black-crossed planes swung over. We hated them as we hugged the bank closely, hoping they would see no movement. They dropped flares over our positions. Then heavier guns ranged on us. But that was just routine stuff.

Bleak rain commenced to pelt down. Oh for darkness! At last the shadows of night closed in. I was finished. One of my Diggers made a groundsheet shelter and put me in. As I lay dazed and half asleep I heard a metallic clatter as Fred Cherry arrived with his Stokes guns. The groundsheet rustled as it was drawn aside. 'Come on, Mitch,' came the skipper's voice, 'our relief is here.'

Weary to the edge of death, half blind with exhaustion, I tottered out into the mud, where stood my waiting platoon. The company filed off over the fields towards the Amiens road. A blustering wind, deadly cold—rain and sleet. Night as black as a wolf's guts.

Each step a fight between the will and body. Can I do it? Crash! A five-point-nine close behind. Crash again. Found myself stepping out in good form. 'First time I knew a flaming five-point-nine to do any good,' I thought.

Across the Albert–Amiens road. Scarred and torn. Broken trees. Wreckage. Into the fields beyond. The man ahead of me was stopped. I stopped.

Spoke to him. He did not answer. I went closer. Didn't look right. Went closer still. A blasted mule standing with his hindquarters to the storm. Passed round it quickly, but had a brainwave and went back. As I expected my next in line was standing patiently behind that misbegotten animal. 'Don't stand all night like a dope, behind that bloody mule,' I said with virtuous indignation.

Had to step out, hoping we were not completely lost in that black, inhospitable night. Finally sighted the wraith-like figures of our advance guard. Into a derelict trench system, sodden, clammy mud. Pottsy and I put down a groundsheet, lay down all standing, tin hat on, one sheet over us. The rain pattered down and flowed under. If he had mentioned twenty-one bob I would have bitten him. Never moved all night.

Dawn brought Good Friday—29 March. Got up out of a pool of water. If any one had pushed me I would have sat down and cried. But we set to work and made a rainproof shelter, and had a feed. The world was better immediately.

We lived under an arch of shells, but had no excitement all day. The skipper came to live with us. We cussed him that night when the runners came bursting in at all hours.

The 30th was another day of rain and shellfire. The 46th relieved us, and we moved back to the valley behind Millencourt. Dugouts had been cut in the bank. The roof of ours leaked all night, but we slept well.

Good and early on the 31st I went into deserted Millencourt. Had a bath and a shave. Brought back a stack of bedding which varied between tablecloths and wheat-bags. Also two sheep and a heifer, which I handed over to the company cooks. Rested throughout 1 April. Wandering into a big house in Millencourt, I found a group of Tommy NCOs. They had a big range in full blast.

'If you come back tonight, sir,' one said, 'you can have a piece of roast beef.'

'I'll be back, all right,' I told them. I was.

They piled my plate high with beef, baked potatoes and onions. There was an enormous stock of crockery in that house. They had not had to wash any yet, and they had been there five days. At each meal they piled the dirty plates in a corner of the room and brought out fresh clean ones from the cupboard. They gave me an eight-pound roast of beef when I left.

Back to the dugout. The skipper and Pottsy went for that meat like wolves. 'Mitch,' they said, finally wiping their mouths with the backs of their hands, 'you're a bloody little angel.'

We sat by the candlelight blissfully postponing the moment of turning in for a glorious sleep. A runner for the skipper. 'Your company will move up to the trenches in support of the 49th.' What a war!

Out into the cold night rain. Hop-over for certain. Up to a trench system about twelve hundred yards from the line. Ferguson led me to a good dugout for two, so we turned in without delay.

On the morning of 2 April the dingbats brought us our breakfast in bed—a thin slice of cold bacon, a tiny slice of bread, and some biscuits. We must be losing!

All day the shells roared overhead in a sustained chorus. Millencourt, Lavieville and Henencourt were getting it hot.

We played poker on credit. I won all round, but never collected. The losers were all stonkered before they handled money again.

A little before dark a plane with our markings dived and pelted us with bullets. Emptied a rifle at him.

'Don't shoot, Mitch, he's one of ours.'

'You tell him,' I said.

Windy, cold night. Guns flashing everywhere. Clusters of coloured lights over the line. Then sleep.

April 3 came in with a furious burst of fire along the front. Up where the Amiens road met the railway, great trench-mortar bombs were bursting to the tempo of a mighty kettle-drum. Brown smoke rolled away in clouds. It was as if a new volcano had suddenly burst forth. Sheets of flame leaping among the chaos lent realism to that impression.

Little Bill Connaughton was at my elbow, 'Nothing can live in that.'

'No,' I said pensively, 'that is why we are here. Nine Platoon. Stand to in fighting order. NCOs check ammunition and issue bombs.'

A runner from company headquarters arrived, 'Stand to arms.'

But someone did survive in that volcano.

Word drifted back that Marines had tried to raid the 46th, and had been dealt with.

Some copies of the *Daily Mail*. The utterly confident tone of that somewhat jingoistic paper was completely reversed. 'Iron Australians,' we read. 'The Australians have stopped numerous attacks in front of Albert. It is expected, however, that the enemy will enter Amiens tonight.' One did not require to think hard to see that the paper was preparing the nation for utter collapse.

A feeling of gloom seemed to pervade all ranks. For our own capacity we never had a moment of doubt. But of what use would be our efforts if others let Jerry through. The harder we fought, the more certain would be our annihilation. Bitter were our thoughts. We blamed bad staff work on our side for the enemy's successes.

At that time none of us expected to live long, and we had a feeling that over our bodies the enemy would march to complete victory. It was a bitter draught. The end of all things. Britain a fourth-class nation bereft of all colonies and greatness. Alien forces in occupation, Australia under the iron heel. And our lives not sufficient price to stave this off.

The blood and thunder of 1915, 1916 and 1917 passed in review before us. All those—our mates—who went west then.

Byrne, Hunt, Gilpin—their names are legion, the finest of mates, the best of men. All for nothing. Perhaps they were lucky to go then. They were spared the coming *débâcle*, when our flanking troops would ebb and we would be ringed with fire and steel. We, too, must die, and in dying look upon the shame of utter defeat. How those men who had gone west would have laughed at anyone who prophesied our defeat.

But the black gloom did not last long. As I read in the London *Mercury*:

> One thing is sure. This crazy round-about
> Destroys the introspective attitude.
> Action uproots the dreamy Hamlet-mood
> And blithely cuts the yellow throat of Doubt.

A little comedy was being played by the roadside. An old French peasant was arguing with Fergy. He would go for his pigs. 'But you will run into the Allemand.' Allemand nothing, he wanted his pigs. Two Diggers firmly led him away.

Later, The Bull, in passing, fixed me with a speculative eye. 'Mitchell,' he said, 'there are some loose pigs by the line. Pork would be very nice, but of course you must not go looking for them.' Clicked my heels dutifully, and coyly said, 'No, of course not, sir.' After dark, I prowled and prowled, but divil a pig did I see! When I finally heard guttural Deutscher voices, decided it was time to return to the safety of my mob.

At midnight our company shifted up to the big bank in close support. April 4 was a day of rain. At noon, the enemy guns opened with an intensity that presaged more trouble.

We were all strung up again by the inaction. Out of the rain came a little rabbit, too young to know fear. It walked the length of my body and sniffed my face trustingly. It shook the raindrops off its fur, and settled down while I petted it. For hours whilst the ground quivered and quaked with the fury of shell bursts, the little bunny snuggled up to me. At times it would quest out into the rain, but would always return.

Captain Carter was wounded in the face by a shell burst that blew in his possie. Up came Captain Norman G. Imlay to take over. He took up the reins firmly. No chance of getting away with anything when N.G.I. was there. I knew him, but worse still—he knew me. 'Mitch,' he said, 'we are for it tomorrow.'

He told me that I was to put my platoon into a trench on top of the bank, either that night, or before daylight on the morrow. Kept very quiet while he decided whether I should go then, or in the morning. Did not relish the idea of standing on my hind-legs all night in the rain. 'And hold the position,' he said, 'unless you get orders from me to leave it. Don't go leaving your men and buzzing off on private business.'

Three of our companies were in the front line. We, as the most battered company, were in support. Studied the map in the skipper's dugout by the light of a guttering candle. And so to bed.

Before dawn of 5 April inferno raged. A runner dived into my dugout. 'From Captain Imlay, stand to in your trench.' Wars should not be allowed before breakfast!

If ever I come out of this I will never get up before ten in the morning. This is the real horror of war—this 'standing to' before daylight. Bleary-eyed, shivering and miserable, buckled my equipment in place. Gas helmet, alert, pistol, cartridges, flare pistol, SOS flares, haversack, map, water bottle, overcoat under, groundsheet over. OK.

Went out into the dark, dripping, foggy night. Hedges and men looked gigantic at close range. Barged into the skipper's dugout. 'Here, Mitch,' he said, 'might as well take your platoon rum issue with you.' Filled my water bottle. Owing to our losses, there was plenty of rum.

Collected my platoon—the whole twelve of them. Scrambled up the steep bank and flopped into the short, sloppy trench. Glared in gloomy disgust at the Somme mist, thickened by the smoke of shell bursts. The rate and weight of enemy fire set old hands talking of Pozières.

In a fed-up moment, I thought of the rum issue. Took a swig and passed the bottle down the line. It came back with a nip in it! So had that, too. The sergeant major blew up at full daylight. Gave him the empty bottle to replenish. Passed that round, too. We stood in great form, commenting on the closer bursts. Hands on the parapet, we stood. We would pick up and examine all the hot, jagged pieces that landed within reach. And there were plenty. A lifting barrage reached us. Five-point-nines landed so close each side that the lips of the craters intersected the trench. Not a man hit.

We could not see a hundred yards for mist and smoke. But the sounds from the front line filled me with alarm. Thudding of German bombs—hand-to-hand fighting. Ragged, fluctuating volleys of our rifle-fire that told of a dwindling defence. Short, stabbing bursts of Lewis guns running like a refrain through the mad chorus.

Could read the battle by sound easily, but nothing I heard gave me any comfort. Inspected my faithful dozen, ammunition, rifles, guns, food. The future was dark. The hours of the morning dragged. The audible tale of the front became worse. From the right rear, a new sound—insignificant to the untrained ear—but it was the slow, irregular tack-tack-tack of a German heavy machine gun.

Sent immediate information to Imlay. His return note was just a terse comment, 'Hold your position.' So the line was broken somewhere!

At 1.15 p.m. a bunch of men suddenly burst over the hill. Some were wounded. Some fell as they ran. Went to meet them. Asked one man what had happened. He pointed to his face. Rags of flesh were all that was left of his lower jaw. Questioned others—47th men. 'Fritz swamped the 52nd. Pushed artillery into the gap and blew us out.' Borrowed a 47th captain's field glasses to inspect a crowd half-right. They were Fritzes. In the confusion I kept the glasses.

One 47th sergeant, resting momentarily in our trench, said, 'You are being surrounded, you will be captured if you don't get back.' Now, as the front line was rolled up farther, came the 48th men. Saw Pavy turn head over heels as he was shot through the leg. Went out to help him up, but he managed to get along himself. Examined him for surplus ammunition, and wished him joy in Blighty.

One 48th company under Captain Cumming, was holding fast. Down the valley on the left galloped Pottsy with his gallant little platoon, to help extricate them. 'Well,' I thought, 'Pottsy may be going into the lion's den, but I am caught in a bear trap.'

Then came back the last survivors of the front line garrison. Bitterly they fought, as though their lives were already forfeit, stopping to swap shots with their pursuers. They fired and moved in a desperate heroic gesture. Hard-faced, they passed into security beyond my trench.

The world had fallen. The Australian line had been broken. Not even pride was left. Tears of grief ran down my face. I did not know that fifteen storm divisions had attacked the shattered 12th and 13th Brigades.

Suddenly as the raising of a curtain the fog lifted. My eyes bulged as I saw at the railway crossing one thousand yards away, lines and masses of enemy—men and guns. The sight of the packed mass of men, wagons and guns made my mouth water. What a target for our guns! Slapped a green flare into the pistol. Cocked, and fired, the pistol kicked against my hand, away hissed the flare. Then another. That was our SOS.

Our barrage came down. Two eighteen-pounders. All that was left with ammunition, or un-hit by German shells. A saga could be written of our gunners that day.

Sound of rifle-fire from my right. Went over. There was a party of the 47th battalion solemnly desperate, making a stand on my flank. Advancing grey-green hordes in front. As the party would fire on one group, twenty others would advance. Stood by the young sergeant-in-charge. My inclination was to say, 'Get to blazes out of this. It is death here.' But there was the job to do, so I said, instead, 'Hold this position if you can. As long as you can hold, we will keep your left secure.'

Here was the apex of a long valley. In the V of our view was the plain ending at the railway. White jets of seventy-sevens as they fired from the railway. The instant burst of the shells, close at hand. Beyond the railway spouted the white flame of countless guns. The quiescent enemy mass by the railway. Hordes of advancing stormers spread all across the plain, constantly closing in.

The whipping cracks of enemy small-arm fire was of a fury

unparalleled since the Landing. 'For God's sake, get down, sir,' appealed the sergeant, 'every one standing up has been hit.' Tried to explain to him that it was not possible for me to be hit. But in deference to the added voices of the men round him, I knelt beside him and studied the enemy movements. I had an obsession during the whole stunt, that so long as I exposed myself freely I was safe, but if I went to earth, I was done for.

Left this gallant, doomed group, with a heavy heart. My platoon was blazing away at the multitude of targets. Scribbled a précis of the situation and sent it down to Captain Imlay. Back came his reply, 'Extend your flank to connect.'

Unwillingly, I spaced three of my precious men across the open between. Shortly after, a salvo of enormous black shrapnel burst over them, eight feet up. We went across. All dead. Went to the flank of the 47th party, most of them finished also.

The jig is nearly up. Did not replace the slaughtered men, but left my remnant of a remnant under cover of the trench. Groups moving up. Rifles smoking. Connaughton chop, chop, chopping with his Lewis. At each burst a party went down. But a dozen other parties advanced.

Futile and hopeless! Tears were still running down my face— rage and injured pride. Sent an NCO across to the 47th. He did not return.

Went over myself. Wiped out! Every man lay face down and silent behind his silent gun. Every man and every weapon faced the closing enemy. Even in that moment I felt a thrill of pride and pity.

Back, and sent a message to Imlay. 'Flank gone. We are being surrounded. Can we retire to better position?'

The reply, 'Hang on—N.G.I.'

'Backs to the wall!'—Backs to hell, and Old Nick reaching out with his pitchfork. We could not hear our own rifles above the din. Only knew by the recoil we had fired.

Could feel the sidelong glances from the men, and the unspoken thought, 'How are you going to get us out of this mess?' 'Poor blighters,' I thought, 'my job is to keep you here till you are done for. Not get you out.'

As we blazed I thought hard. By nightfall the attack would have swept far beyond us. Company headquarters would be swallowed up, too. We will keep this ring of attackers back. I will have two or three men left by that time.

So with darkness we will slide into the grass and crash through the weakest part of the ring. Then join up with some harried group and fight as seems best. With my mind made up, we carried on the war. On three sides they closed in. Only the way to company headquarters was open.

Suddenly a runner dived in, and I read the message, 'Retire to the line by the aeroplane—N.G.I.' Did not know where the aeroplane was, but passed it on as I got it.

Sent the men back in three sections. Connaughton I left with me to cover their retirement. All the visible enemy in our short field of fire he shot down or drove under cover. With one last drum left—he looked a question. 'Sweep the ground with it.' He did so. 'Now you get back.' He looked at me distrustfully. 'I'll wait for you,' he said.

Abused him, and ordered him back, though I would have sooner patted him on the back.

I intended to utilise this last opportunity for a glance over the valley, so that I might take back the very latest information. Connaughton started. I moved to the right, where I could see over the ridge. Fifty yards away five big capable-looking stormers rose slowly to their feet. Their rifles swung to their shoulders, as by an order. Could see their eyes, set grim expressions, and every article of equipment. Changed direction from a direct line to them to a line across their front. Hard to hit that way. Nothing seemed to matter much, so did not run. Watched them as each rifle puffed, and thought of putting my fingers to my nose. 'Bloody rotten shots, aren't you?' I said confidentially.

A depression led from in front of my old trench to the left. As I was waist-high above it, they tried again. Never heard their rifles or the bullets above the din.

Down the bank once more, and out on the lower plain. Futile bullets pecked the ground as I trudged. What did it matter? Only a question of today, tomorrow or the next day!

There was the aeroplane. To my delighted eyes there stretched a well-sited, new dug trench lined with capable-looking Australians. Furtively wiped the tears from my cheeks with the back of my hand.

Eager questions assailed me. 'Where is he? When is he coming?' Pride came back. The world dizzily reoriented itself. 'Massing over the hill,' I replied, 'here in about twenty minutes. But we've got him now, we've got him!' Reported to Captain Imlay, where I found him walking along the parados.

Wreckage of platoons, companies, battalions, engineers, pioneers, waifs and strays, all stood to arms there. Sorted out my platoon and led them to the extreme left, where there was a gap. Some Tommy Vickers gunners came with me.

A roar of small-arm fire came from the right. A 13th Brigade battalion—the 49th—swept forward into the gap. We watched as they swung along with irresistible momentum. The ranks thinned as they went. Here and there groups shot and stabbed. Ahead of them ran field-grey figures. The gap is closed by good Australian bayonets!

No further attack came from Fritz. On the skyline from my old position bunches of enemy dug in; eighteen-pounder shrapnel bursting white among them. Strings of machine-gun bullets zipped round us. We replied with Vickers and Lewis.

Darkness, and orders to move back. Took my platoon to battalion headquarters. But from there we were sent back again to a position alongside the Amiens road. All night we dug. Partly to keep out the cold, partly to prepare against the storm of aimed shellfire expected with daylight.

All day on the sixth we waited tensely for the hail of shells that spelt continuance of the offensive. We were swapping machine-gun compliments with the ridge opposite. We must have caught some of them, for they put up a double green flare, which I had noticed meant stretcher-bearers.

Now, our SOS was two separate green flares. So down dropped our gunfire on them. And down came their gunfire on us—the worst I ever experienced. Whizz-bangs fired from short range hit on their shoulders, bounced twenty feet in the air, and burst with deafening howls. Big shells punched the rocking earth with appalling fury. Smoke rolled in clouds. Had a bad attack of wind-up, and the taste of death was in my mouth. If I live through this, I thought, as I lay in a heap, I will never be any good any more. Ten shells a second, I calculated, landed on our hundred yards of front.

Above the din came the approaching roar of some great howitzer shell. Its sound of travel muted even the bursting of the five-point-nines. One crashed the bay on the right where Vickers gunners were. A still, small voice kept saying within my head: 'This is death.' I lay still, idly watching the small burning balls of powder eating holes in my sleeve.

Lance Corporal Siekamp carefully brushed the sparks off. I waited for the crushing trench walls to leap on me. The end of the world! In a sheet of flame, with the roar of chaos, the next left bay, holding my platoon, went.

'A job of work.' Scrambled round the corner. Where my platoon had been, was charred, tumbled earth. No trench. Back in gasping haste to Siekamp. 'Dig this end—quick—quick.'

Back again over the top of the grave. A machine gun opened on me as I went. Grabbed the first man I came to. 'Come up and dig these men out.' He looked at me slightly bewildered. 'But there was no one in that bay. Sergeant Hatcher said a shell would come in, and shifted us out just before it landed.' If I had seen Hatcher bunching those men I would have blown his socks off. But now I would have kissed him.

Went back, relieved and happy. The Vickers gunners dug out their men dazed, but unhurt. They were still spitting out dirt when last I saw them. Slowly the fire died. The 2nd Division came up and relieved us. We assembled our weary few and marched back.

Next morning we marched past The Bull as he sat statuesque on his big charger. Heads up, we went, chests out, unshaven, muddied, torn and bedraggled, but happy. A grin split his hard dial. 'My God, Mitchell—you look rough.'

Grinned back—saluted decorously, and marched on.

A day of rest in billets, then a swift round of refitting and reorganisation. Gaps in the ranks where trusty mates had stood, and whose places no newcomer could fill. Many times I turned at the sound of a voice I knew, only to find that it was a trick of imagination. For the dead do not speak in the broad light of day, or stand by one's side as the wrecked platoons and sections are clubbed together. Imagination is not good for a soldier. We bent our minds to the job in hand, lonelier and lonelier as marched the years of flame and smoke.

One day as my platoon was lying idly in the grass of an orchard, I read them the newly received 'backs to the wall' order. Still, they were, as men who take their rest when they can. Capable by their training and pride. Fatalistic by their experience, they listened quietly.

'The enemy has attacked in overwhelming strength . . . gained initial successes . . . We have our backs to the wall . . . Many of us are tired . . . Positions must be held to the last man . . . Believing in the justice of our cause . . .'

'So now, gentlemen—you know,' I said carefully folding that historic document away.

'Bull dust!' said someone casually.

In a few days our faces were turned again to the line.

The distant whiff of gas from Villers-Bretonneux and the slam of shells wrecking the town.

A Digger sidled up to me.

'Did you hear about the new tin hat issue for the Aussies?' he asked.

'No,' I bit, 'what are they?'

'They are giving us tin hats turned up at the side. We won't need our felt hats any more.'

'I think you are right,' I said thoughtfully.

A big shell crashing into the field on our right seemed to confirm it.

Fugitive lines of Kipling were going through my head. They came to me suddenly as we entered the stinking wood by Villers, and slung our gas helmets alert:

> Our world has passed away
> In wantonness o'erthrown;
> There is nothing left to-day
> But steel and fire and stone.
>
> Comfort, content, delight,
> The ages slow-bought gain,
> They perished in a night,
> Only ourselves remain
> To face the naked days
> In silent fortitude
> Through perils and dismays
> Renewed and re-renewed.
>
> Though all we knew depart
> The old Commandments stand—
> 'In courage keep your heart,
> In strength lift up your hand.'

Again a shell slammed hollowly in the silent wood and the renewed stench of gas, dead men, and horses came to us.

16

The Vin Blanc sector

Behind our support trench was the wood that flanked Villers-Bretonneux.[1]

Villers standing in gloomy grandeur on our left, smoke rising from shells and many fires—looked the very spirit of undefeated France.

All about us lay the dead, pitifully boyish-looking Tommies who had been driven out of Villers. Among them were the equipments of our 13th and 15th Brigade men who had died in the recapture of Villers and had been buried. The haystack-like shapes of stalled German tanks showed on the skyline.

Near them were the more graceful types of our whippets, also out of action. A great and decisive battle had been fought here two days before.

The price to the enemy was shown in the grey-clad clusters of dead. In front of us was the International Post, where in the firing-line our men mingled with the French of the Moroccan Legion.

Big soldierly Frenchmen passed us in chattering groups. By day and night, their seventy-five's raved with Gallic fury.

A Digger came to me with a sandbag, half filled. 'I found this by a dead bloke. Have a look over it.' He emptied the bag on to my bunk. Very few things contained so much concentrated tragedy as the contents of that sandbag. They were all letters, unsealed and uncensored. Some of the letters were pierced through and crimson-stained.

The history of these letters formed in my mind with swift certainty, I could see everything clearly. These were the letters written by our 13th and 15th Brigade men before they were rushed into the attack. Without a chance to post them, they had carried them on to battle. And they had died. The unknown gatherer had been struck down during his kindly task.

These letters were the last words of men, who in desperate battle had in dying saved the Allied front. And these were written to those who were dearest to them.

Now, the sacred duty had fallen to me, from the hand of death, to deal rightly by them. Long I pondered the problem.

It would not be fair to just frank and send them on. False hopes might be raised that the sender still lived. I knew that these letters would only have been taken from dead men.

That afternoon I spent in writing a short explanatory note on each letter. I strove for words to ease the blow, yet did not attempt to raise vain hopes.

It was my duty to read each letter to see that no military information slipped through.

War-hardened as I was, the task shook me—these last lines

of the fallen. Cheering words to mothers in far-off sunny places, loving thoughts to wives, to children, and sweethearts. A little of the longing of the writers crept through. Sometimes there was a hint of the knowledge of the approach of the reaper. My eyes were wet, long before I had finished.

Returning with a fatigue party, I found my batman at my possie entrance. 'What would you like?' he asked, and then reeled off the names of eight or ten different wines.

'Give me anything that's going,' I said, 'but do it quickly. I'm dry.'

'It's dinkum all right.' Tom went in and turned back the blanket that covered my pillow. For a pillow were a dozen bottles of wine, labels upward, and each label was different. We drank from mess tin lids.

Next day, Captain Imlay sent me up to have a look at Monument Wood, which we were to attack in a day or so. My path led me past the corner of Villers where the dead of four nations lay thick. In some shell holes were German equipments and bloodstains, in opposite ones British equipments and bloodstains.

A German field gun lay wrecked beside a wrecked building. Through broken windows could be seen set tables and made-up beds.

But I pushed on, up the railway cutting, climbing the bank by a stone bridge. Through the back door of a lath-and-plaster cottage I went, and cautiously climbed the stairs. Where the plaster had fallen, through the lath spaces could be seen the German line and all beyond. These walls would not stop a bullet, so I set myself ready to roll downstairs if a machine gun opened up.

Through the slits I trained my field glasses. I was looking down on to the German garrison, a hundred yards away. The glasses brought them to within feet of me. I studied closely the features of the men I hoped to kill, and whom I hoped would not kill me. We bore no personal hatred, but considered that their elimination would atone for some of the losses they had caused us. No squeamishness ever clouded our sights at the critical moment.

I saw as much as I could, then carefully climbed down, crawled below the line of the windows, and slid out the back door. Did not feel safe until I was below ground-level.

On the top of the bank was a post, held by bored-looking 45th men. I was dry.

'Got anything to drink?'

'Not a thing,' they said. 'No tea, no water—nothing.' As an afterthought, one said, 'There is some red wine in that tin, if it's any use to you.'

A two-gallon petrol tin was three-quarters full of neglected claret, a very sound wine. So I quenched my thirst.

A little farther along was another post high up on the crest of the cutting.

Two men signalled me to come up. After clambering up an almost vertical forty-foot clay wall, they told me why they had called. Would I try this wine? Something extra special. I did. It was.

Down where the rail-cutting dies out on level ground were four Frenchmen. Their tunics bulged. Necks of bottles poked from every pocket. Their hands were full.

Two hundred yards away, five-point-nines were blasting the railway track.

'*Ah! Officier d'Australie.*' Would I have a drink with them? I always defer to the Frenchman in the judgement of his native wines. Their choice was nectar.

Would I accept four bottles? Too right I would—'*Avec plaisir, messieurs.*'

I swayed blithely along the track that led to my trench giving a passing word of condolence to a German that he could never again drink of the wonderful wines of France.

A debonair French officer and *poilu* were on the path in front. They waited. Would I do them the honour to drink with them. Delighted! Now would they honour me by drinking with me. But certainly. The bottle passed from nation to nation. It was not exactly a compass course by which I reached the trench.

'Have a drink Mr Mitch?' asked Tom, my faithful dingbat.

A day or two we stayed there. Heavily they shelled us at dawn and sunset. At odd times big shells would explode in the forest behind us with a sound like a giant door slamming.

Once I was watching a barrage tearing up the country two hundred yards ahead. A bird flew fast over my head. In surprise that there should be a bird in all this shelling, I turned my head quickly to follow its flight. It landed just behind, and exploded. It was a shell!

By night, the rockets spread in their multi-coloured sprays along the French front. Their artillery rose to furious drumfire every hour or so. One would think that there was a full-dress offensive going on all the time.

Along our front was quiescence, only the slow thunder of our guns, as they systematically flayed tactical points. Our slower and more methodical gunfire, probably cost the enemy many times more casualties, as prearranged targets were constantly engaged.

At midday on 2 May I received a batch of fourteen reinforcements to add to my fourteen platoon members.

These men were all too old or too young. Few of them were of the physical standard to which we were accustomed. Some of them had been civilians in Australia three months before. Most of them had been intended for non-combatant units, but owing to our losses, they had been pushed up to us.

I set about musketry instruction.

When I ordered them to load, two of them tried to push the clips as well as the cartridges into the magazine, so I moaned feebly and handed them over to my toughest sergeant.

My trusty Tom thrust a half-dixie of wine into my hand. Refreshed, I went back to the teaching of parade-ground elementals, within sight of the enemy wire.

I was sorry for these men, that they were to be thrust into a night attack against a seasoned enemy, but I was sorrier still for myself.

17

Monument Wood and an unofficial armistice

Just after midnight on 3 May 1918 we filed out of the reserve trench and over the railway. We were to attack Monument Wood at 2.20 a.m.

I was in a bad temper. Why, thought I, should I be afflicted with an untrained rabble in my fourth year of war; Anzac leave months overdue, all for a rotten little attack on a narrow sector that would draw a concentration of all enemy artillery within miles.

Could visualise the big hefty Hun artillerymen swinging the trails of their seventy-sevens and five-point-nines, saying, 'Komm, we will blow these verdant Englishers to hell.'

As we trudged over the sleepers to the rattle of equipment and the sound of bumping of rifle butts, I pondered Kipling's 'Islanders':

Sons of the sheltered city—unmade, unhandled,
    unmeet—
Ye pushed them raw to the battle as ye picked them raw
    from the street.
And what did ye look they should compass? Warcraft
    learned in a breath?
Knowledge unto occasion at the first far view of death?

Reached the railway bridge near our hop-over point. A mob of elephants would have climbed the bank more quietly. The recruits had not developed their eyes to night work. They stumbled and fell over obstacles that we old hands could see clearly. Poor blighters—it must have been a black night of fear for them.

A guide met and led us over the front line trench. He immediately mixed my men with McDowall's in the dark; then mixed us up in a lot of barbed wire. My language should have melted the wire.

Placed each man flat with his head pointing to Fritz. 'When we charge go that way.'

Didn't take long, but the left platoon was moving about looking like haystacks in the light of the flares. They collected. Several machine guns opened, and they went down like wheat before the reaper.

Flares were going up from the enemy like fury. He might just as well have issued us an invitation and made it quite formal. We found later that he had packed the line with Jaegers and had one machine gun to every two of our men.

At 2 a.m. we were settled down and the playful Jaeger was parting our hair with machine-gun ricochets, just to show what he could do if he tried.

A flare dropped against my ribs and still burned. The hard white light must have shown me to the wide world.

The heat was penetrating, but I was scared to bat an eyelid. Started counting the tenth parts of seconds till a shower of bullets would arrive. But the flare went out and I was still whole.

2.10. Comparative peace. 2.13, 2.14, 2.15. The whizz of our shrapnel. Six eighteen-pounders fired for three minutes, then stopped. The only harm they did was to blow up several of McDowall's men. Nine platoon had had no casualties—yet.

We were astounded at the poorness of the barrage. Just enough to wake Fritz up properly.

Zero hour was 2.20. The illuminated dial of my watch showed 2.17.

We had failed already. Half hoped that someone with brains and sufficient authority would call the show off.

2.18, 2.18½. Ten seconds to go. Blast these little hopovers! Five—four—three—two—one. Zero.

Raised my head. Not a move anywhere. If we are wise we will lie low and say nowt. Ten seconds and no move. Imlay must be gone or he would have set things moving. Fifteen seconds. McDowall's voice. 'Advance C Company.' Blast it! That's torn it. 'Advance nine platoon.'

All the typewriters in the world going together. A dozen flares over our heads. A line of bursting bombs at the Fritz wire. Bullets sizzling, squealing, and buzzing.

An enormous Fritz officer plain against the light, galloping along his parados, yelling fire orders in a voice that outdid the bombs.

'Ruddy little hero, aren't you,' I said to myself, 'cantering across shell holes to do battle for your king and country when you would sooner be at home in bed.'

Arrived in front of the Fritz wire. It was picked out in showers of sparks from end to end by the German machine-gun bullets. It was an untouched and perfect barrier.

Looked around for my platoon, to give Fritz some of his own medicine, but there was not a man above ground.

'Well I ain't no thin red hero,' I thought, and slipped into a juicy, deep shell hole.

A sudden tattoo of bombs and rifle-fire forty yards to the right. It was Captain Cumming and three men who rushed vainly at the enemy trench. By the light of bursting bombs I saw them fall.

Then I took stock of the enemy line and what I saw made me rage again. He had had the cheek to hoist his machine guns into the open in front of the trench. The crews sat and knelt around them—big black blobs. The riflemen stood between, firing from the hip. Every seventh or eighth man was throwing bombs like clockwork. They were bursting behind me.

I had brought a rifle and bandolier.

Bull Voice, their officer, was still dashing up and down giving orders. Took a snapshot at him before settling down to serious work.

The nearest gun was thirty feet away. No need for sights at that range. Gave them a magazine and another. They went out of business. Started on the next until the fifty-cartridge bandolier was spent. Just at this stage, Tom Davis, my batman, arrived with a bag of rations, a corporal, and a reinforcement. Sent the corporal back to dig up any rifle-grenadiers he could find, keep them well back, and drop Mills into the line. He did so with excellent results. A Fritz screamed with the first burst.

I took the reinforcement's spare bandolier.

The reinforcement let out a yip and sat back in the shell hole. 'What's up?' I asked, far too busy to knock off my twenty-to-the-minute shooting to have a look.

'I'm hit.'

'Where?'

'In the arm.'

'You must have tin pants on. Five minutes in action and you get Blighty. Hop it.'

He hopped.

With a rush and a clatter, my Lewis gunner arrived. 'Now,' I said, 'we will really do something. Gimme the gun.'

I flattened the bipod to keep it low, took a deep breath, then let go.

Shades of persecuted Loots! The stupid cow had put on a drum of anti-aircraft ammunition—tracer one in four.

A line of light from the gun-muzzle showed our position to the wide world. As the last bullet was leaving the barrel, I was sliding back on to my sit-down out of harm's way.

Dante knew nothing. Every gun converged on to our shell hole. One or two machine guns can make things unpleasant but when twenty converge, it behoves the wise to emulate the rabbit.

Bombs landed all round the lip of the shell hole, but none came in.

Began to think that perhaps we had outstayed our welcome. Also worry about what daylight—now not far off—would mean to our scattered remnant.

So scribbled a message to brigade headquarters: 'Attack hopelessly held up on uncut wire. No chance of success. Can I have permission to retire the company?'

When the machine-gun fire ceased I sent Tom off with it.

Left alone again I began to worry hard. Not much time left, and only one thing to do, retire. I will find another officer and share the responsibility with him. So hopped out and down the line.

The things I saw would have made an angel weep. One reinforcement was using a small mound for cover, but he was on the Fritz side of it. Rectified that. Another was lying side-on to Fritz. Another was as flat as a snake alongside a deep shell hole. Suggested that he get in the hole. He did. Next time I passed he was as flat as a snake in the bottom of a shell hole. But not a sign of any other officer.

Stopped in amazement in an open space at the sight of a man torn to rags by machine-gun bullets. What I might have done then was problematical, but Fritz intervened.

A sledgehammer hit my left foot and seemed to knock it off. 'What ho!—a Blighty,' said I, and hopped on my good foot to the old front line.

'Any officer?' I asked. 'Here's Mr Clarke,' said a voice.

There was Ginger Clarke all right, flat out on the floor of the trench, shot through both arms. He looked very pale and done. 'You hit?' he asked. 'Yes,' I said, 'I've got one in the foot. Can you walk?' No, he could not. Spied long Sam Siekamp. 'Carry him out, Sam.'

Inquired again for officers, but they were all gone. Even the 45th officer in charge of the front line garrison had been shot through the head watching us go over.

No wonder there had been no impetus in the attack. All of our officers and most of our men chopped down before they had gone ten yards; I had lost Sergeant Rundle—a splendid soldier and man.

All right, I thought, I must be the boss here now. I will bring the men in and face the music later.

A runner: 'Any officer?'

'Yes. Here.'

'Message.' I got down into the trench, struck a match, and read it. 'Advance at all costs—D.A. Twining, Adjutant.' I turned the air blue, pink and saffron, and threw the message away.

Was heaving myself out of the trench to withdraw the company when there was another voice.

'Any officer?'

'Yes. Here.' It was young Arnold, MC, DCM, MM, our intelligence officer, nicknamed Ickey.

'That you, Mitch?'

'Yes.'

'Where is Captain Imlay?'

'Hit.'

'The others?'

'All gone.'

'You hit?'

'Yes.'

'I've brought orders for you to withdraw the company.'

'Just what I'm —— well going to do.'

'All right,' says Ickey, 'I'll help you.'

'You —— well won't,' I said. 'You don't know where to go and will be killed.'

But he went out in his usual untroubled way to some flank troops.

The east was very light now.

So out again I went. Stirred each man with my toe. 'Hit?' If he answered and it was 'No,'— 'Back to the line.'

Half-light and a shower of bullets ended the business, so I dropped into the front line.

Then it dawned on me that I had a Blighty. Carefully, like a mother with her first babe, I took my boot off.

Another blanky sell. The bullet had struck the iron heel-plate and I did not have a scratch. I consoled myself with a slab of chocolate and wine out of my bottle.

After setting day-posts to guard against surprise I was dozing peacefully, when a tattoo of shots and a call caused me to look over the top. A man had hopped out of a shell hole and into the front line.

Then there were some more shots. A dazed looking, bespectacled reinforcement ambled obliquely across our line. He was about eight feet from my section of the trench, but seemed to have no inclination to get in. Called out and beckoned him furiously to come in. Half a dozen Jaegers were potting at him.

He stopped with his mouth open and looked at me. Then he collected, spun around, and dropped. A sergeant with an expression of vast disgust, reached out and hauled him in by the foot. One through the shoulder. Just a nice Blighty. Little wounded hero. They could only hit the heel of my boot.

Thoroughly peeved, I yelled to the shell holes: 'If any one else tries to move before dark, I will shoot him myself and save Fritz the trouble.'

They must have taken me seriously, for no one else moved.

The sound of voices awoke me once again. A party of our stretcher-bearers appeared over the railway bank. The leader carried a white flag.

Held my breath for fear they would be shot down. Fritz was a gentleman. They went unscathed, not a bullet was fired from the enemy trenches, a short one hundred yards away.

Then an astonishing thing. Full length out of the German line rose an officer—our old friend of the Bull Voice. He called: 'Do you want to surrender?'

A chorus: 'Surrender be ——!'

Again our friend: 'I do not speak French. Speak in English.'

Just as I was debating whether he had a sense of humour he marched calmly toward our line, large as life and twice as natural.

My brain fairly buzzed.

'Can't let him come here and see our weakness. Can't shoot him because our stretcher-bearers would be shot in turn.'

'He must be met in the middle. By whom? You, of course, you silly cow; you are the only officer left!'

With a sigh of resignation I heaved myself out of the trench and marched toward him with all the dignity that is possible to one who knows that he may be snapped short in mid-stride by a bullet. I could see very close now the line of deep helmets topping heads that gazed at me in frank curiosity. Soon I was face to face with Bull Voice.

We saluted. He, flat handed in the German style. Both very formal. 'What is it that you want?' he asked with an air of a god dispensing an inconsiderable favour. 'These,' I said, pointing to our wounded all round us.

'Very well,' he said, 'I will give you twenty minutes. If we fire three shots in the air we will continue war.'

'Three shots,' think I, 'time to dive into a shell hole.'

'Very well,' I said, 'I will not go farther towards your line than here, and you do not come closer to us,' for I was anxious to keep him away from our line.

'Yes,' he said.

My troubles were not over. The new hands seemed to think this was a regular occurrence, and that the hatchet was buried. So they started to swarm out of the trenches.

I made some most pointed comments and they got back in again. Keeping Bull Voice away from our line, and looking after wrecked C Company and a platoon of the 45th was trying.

But to do him justice, Bull Voice was the soul of honour, integrity and generosity throughout the whole proceeding. He was tall and handsome, well over six feet, and did not look more than twenty-two. He sought no small advantage—as I should have. I should probably, in his position, have stipulated that I take the lightly wounded and he the severe cases.

However, 'One man,' he said, 'I will keep. He is on our parapet, shot through the foot.'

He then changed his mind and gave him to us. He gave us Captain Cumming's body—wristwatch and papers intact.

Shades of Ned Kelly! Could you imagine an enemy officer in our lines being unrifled? Besides, the papers in his possession must have had military value.

Fritz started stretcher-bearing, too. Counted with satisfaction eleven being carried away from the scene of my operations.

Stretchers had all gone and not yet returned. So set a party to work to rip the doors off the cottages behind us, use them for stretchers, dump the casualties at the railway bridge, and return.

In this way the work went on swiftly. Bull Voice and I strolled up and down together. We talked of Cabbages and Kings. He led me to one of our men near his parapet.

I looked down into the trench full of square-built, stocky looking Jaegers. A queer sensation. They looked at me in apparent curiosity and friendliness.

Then, I think, 'All this generosity going to waste, and nothing in return. Must do something.'

'Oh,' I said, 'there is a dead H— German near our lines that you can have.' (Nearly said 'Hun' to him; just caught myself in time.)

His eyebrows went up in surprise. 'One of my men?'

'I don't think so.' He was a fortnight dead and humming to high heaven. I was getting rid of him for our sakes.

'If you will give me four of your men, I will get him for you,' I said. My men were fully engaged.

A volley of German words, and four Fritzies climbed out and came to me with friendly grins.

So I marched off in charge of a party of enemy.

My boys vastly enjoyed the joke. Out of earshot of the officer, these Jaegers turned to me eagerly and said, 'Cigarette?'

Gave them a packet of Red Hussars, a most unpopular issue cigarette.

'Darn lousy trick even to play on Fritz,' commented the boys.

With crinkled noses they rolled the corpse on to the groundsheet and marched off. I could get on with those Jaegers.

On patrol with Bull Voice again. One of our men came up. 'There is a wounded man just over the road.'

Over the road might have been the next country for all we knew of what had gone on there.

As a matter of fact, Charlie Stoerkel, MC, our battalion fire-eater, had broken through and captured a battalion headquarters there.

Bull Voice and I stood by the road. I had many qualms, but stuck close to him. A new vista of firing-line opened up, both Australian and German. And they did not fire on us. We both stood sentinel, beautiful targets, while our bearers raked in some more wounded from over the road.

The twenty minutes of grace had stretched to two hours. All the wounded had been removed long since. Unwounded men in shell holes had been solemnly rolled on to doors and carted in.

Now even the dead were removed and placed behind the buildings.

Quietly I had passed word to my men, and they were all back in the trenches, keeping careful armed watch.

I turned to Bull Voice: 'I thank you for your generosity. We have all our wounded. We had better continue the war.'

'We need not start yet,' he said.

Visions of eighteen-pounder shrapnel, dirty stuff that sweeps the ground like a vicious broom, crossed my mind. Everyone but ourselves on both sides was now under cover and standing to arms.

And also visions of some inexperienced youth on either side wishing to pick off an enemy at forty yards.

'No, thank you,' I said, 'I think it better that we continue war.'

We stood to attention—face to face. He saluted flat-handed—I with the palm outward.

We turned right about and marched slowly back. I took my time, feeling that the dignity of the AIF rested on my inadequate shoulders. No flaming Fritz was going to make me look windy. Reached the parapet. Out of the tail of my eye I could see Bull Voice gazing round. I looked about again. Another glance showed that Fritz was still standing there. 'Blast you,' I said, 'you win.'

So I stepped down.

Then, and not till then, did this German Imperial officer step down.

I led the remnants out that night, anticipating court martial for fraternising with the enemy. But I was quite contented, knowing that the wounded had been saved.

But no one knew anything—officially. Heard later that our artillery observers were worried to bits. They could see German tin hats in No Man's Land, then British. So they held their fire. Or Bull Voice and I would now be pushing up daisies.

18

Slaves of the trenches

This is a little of the tale of the long endurance of the AIF in 1918. From March to August were we kept in the forward area within range of the ever noisy guns. They were anxious days; days that saw the swing from defeat to complete victory. Our men paid their full share of the price in blood and endurance—the tension of living constantly under the shadow of death.

The Diggers had a theory that Haig had made a bet with someone that he could break the Australians' hearts.

This book is all too short to allow of an adequate description of those months.

War-weary as we were we did not become depressed and there were some happy interludes. There was none of the slimy horror of the winter of 1916–17, nor the fever and starvation of Gallipoli. We felt at last that decision was in sight.

Not for a moment did we lose that sense of personal

superiority over the enemy, without which no nation can endure in the ultimate test of war.

Five days were we given to rest, train and refit after the Monument Wood attack. Then forward again to where the fat smoke trees grew in thunder on the ridges.

A glorious spring evening; it seemed terribly wrong that we were marching to the fighting in such surroundings.

Corbie, half-hidden in the valley amid the trees, looked intriguing while we waited for night outside Villers.

A guide led us through the corner of the forest. Shattered shell dumps were all about, wrecked tanks, dead horses, the reek of stale gas and a real old Gallipoli stink.

We walked through silent, empty Villers, our footsteps echoing ghostly from wall to wall. Debris crunched beneath our boots. A stray bullet spanged off a building and howled away.

From the dead town we marched through the wire-strewn waste beyond, and to the trenches.

Guy Bonython, in charge of the relieved platoon, took me round with unusual thoroughness. The ordinary hand-over procedure is 'Sign this. We're off. Sailor's farewell.' But Guy and I went out on a patrol almost to the enemy posts.

When he had gone I stood and took stock of things.

Just across the road, on my right, were the aeroplane hangars, held by the enemy.

My men were so few and widely spaced that there were intervals of up to eighty yards between posts. Under these conditions our continuous trenches seemed to me to be a menace, affording a covered flank approach for attackers.

A delicate young tree stood in No Man's Land. A German flare dropped beyond it. A fairy tree it seemed then, when each leaf shone as burnished silver. The startling beauty was eclipsed in utter blackness as the flare died. 'Toc-toc-toc,' went a Fritz gun. 'Ping!' went a rifle-grenade.

I was unhappy, wandering from post to post where split-up groups stood or sat in patient boredom, near the sheeted outline of Lewis guns.

The long empty bays made me vaguely apprehensive. Nothing would be easier than for an enemy party to slip into our trenches, and lie in silent wait.

All I would see, to prove that they were not our men, would be the gleam of lunging bayonet or the outline of upraised club. Too late then to go for my pistol.

Sometimes I gave up the line patrolling as hopeless and dangerous, and would spend an hour or two of the night sitting in my dugout. But then my conscience would prick me, and out again would I go.

Suddenly the solution of my problem occurred to me. I would do my rounds with pistol drawn, an unheard of thing.

With renewed confidence, I roamed those long empty sections, the bays where the darker shadows lurked. Secretly, I was tickled at the shock any ambushers would get. Instead of a surprised man without a weapon in hand, they would meet an instant shower of big lead slugs.

When the failing light of next day made the approach of a runner easy, a message was brought to me.

'Secret,' it was marked, 'do not divulge to other ranks.'

The message from brigade headquarters went on to state that positive information had been received that the enemy would attack at dawn, four days hence. Masses of artillery and troops were observed to be concentrating on our front. We would not be relieved until after the attack but were to hold our position to the last man.

Four days to live! Oh well, it had to come some time. I drew my men into more compact, self-contained groups and centralised ammunition supplies. I saw to it that with each group was a man of outstanding fighting quality. My own personal preparations were simple.

My flare-proof dugout had only one exit. I placed the SOS rocket in a rifle that stood outside the entrance. The blank driving charge was in the breech. The magazine was fully charged with ball cartridges, so that I could fight on after notifying our artillery.

No, I decided that there was nothing more that I could do. I would hold my men compact for mutual support. We would be outflanked and surrounded of course—if the artillery preparation left any of us alive.

A mouth organ, long ordered from England, reached me. At each succeeding dawn, at that time when the night watch ends, and the fewer day watchers take post, half a dozen men would assemble in my dugout.

Sergeant Halliday would play to us. We would sing the choruses softly. Those little concerts were unforgettable. There came the last dawn before the attack, and what I thought, would be the last concert.

I slept untroubled till the sun slanted hot and steep in late afternoon.

The world of war was quiet and unhurried. The usual slow persistent gunfire sounded over the land. I judged that it was time to break the news of impending attack.

'Oh, sergeant,' I said to Halliday, 'Fritz is going to attack at dawn tomorrow.'

'Must be getting game,' he said, 'to come at us again.'

The news was received everywhere in a matter-of-fact way. Gunners tested the recoil mechanism of their guns, and put more panniers of ammunition close to hand. The needs of the hour would be met when the hour came. Probably therein lay their strength.

The night came that was to herald the dawn of attack.

Far out beyond the reach of hope or fear I listened through the minutes for the uproar that would herald the avalanche.

Tom and I prowling out a long way into No Man's Land heard guttural voices, smelt cigar smoke. We heard nothing that pointed to the massing of men.

Slow marched the hours. Dawn, grey and dim, made the world take form. Full daylight flooded the land. Sergeant Halliday played the loved old songs to us. We sang, low-voiced, that we might not draw fire. Then we slept soundly, neither pleased nor sorry, bitter nor hopeful.

One night, out of the rear, came Staff Captain Jack Stabback. With him trailed an American officer, silver bars on his shoulder straps.

He introduced us. This American was a clean-cut, eager type, and impressed me most favourably. He handled a German rifle that had been standing in the dugout.

'Would you like it?' I asked. He was incredulous that I was really offering him such a fine trophy. 'I can get more if I want them,' I said. I did not explain that I could have filled a truck with them if I so desired.

He was hard put to it to express his thanks. They were cut short by the whistle of a shell. More shells came in a hail, exploding all about us. 'Our guns!' I said to Stabback. I directed them to keep against the back wall of the dugout and dived out into the trench. Just above our heads was the flashing of bursting eighteen-pounders.

That I lived to cover the ten feet of straight sap to where the front trench ran cross-wise, still amazes me. The leaden pellets flayed the ground in stinging squalls. The displaced earth showered all about. The howling and thudding of shell-cases made a hellish note in the din. Resinous smoke billowed round our position.

Men crouched low, passively waiting the passing of the storm.

I found my platoon runner. No telephone was in my section, so I sent him off into the shell-lit night to company headquarters to tell them that our guns were on us. All the time I was raging with helpless fury.

Howitzer shells commenced to drop about us. Our trench was being blown in here and there, but there was a lot of trench, and few men. The beautifully burst hails of eighteen-pounder shrapnel were blasting our parapets.

After fifty-five minutes, the fire ceased. I went in to my guests and entrusted Stabback with a very definite message for brigade headquarters.

My runner returned with the expression of a man who had seen a ghost. I felt rather sorry for having sent him out in that. The odds were against his getting through.

The barrage had been fired out to the bitter end. To queries at artillery headquarters as to whether any guns were firing on our sector, the answer was 'No'.

It transpired later that the guns made the slight mistake of firing fifteen degrees left, instead of fifteen degrees right of sector.

But I was determined on satisfaction. Each night a report of work done had to be submitted. My works report for this night stated 'One ton earth removed from Private Jenkins. Buried by our own guns.' I had happened to see a very disgusted Jenkins crawling out from a blown-in piece of trench, coughing and spluttering.

The works report next night stated 'Forty-six yards of blown-in trench excavated (blown in by our own guns).'

Next night it was a fictitious amount of blown-up wire re-erected, the guns again blamed.

When relieved we shifted to a bank beside Villers. All through the days aircraft struggled for mastery. It was a common sight to see planes falling, the pilot twisting in air beside the machine in the race to earth.

By night the grumbling bombers would make an outline of blacked-out stars. Aerial bombs would hiss down and spray out flame and sparks. Around Amiens would the fingers of the searchlights sweep the skies, crossing and recrossing. It looked like London on an air-raid night.

One night the guns fell silent. We woke up at the unusual state of things. Someone started counting off the seconds. Fifteen seconds went by. 'Woompah!' went an eighteen-pounder just down on the flat.

'You lousy cow,' said someone, 'you would start the war all over again.'

Villers-Bretonneux was a source of unending interest to us. Wine could still be found there. But we were rather surprised one day to see walking toward us a little top-hatted gentleman immaculately clad in a tailcoat and striped trousers. He was escorting a buxom blonde, who wore only frilly underclothes. She slapped his face at one stage. They embraced and made up. Our men stood beside their dugouts in wonderment. Soon we discovered that it was a pantomime put on by two of our Diggers.

There were vast stores of clothing in the factories. Most of our men decided that new bloomers were preferable to lousy underpants. Later, there were some comic happenings when some so arrayed were sent, wounded, to hospitals.

One day I was wandering in Villers. There was a great sound of revelry in a château. The big ballroom was crowded with officers and men. Self-appointed barmen were serving wine faster than any barman ever worked in a six-o'clock rush. The piano was being played furiously.

Two officers were step dancing on top of the piano. One jumped down via the keys. The other leaped over the heads of others, and clung to the swinging chandelier. The chandelier came down with a crash, and he was pulled from under the glass pile, unconscious. Another went out cold from accidental contact with a high kicker. The casualties were dragged aside, and left to recover at leisure.

A whizz-bang hit the tail-end of the building. Men laughed as at a priceless jest. A piece of shell smashed a window and thudded against a wall. Men passed the hot bit of steel from hand to hand, laughing at the haste of the recipient to pass it on without being compelled to drop it.

Back at our position, the company sergeant major called me over to have coffee with him. He had an expensive silver coffee service set out.

One night the vanguard of the 3rd Division came up and relieved us.

Through the darkness we marched back towards Amiens.

Dawn showed the summer glory of this fertile country. Breast-high rustling wheat was all about. The waters of a swamp pictured the glory of trees and sky. Some horse transport drivers lay asleep under their blankets, beside the road. Our weary wags were soon in full voice, 'Wake up, the Boche has broken through. He's just behind us.' They sat up suddenly.

'Get up and pay for your bed.'

'Come on, get out, the horses are singing out for a feed.'

We billeted in Rivery, a canalised market-garden suburb. Numbers of gondola-type boats were available. We soon seized these and organised sports and business.

Parties brought in boatloads of green vegetables. We swam and skylarked for the few days of our rest. Americans were crowding into these back areas in ever-increasing numbers. One afternoon I fraternised with a party of US Engineers, donned one of their tunics and prepared for a sortie into forbidden Amiens. Diggers addressed me as 'Yank'.

We set out and crossed one of the Yankee-guarded bridges. An empty town is a weird place. There seemed to be ghost voices following down all the deserted streets and alleys.

The giant shell that burst overhead was no ghost. Nor was the plane raid, and the thundering bombs that shook the town. We returned carrying many bottles of champagne.

That time was too good to last long. One morning at 3.30 a.m. we were again headed up the line.

That afternoon I selected a luxurious roofed dugout at Daours Bank near a bend of the leafy Somme.

Someone had covered the clay wall with tapestry, and the floor with carpet. A folding table and six chairs furnished the place.

Tom, fresh from a foraging trip, tacked up a number of large photographs of femininity in the raw. The dugout was soon a show place. Various officers came to view my art gallery, always taking away a souvenir.

It was no unusual thing to see Tom dive in the entrance, pull down several of the best, and put them out of sight. If I questioned him, he would probably say, 'Just seen the Major and the Doc headin' this way.'

A big high-velocity gun would shell our position at times.

We got much entertainment from the sight of the shells that landed in the Somme. The snowy white spire of spray would rise as though it would never stop. Then it would dissolve in rainbow shades.

These days in support were taken up by many working party jobs, wiring, digging and all manner of defensive work. We would roam, in our spare moments, through the deserted towns. We would enter any house we thought fit, and acquire anything useful to us. Many games of billiards we played as unbidden guests.

One day I found myself alongside an English artillery officer in a support trench. He was watching a shoot through his glasses.

I questioned him on a thing that was uppermost in all our minds. 'When will the Hun again attack here?'

His answer, given quietly, without pause for thought, was one of the many tributes the AIF received in that year, 'Not until your people go.'

Some nights we would wake and listen to a torrent of gunfire, wondering whether dawn would find us in the heart of the storm.

Our crowd was detailed for salvaging. This was one form of work that the men heartily enjoyed. My exhortation ere they went off, ran something like this: 'Don't lift anything that has an owner. Don't salvage any live ammunition from guns. Don't lift any buried cables that have men on the ends.'

They promised not to do so, but word drifted back to where I was hopefully writing another Air Force application, that some of them were sitting behind a battery asking the gunners to fire, so that they could salvage the cases.

A typical evening is described in my diary of 15 June:

A warm, windy day. In the evening Fritz strafed the road alongside with four-point-twos and then, damn him, he switched to our trench. The transport is flying along the road for the lick of its life, horses flat out, drivers bending low, limbers swinging wildly.

Night is calm and clear. Bombing planes drone above shutting out the light of separate stars. Plane signals are going up in the Hun lines. An early light wavers down behind the dark mass of Villers. A gun barks occasionally. Somewhere, high up, a shell whines shrilly.

An engine is puffing over on the left. There is the rumble of transport wheels on distant, busy roads. The drone of aeroplanes grows louder. A succession of heavy, flat crashes. Bombs for our main roads. Bed for me.

Soon we were shifted closer towards the line. We marched with full kit through broken Aubigny, and along the mirroring canal, poplars shading our way.

On one old wall by the water was a painted arrow, pointing to a crude map of Australia. In careless strokes from which the paint ran and smudged were the words, '13,000 miles to Griffiths Bros'.[1]

It was crude, but somehow it left us silent for a while.

At the foot of a steep bank we dug positions for our cookers, and then dugouts for ourselves. After their digging, the men moved off to the nearest village, to salvage materials for roofing.

It was 2 a.m. when we settled the cookers in place and went to bed. Breakfast in bed at 10 a.m., tinned stew and tea. From my bunk, a little up the bank, I could see the fields of wheat and barley that stretched across the valley. Patches of vivid poppies were everywhere. Little clusters of trees spread across the land. Some cottages, white-walled and red-roofed, nestled among the fruit trees. Close observation would somewhat spoil the picture by the discovery of gaps in the tiles.

Farther to the left, from among masses of trees, gleamed the vivid roofs of Vaulx Sous Corbie.

Night after night we would go up the line, wiring, digging, patrolling. Once, I swear a whizz-bang went between my legs. We developed the eyesight of cats. Even the moonless night, when drizzling clouds hid the stars, never seemed darker than a night of full moon to the average sight. We could see men at three hundred yards clearly. This increase in night vision was to be expected, for we were become creatures of the night, sleeping by day.

Infinitely stranger was the development of an instinct that told me when and where shells would come. I never questioned my personal instinct, never tried to overrule it by logic. Moving about in the open, subject to hails of instantaneous fuse shells, trouble would rush screaming from quiet skies any fraction of a second.

Deeply bitten into our lives was that sudden scream, the too-illuminating flash, the roar, the outcry of wounded, the silence of those who would never speak again, the stink of explosives.

It was the modern sword of Damocles, ever above our heads.

This one night is an example. We left our billets at sunset. At battalion headquarters, we had drawn our implements and wire for a front-line job. The night was moonlit, still and warm. Overhead was the continuous drone of bombers.

There came the crash-crash-crash of aerial bombs up ahead, showers of flame and sparks; the moon shone on rolling waves of smoke.

My laden men strung out behind as I set a slow pace. To our left lay the communication trench called Whizz-bang Alley that led towards the front line at Sailly-le-Sec.

A man reeling towards us called for stretcher-bearers. Two stretchers and two bearers were in my party.

The bearers set to and bandaged him. Shells began to drop near, so I sent my grouped men into the sap to wait.

The casualty told us that aerial bombs—the ones we had seen explode had caught his company, that scores were killed and wounded. Were there any stretcher-bearers there? Yes, a few, but they could not cope with the rush.

He went off alone, and I sent six men with my bearers to help.

When I saw these bearers again they told me the place was like a butcher's shop. A company had been caught by a bombing aeroplane in a sunken road. Twenty men were killed and forty wounded.

I made my way very slowly along the sap. Every now and again long-range machine-gun bullets would come in whispering strings. Lilies of light marked the front line as far as we could see to left and right.

The trench ended about three hundred yards from the line. Ahead of us was the bare space called Mad Acre. Not a bit of cover was out there. Instinct told me that shells would soon be falling there, so I ordered my men to make themselves comfortable a while in the trenches. In the time that it would have taken us to reach the middle of the field, there came a rush of shells. Mad Acre was ripped and torn for a crazy five minutes.

'How would we look out in that?' I asked my sergeant.

'It would be tough on the poor blinkin' burial party,' he said.

My batman chipped in, 'There'd be rolls of wire, mallets and arms and legs flying.'

They were a hard-bitten crew.

The shelling ceased. The smoke rolled slowly across the field. My instinct still held me fast. Someone, anxious to be done with the job, suggested that we push on. 'You're comfortable,' I said, 'so shut up.'

In the time that we would have taken to reach the centre of the death-trap, down came another hail of flame-driven metal, snarling of destruction and doom.

'I dunno what you know,' said the last speaker, 'but whatever it is—you'll do me. In future, I'm sticking to you like mud to a blanket, and if I open me trap again, I give you full permission to put your foot in it.'

I knew without any doubt which was the last shell. 'Come on,' I said. 'Move fast.'

They needed no urging. We strode out through the lingering smoke. As we dropped into the front-line trench, Mad Acre was again deluged.

As the prophets foresaw a sticky night my men were not

put on wiring in the open, but set to digging a sap. Some Yank officers had come up. I took one in hand, and we walked to the right, where the high land overlooked the Somme Valley.

He was worried. 'I don't know when to duck, Aussie.'

'You'll learn,' I told him.

Just then came the fearsome stockwhip sound of a machine gun that the French call *claquement*.

The noise is terrific, but by some trick of sound, one is never under fire from that gun so heard. I do not know what the scientific explanation is, but there is nothing to worry about.

The Yank was on his tummy.

'You don't get down for those,' I yelled above the din. He got up with a puzzled expression.

We walked on for a while, outlined stark on the skyline.

There came the soft hiss of bullets close round us, each making less noise than a big mosquito. I got into a shell hole and looked up to see the Yank still standing and gazing round.

'Come in America,' I said. 'If you want to see much of the war, this is where you do get down.'

He got in: 'It sure has me beat how you work it out.'

When the machine-gunners' attention was turned elsewhere, we strolled on. With horrible suddenness a whizz-bang arrived from the left and made a fan of flame on the bank below us. We both dropped and crawled into a handy length of trench. More shells came as we crouched, the hot breath of the smoke rolling over us.

'There didn't seem any doubt about that lot,' said the Yank.

'No,' I replied. 'Your instincts were sound that time.'

Farther along we met another platoon of our company, busy wiring. The platoon officer was gazing out over No Man's Land.

'Hey Mitch!' he called, 'come and have a look.' Out about a hundred yards were two Fritzes, walking back into their lines.

We felt indignant. 'Game to go after them?' he asked.

It was a nice night for it, and we both felt fit, so we galloped out, pistols drawn. We seemed to be catching up, when they disappeared into a trench.

Bailing up a couple of stray Fritzes in the open, and attacking a trench position are two different things, so we turned back. A newly placed trip wire brought me down as I neared our trench. Some bright youth in the trench chose that moment to challenge, 'Halt, who goes there?'

'Hindenburg and the Kaiser, you bloody fool,' we told him.

The Yank officer appeared to be trying to reconcile the facts of the trenches with the fiction of the instruction books. He was a very silent man as we strolled back.

No sooner had we reached our own busy party, than there was a flash and roar from behind, a great whispering overhead.

Then, I remembered that our people were putting projector gas over this night.

There came a pattering sound over the German trenches. Voices, fear-edged, rose from their lines.

'Gaaz, gaaz, gaaz.' A wall of gas billowed round. The shouting ceased. Their machine guns ripped No Man's Land, raising showers of sparks. Trench-mortar bombs earthed, shells raced overhead, biting into the waving wheat. We kept low till the storm blew itself out.

When comparative peace reigned, we left that not-so-nice sector, nor waited on the order of our going. We disdained to use the delaying trench, except when driven in by near shells.

It was daylight when we reached our dugouts. Our friend

the enemy had been paying some attention to the place during our absence. One cooker had been blown up. That is the worst of living near cookers. Every enemy airman, when he sees the two-wheeled contrivance with the tall smoking chimney, marks the position on a map and hurries back with the information for his gunners that he has located a battery position.

And so it happens that the poor, greasy and unwarlike cooks get a bad time as they ply their peaceful trade.

My dugout was wide and exposed. But near it, in the steepest part of the bank was a narrow slit, into which I calculated it would be impossible to lob a shell. I had marked that place for a refuge if we should be heavily shelled.

During the day shells woke us from our hard-earned slumbers. They were dropping all about, 'counter-battery work on the cookers', I heard someone say. 'The babblers'll declare war if Fritz isn't careful.'

Shells were getting close. I remembered the safe and unoccupied crevice, 'Blast 'em,' I said and turned over and slept between the bursts. Late in the afternoon, my sergeant poked his head in the entrance: 'One shell was pretty close to you.'

Went out and looked. My chosen refuge was ten feet from my dugout. An instantaneous fuse shell had dropped right in it.

It was blackened by smoke and riddled with fragments. If any one had been in it, he would have been mincemeat. Either my laziness, or my instinct, had saved me that time. One man wounded in the leg was our only casualty.

There were many strange ways of getting wounded. One night my platoon was deepening a deep sap, well back from the firing line. There was nothing coming over. One of the men down in the trench was new, just over from England. There had, for a long time, been only the thudding of picks, scraping of shovels, and a spasmodic macabre banter. Suddenly the new hand called out in a voice that was high and querulous, 'I'm hit!'

I walked over and looked down. All had stopped work in surprise. 'Where are you hit?'

'In the leg,' he said.

If he had said somewhere high up, I might have given it a second thought, but instead ticked him off for imagining things.

Sergeant Halliday slid into the trench, examined him, and said: 'By Jove, he is hit. A beautiful little bullet in the leg.'

I walked round while the bearers put on a bandage preparatory to taking him away. I was delivering a profane, but inspired dissertation on men who could collect Blighties a mile behind the line easier than others could get their rum issue.

One Digger cocked a humorous eye upward, and, referring to Monument Wood, broke in on my monologue, 'No damn use you wandering round up there, you won't get a Blighty. They couldn't even hit you with fifty machine guns.'

I had a very distinct grievance. Why shouldn't I get my share of cushy Blighties like the others? But that mob of mine gave me no sympathy. They knocked off work to advance their individual theories. None of them was particularly complimentary to me. When one prophesied that I would get a big shell all to myself in the last battle of the war, I laughed with them and set them to work again.

'You might as well have let him live,' growled someone to the last speaker, 'and then we'd still be arguing instead of working.'

That slight casualty was the only one that occurred in working parties under my command during the whole of 1918.

Since the last months of 1917 small drafts of 1914 men had been returned to Australia for six weeks' leave. It seemed inevitable that the war must drag into 1919, before which time the weight of the armies of the USA could not be felt, although already their specialist units were crowding the back areas.

In our battalion were a few men who had gone overseas in 1914, and most of these had been invalided back to Australia at some time. Now that The Bull was brigadier, I headed the list by merit for Anzac leave. This brigade was a sister brigade to the 4th Brigade, which had been in the Landing. But the 4th Brigade landed some hours after the 3rd Brigade to which I then belonged. So, most of our Anzacs having been 4th Brigade men or Light Horse previously, I was on top of the list by right.

Not that it did me much good. A few privates and NCOs were sent from the transport and other non-fighting sections, and my name still remained in place on the list. Visions of Australia were as of some distant glorious view of heaven, certainly too wonderful to be taken seriously.

In addition to my chance of leave to Australia was my chance of transfer to the Flying Corps. Repeated applications had been sent in and I had been medically examined. Now I just waited the call that would order me to pack my gear, and enter a wonderful new world. And I would have preferred that to Anzac leave. I more than suspect that several requests from the Flying Corps had been quietly pigeon-holed at battalion headquarters.

I was also a trained raiding officer.

With this combination of possibilities, a peremptory summons to battalion orderly room caused me great speculation.

Several such summonses I received. Each time the adjutant gaily ordered me to take out a fighting patrol to prospect certain areas of No Man's Land, and, if possible, secure a prisoner or two. With my chosen men so highly trained and well tried, these jobs presented no special trouble or difficulty. We knew the dangers from our own artillery's short firing, but by ascertaining the times of their shoots, we were enabled to be under cover and avoid casualties. Sometimes we returned to our lines through gaps in the trench system, and had to send back information to the front line that we had come in. These expeditions were not in any way unpleasant, and served to break the monotony of life in the forward area. A big whisky at battalion headquarters was my right, on returning.

There were nights when we filed over the two planks of the barrel bridge that spanned the dark-flowing Somme heavily laden with U frames; the bridge would rock and roll beneath. Usually, someone's load would splash into the water as he let it go to save himself. The men would rest their timber and grin, there in the shadow of the tall poplars that lined each bank. Carefully I would have to climb round each waiting man, to get past him without pushing him in.

There I would find a man lying on the planks, holding grimly to his load of timber against the pull of the current. Finding insecure footing on the submerged barrels, water lapping about our knees, the sergeant, corporal and I, working one-handed, would retrieve the awkward load, and the line would sway precariously on towards the far bank.

'Won't need draughthorses in Australia if any of us get back,' someone would growl.

Our greatest trouble in this nocturnal existence was the presence of men whose sight was not adapted to night seeing. There were usually one or two in a platoon. My place was at the head of the file of men, picking the route, deciding when cover should be taken, and so on.

Suddenly word would pass up from man to man that part of the column was lost. For in these night marches each man watches the man in front. A man who breaks the link is followed by all behind him. Many hours were spent in unhealthy, well-shelled places, searching with great profanity, for a lost tail.

The unseen has many fears and perils. These short-sighted ones would stumble and fall in all manner of places that we, the more fortunate, could avoid. If they were at all nervous, the unseen terrors of snarling nights must have been most fearsome to them. The physical toll for them must have been doubled. We, the platoon commanders, left them at home if we could. If we had to take them, we placed them on the rear of the line. Then, when they got lost, they lost only themselves.

Thus we avoided late arrival at rendezvous points and were never caught by the coming of daylight within view of the enemy trenches. But we never took these blind ones out on patrol.

The Digger was always prepared to give his best in a clear-cut issue, but hated any manner of futility and humbug. An officer who set his men to work digging holes and filling them up again would have had a justifiable mutiny on his hands.

The only way to manage Australians and get the best out of them was to take them fully into one's confidence. 'Here is the job,' we would say. 'When it is done we go home.' Even though the work was triple that calculated as a fair thing, it would be completed ahead of schedule.

One night a big party was ordered up for the digging of a communication trench. As Lieutenant Swan[2] was sick, I lumped his platoon in with mine, and set out at dusk. Rumour, not always the lying jade, had it that we were to work in a very hot spot.

We filed across the barrel bridge with its one taut hand-rope. Engineers served our men alternately with pick and shovel as we filed past a tool dump. Sappers walked at the head of each platoon, up a long hillside. Two full paces were stepped out for each man as his job. I roved round and sniffed the air. The stink of high explosive was evident everywhere. Starting at the head of my platoon I told each man, 'Pick out a shell hole to dive into when Fritz strafes. Don't wait for any orders from me. I'll be there first. When you hear the first shell—jump.'

No sooner had I reached the last man than the howl and explosion of a shell followed. There was a clatter of running men, but no confusion, as each man had located his cover beforehand. For five minutes shells rained all about, then stopped. Men were hit ahead and behind us, but none in my two platoons.

Stretcher-bearers moved off to the rear.

The skipper came down. 'We are right on Fritz's SOS line!'

So I passed this word along as extra incentive to the Diggers to live up to their name. They dug like furies. Every twenty minutes came a fresh blast of shellfire. Soon the men were able to lie down in the cover they had dug for themselves.

As I stood beside a nice deep shell hole watching the progress of the work, I heard a Digger growling, 'I'm going to swim the Somme on the way back.'

'Why?'

'That first shell hole I jumped into turned out to be a flaming latrine!'

'Which shell hole was that?' I asked.

'That one you are standing alongside of.'

So I took the hint and stood beside a newer and therefore more sanitary one.

Throughout the night the spasms of shellfire continued. More casualties occurred, until my own stretcher-bearers were called on to assist other platoons and companies.

At last the skipper came down with orders, 'Platoons move off independently in fifteen minutes.'

Delay in mustering would be fatal to someone. My sergeant and I moved along to each man, 'Get equipments on. As soon as the next shelling is over, be ready to hop off at the toute.'

The next shelling came at the expected tick. The last delayed shell crashed, and my line was striding out at five miles an hour. At our heels came the next shelling. There were calls for stretcher-bearers, but not one of our men received a scratch for the night of work.

Picks and shovels clattered on the dump. The barrel bridge rocked again beneath us. The rumbling night birds were passing overhead, to be safe in lairs before dawn would expose them to the gunners. We strolled in little groups along the towing path, the tension gone.

Someone asked: 'What'll you say when your kid asks, "What did you do in the Great War, daddy?"'

'I'll tell him I was a big mug buck navvy,' answered another.

'I'll knock the little ——'s head off if he wakes it up,' contributed another.

Extravagant word pictures were painted by some as to what they would do in their great leave that was the war ending.

Vivid and humorous themes would be expanded, until someone would say, 'Shut up you lot of mugs. You'll all be pushing up daisies before the war is over.'

At our dugouts, in the new daylight, food would be waiting, and someone would call out, 'Hey, Mr Mitch, is this supper or breakfast?'

19

Last turn in static warfare

Step by step we moved up towards the front line. Just after the midnight that ushered in Sunday, 30 June, we moved up to the line to take over.

At 1.30 a.m. the outgoing garrison had tramped away. Part of the Western Front was in my charge. A wheat crop was on our right. In front smooth and level, the grass stretched to the German parapet, a hundred yards away. Then night crept slowly by. Time never lags so much as in the front line.

To pass away the hours, I was playing with a Lewis gun, practising the firing of single shots. Over the way a Fritz imitated me. Then I started pom-tiddly-om-pom pom-pom. He imitated that too. Everything I thought of he copied. Then I got bored, found a rifle with a grenade attachment, and fired a Mills across to the position that he was firing from.

'That shut the cow up,' I said. There was the sudden ping of a rifle-grenade. He had copied that too.

'See if he can follow this,' said Halliday, and fished out a phosphorous bomb from a case. I reloaded the rifle with a blank, carefully slid the bomb into the cup, and withdrew the pin. 'Pop.' The bomb was away.

The bomb burst brilliantly above the trench, spread like an umbrella and the glowing spray descended.

There followed a terrible yell. At that moment, a runner arrived with a message for me. I took it into my little dugout to read. In a few moments, three men plunged in to avoid the descending phosphorous stream from a return bomb. The un-principled square-head had copied that too.

In the hour before dawn, we all stood to arms and watched the slow lightening of the sky.

There is something in trench-holding that is particularly nerve straining. One knows that, come what may, we must stay and take it. In moving about the forward areas, we would run into trouble, and be soon out again.

But, at the back of a soldier's mind is always that lurking dread that the enemy artillery will concentrate on his trenches and wipe them with their garrison out of existence. Nothing is more fearful than a heavy barrage. No soldier worth his salt, fears the actual attack of the enemy.

Cool men handling infantry weapons can easily beat off ten times their number of enemy.

There was unquiet rumour of action in the air. We did not know at what moment a runner would dive in and tell us to attack at short notice.

Here is the diary entry of 3 July:

The day posts mounted at daylight. I crawled into my dugout to gain what sleep I could, and slept fitfully till 2 p.m.

Then, sounds of a spiteful trench-mortar barrage on the left stirred me to get up and look. The smoke was billowing round our left platoon. Our Lewis gunners stood ready to draw lines of protective fire to shield our neighbours.

All the afternoon, the sky was thick with planes. The tattooing of machine-gun fire, aircraft and anti-aircraft, is continuous. The sky is flecked all over by the smoke of anti-aircraft shells. Bits of shells sizzle down to us. One plane spun cleanly to death. Two others burst into fierce red flames and raced comet-wise to earth.

All day, the shells have been roaring over our heads, going each way.

My two stretcher-bearers are down, Hergstrom killed and Ericson wounded. They were good men.

The sword is for ever over our heads.

An occasional rifle-grenade bursts a few feet away. I tried to read or write. The grey trench walls that may be the walls of my grave, stare blankly at me. I just sit and think. The larks are trilling gaily, and the sun is warm.

The colonel and the skipper came up, and ordered me to take out a patrol forthwith.

My orders were specific and detailed.

I was to take almost my whole strength, and Lewis guns, go out to a flank, jump a supposed machine-gun position, and find out, if possible, how it was that the headquarters scouts were cut up the night before.

They did not wait to see the job done, so it was done with modifications.

The experienced patrol officer remembers certain things. Take out as few men as possible. A lot of men mean a lot of noise, and are a lot of target. Only take trusted men, with good night eyes, who can move quietly. So it was only Sergeant Halliday, Tom Davis, and I who stood on the parapet and looked a moment at dark sweeps of countryside, ridge and gloomy valley, black blurs of forest. Our eyes picked out much detail, looking just above the skyline for best results.

There was not a speck of light anywhere, save where low-hung stars merged into the skyline. Out there was death for the unwary and the unlucky. To us it was just another everyday job.

A dead German lay on his back in a shallow shell hole ten yards out. Beyond were other dark objects. Any of them could be live men with ready rifles or bombs in hand.

But, if death came tonight it would not come tomorrow.

We walked forward, the others with rifle in both hands, finger on trigger ready to meet any emergency. My pistol was out.

At thirty yards, we bent low; at sixty yards we crawled, each at the point of triangle. Tom on the left, moving parallel with the edge of a wheat-crop flattened suddenly and faced in towards the wheat-crop. His outline was tense. After much patrolling, ideas flash from one to another without need of words. Halliday guarded one flank. I wriggled to Tom's side. Ears must work as well as eyes. He was looking intently into one spot. Our mouths were open and breathing controlled to give the greatest aid to ears. The smell of tobacco smoke drifted out from the wheat. Someone coughed. A rifle smacked twenty feet away, the bullet, striking by Tom's side, howled, ricocheting viciously in air till it trailed into silence.

The wheat waved and rustled before the blast, and was still again. We heard the bolt snick as another cartridge was rammed home. I knew that Tom would stay there to guard against ambush, keeping rifle and bomb ready, so signalled to Halliday to move out farther to right and wait. If I struck trouble farther ahead, I had two trusty rifles to fall back on.

Cautiously I squirmed away. For if we tried to enter the wheat, the rustle would betray us to the waiting machine gun and bombers.

No twig must crack beneath hand or knee. No sudden move must advertise my presence to unseen watchers.

Each hand and knee came down separately feeling first where it must take the weight. Sticks and stones were placed carefully to one side. Out to my right front was the place I was to examine; the real work just beginning.

It was quite comfortable out here. The superiority complex of the AIF working in full blast.

That black object over there, I wonder. A Fritz or a bush?

Absolute stillness as seconds and minutes loiter by. If it moves I will shoot, and cannot miss. If I shoot, and it is a dead man or a bush, No Man's Land will be lit up by a dozen flares, and machine guns will make it a zone of sizzling death. But, I could not stay there all night, so I tried a small stratagem. My questing fingers located a stone. If I throw that to land near, any man born of woman must make some movement. I threw. No move, perfect stillness. Found a clip of cartridges in my pocket, and threw that. It landed dully. Still no move, I wriggled forward.

It was a bush.

The ground sloped down to the right in a steep bank. A trench made a black line at the base.

If I climbed over the skyline made by this bank, I should be a mark for the wide world. If that trench were occupied I should be shot to ribbons. My black hair rose and tingled sharply beneath the weight of my tin hat. Farther and farther spread the area of sensitive skin, nature's warning to man that danger lurks in darkness. Gloomy moor and upland stretched away as I looked outward. I could see clear the upthrown chalk of further defence lines.

But below, in the shadow of the bank, that trench loomed dark, mysterious and deadly. It seemed to challenge me to come down, to come down to my grave, and beyond.

In that moment it seemed to me that dead men, vicious and unresigned, lurked there waiting to drag me down. A mad desire possessed me to leap down and defy its garrison, dead or alive.

I threw things to provoke any guards to fire while yet I could get away. But only a stony dead silence followed the thudding of the clods.

And then I admitted to myself that I was scared to go down the bank and would rather welcome the comfortable trusty Tom or Hal beside me.

Relieved and cheerful at my decision I edged away from the bank, and along the high ground towards the German line. I was a long way from home, and a man is a long time dead. Time I turned back.

Just a little farther. And even as the swimmer, defying sharks, makes out to the next line of breakers, I went on. Might be able to meet and bag a wandering Fritz yet.

There was an even spaced line of smudges; not bushes, not dead men. Soon I saw that it was a big fighting patrol, about twenty-five strong.

While I watched they rose to their feet and ran towards me. Hot and urgent sprang the wish to turn and fly. Cold reason took prompt possession, reason and admiration for a cunning foe. I now knew how it was the scouts were cut up. This big party did the same thing last night. Their plan was to dash toward a smaller party. The little party would run back to escape them.

Back where Tom waited, was their machine gun post that would draw a bar of fire across their track, when running feet were heard. These Fritzes would stop short before they ran into their own fire. How neat!

I stayed fast, hoping that they would stop before they reached me, but ready to empty my squirt in their faces, and roll a bomb forward to upset them while I got away.

They loomed higher. It was time to shoot and go. They stopped and dropped twenty feet away.

Inch by inch I wriggled backward, careful not to move left or right. The steady diminishing of an object may be overlooked, but if I turned side on, the increase in size must be noticed, so I dared not turn. They became faint now to my eyes. I turned and crawled to a deep shell hole, got my breath and moved over to Halliday. 'Big bunch of Fritzes out there. We'll put the draught up 'em. Go and get the boys and we'll plant them in that shell hole.'

The darkness swallowed him as he moved back.

I collected Tom and sent him halfway as a guide. There was much thudding of boots and rattling of equipment, and my party commenced to arrive. Each man settled himself firmly while I pointed out the faint line of blurs.

'One bomb each. Lewis guns one magazine. Riflemen five rounds of rapid fire, when I say go. Then keep down. All set?'

Heads nodded 'Too eyes right.'

'Go.'

There was the click of the release springs as the bombs flew. The Lewis guns leaped to stuttering life, the rifles spat hurriedly, bombs crashed. A terrific racket.

Their allotted firing done, my party crouched below the lip of the shell hole. Enemy rifles and machine guns leaped into full chorus, bombs raged and flamed across No Man's Land.

Flares jostled each other. The faces of my platoon beneath the helmets showed clear, and clean cut. The old hands were grinning cheerfully knowing that all this fury was wasted on us. The new ones were not so sure.

Trench-mortar bombs woke the night, far to left and right machine guns rattled. We certainly had started something.

The machine gun at our flank opened biting at the edge of the shell hole, spraying us with stinging showers of dirt. Halliday threw two bombs. The guns stopped in mid-stride. Shells roared and crashed, bullets wailed, hissed, and sizzled. But not a bomb or shell landed closer than twenty feet.

Slowly the fire diminished and died.

'Get ready to move back. Don't make any flaming noise if you want to see home and mother again.'

Our way led past the shell hole wherein lay the dead German. The line stopped and I could hear an excited voice, and someone swearing disgustedly.

One new hand, his first time out, stood rigid as if frozen, or under some psychic spell. His bayoneted rifle pointed at the corpse, but he lacked the power even to press the trigger. He could only speak in little disjointed sentences.

'Look, look, he's looking at me. He moved. He moved. He's looking at me. He moved.'

The others were grinning at the little tableau. But No Man's Land is no place to stage comedies.

I heard one say, 'What's wrong with his nose.' Tom replied, 'Poor dope must have a bad cold.'

We pushed the paralysed one along, and movement restored his physical powers, but on his face was a strange staring look for a long while. We jumped down into the trench. The patrol was over.

A little before the next dawn I had a visitor from the left platoon. He had come over to inquire about the racket. Just then, roaring out from the direction of Germany came an enormous ball of flame. Its roar of travel was beyond description. A cyclone could not produce so much sound. It lit the world in a hard white light. Whether it was a close meteorite, or a new type of flame shell, I do not yet know.

As it raced above us, our visitor, spellbound, followed it with his eyes, and toppled backward into the trench still watching it.

20

Front stalls for a battle

Rumours of attack became more than rumour.

There was to be an attack on the right of the river, something that would show Fritz where he got off. We were not to be involved in it, but, being on the flank, could expect our share of the backlash. There were to be Yankee troops mixed with Australians.

Such was our news of the projected battle of Hamel. The full importance of this battle was not realised until after the war, for it was made the model for the great battle of 8 August.[1] That day John Monash tried out his theories, and proved them good.

A raid was to be carried out on our left to synchronise with the main attack. Our own artillery had been shooting short for months. We expected trouble.

Midnight of 3 July came and went. We waited in alert tension.

Keeping close touch with my posts I had gone to my isolated right post, along a track through the wheat. In my absence from my platoon headquarters a message had come, and batman Tom Davis proceeded to bring it to me.

So it happened that on my return I saw men clustered on the track. As I got closer I could see that their attitudes were tense, their bayonets levelled at a silent figure in front.

They were standing in dramatic attitudes that amused me vastly. Soon I knew that they were a patrol from one of our support companies. They were starting their job by bailing up my batman. And I had long wanted to score off the Loot in charge of that patrol, so I pushed past the rear to where Tom casually fronted a hedge of bayonets.

'I would suggest,' I said to the officer, 'that you delay offensive action until you get beyond my posts. If you care to go out that way,' with a descriptive wave to the right, 'you might meet Fritz. Come on, Tom, don't muck about here all night.' And we walked off.

After a little silence, Tom said cheerfully, 'I put the wind up them —— company mugs!'

'How did you do that?'

'They were as windy as hell. They poked their bayonets at me and kept on saying—'Who are you, who are you?' The officer bloke couldn't hold his squirt steady.'

'Well?'

'And I wouldn't say a bloody word.'

Away down by Villers-Bretonneux there was heavy gunfire. The night lightened slightly as the moon rose. Someone said that he thought the stunt was off.

At 3 a.m. our guns opened in a sudden terrific blast. The noise seemed to rend earth and sky. The air was filled with the rush and screech of shells. Columns of flame spouted up from the Boche lines all along our front. Showers of liquid-fire shells added to the inferno. Over the way, machine guns opened, raking our parapets. Trench-mortar bombs exploded near our trench. Our own shells started bursting round us.

Flares shot up all along the enemy lines, the light of them playing on the billows of smoke from within which rose constantly renewed fountains of flame. The noise-saturated air beat on us. The ground rocked unceasingly.

A mad elation took possession of me. Seizing a rifle I blazed towards the German parapet. Halliday came up out of curiosity, 'See anything?'

'No, Serg, just shooting to keep happy.'

The infection seized him, and he, too, opened out in rapid fire.

Other questioners came up, and Tom Davis answered on our behalf, 'They're just fillin' in the cracks in the barrage.'

Our men then started out on a private war, sending over rifle-grenades. To add to our enemy's unhappiness his own minenwerfers started to pelt his front line. A big one landed slap on his line. Up shot a green flare, evidently his private signal for short shooting.

Another minenwerfer landed right on the spot from whence the flare had risen.

A group of heavy shells made us crouch in the trench bottom for a time. I made my way along my trench, keeping low, to see how my command was faring. Not a man had been hit. Each had some comment to make on the display.

I suddenly realised that it was growing light, and made my way the right of our position.

There, on the far slope of the river was the beautiful and

terrible panorama of battle. A fire was burning furiously in Quaire Wood. The death-hedge of our barrage was a long way into Germany. The squat, dark shapes of tanks could be seen crawling over the terrain. Lines of our men were advancing steadily. Occasional shells burst among them. Overhead were our planes in swarms, holding unquestioned mastery of the air.

One tank was nearing a post from which red flares were rising, one after another. Alarm could almost be traced in the course of each flare. Some gallant enemy soldier was keeping his rendezvous with death. The last red flare went up when the tank was only a few feet away. There were no more flares from that place.

I went back to platoon headquarters.

A Minnie burst out in front, and a piece hit a man beside me, on the elbow. It did not penetrate, and I left him bewailing his luck.

A cryptic message came from battalion headquarters: 'Prepare to be relieved tonight. But you are not going out of the line. Unit relieving unknown.'

That was something to chew over. Evidently we were to attack somewhere.

The turmoil died down. We left our day posts in charge and slept. A little after midday the feeling of unrest drove me into the open trench. Was just in time to see a German shell drop on their own trenches.

Up shot a green flare. The next shell landed halfway to us. Up went another green. I knew where the next was going to land, dived to where some enemy flares were stacked, and selected a green one. Down came the next five-point-nine with a thunderous roar, just in front of our trench.

Up went my green flare. The next shell landed fifty yards in rear of us. For safety's sake I put up another green flare.

The boys gathered round in unstinted approval.

One of them was heard to say later, 'Our boss gives orders to the Fritzy artillery.'

That is all right, when you can get away with it. But I know of men, who, by selecting the wrong flare, have innocently drawn down on themselves a full-dress barrage. Their popularity quickly became a minus quantity.

The remaining hours of the day dragged. I was left to conjecture into what we would be thrust. The thunder of artillery punctuated the minutes. Sombre night closed in. Around midnight there were accoutred men standing on the parados. They were a 54th Battalion platoon come to relieve us.

I explained the situation to a keen young lieutenant, who was typical of the breed. He signed the necessary documents, and we were gone.

At company headquarters I was directed back to the place where we were to stop the night.

By the light of a torch I identified the map reference, men circling to conceal the gleam.

We were on a gently sloping hillside, dotted with low bushes. There was not a sign of a dugout or trench, no shelter but the bushes.

'I'll eat my tin lid,' growled a Digger, 'if they don't think we are bloody wallabies.'

Daylight came and went. Near midnight came orders to move forward again. We marched beneath the poplars, along the tow-path of the Somme.

The water reflected the pulsing glare of a heavy barrage up in front. Strange and beautiful were the reflected patterns that came and went below. Across the water was the blur of the building on which was the distance to Griffith Brothers.

As a gesture in the face of sombre fate my platoon sang song after song as we strolled along without urgency. I read it as a very gallant *beau geste* to show that their heads were yet unbowed, and my warm pride in them rose even higher.

The barrel bridge lunged beneath our feet like a cantering horse. A tower of snowy spray from a plunging shell overtopped us. Like a dew the dropping water made us gleam in the reflected flare light.

Closer to the devil dance of the enemy barrage, we filed up a sap to a cross trench. Along it were new roofless dugouts. My men dumped their gear and quested out to salvage material for roofing ere the visibility of dawn should hamper movement.

In the first light, Tom located a potato patch. He rooted round among the shell holes and came back with a bag of young potatoes to pad out our rations. All along the trench men were boiling mess tins full of them.

Close to our position was a large farm with its shell-gapped outbuildings. Hundreds of pigeons lived there. Each time a shell burst near, the pigeons rose in alarm.

Several times I watched Colonel Murray, VC, enjoying himself. He would wait in the courtyard with a shotgun he had salvaged from somewhere. He would not shoot at the pigeons as they strutted and preened themselves on the roof-ridges, but wait until a close-bursting five-point-nine would send them into the air. Then, 'crack-crack' would go his gun. Buckshee for the mess.

At nights there would be line-straightening stunts when the artillery would crash like the opening of a mighty orchestra, and the world would be lit by flares and sky-signs in the mad but organised tumult. Then, the war would settle down to the usual grumble of man-made thunder.

The green hot days were made spectacular by the swarming disputing aircraft, the trail of flame and smoke that marked doom on high.

There was always something to see. The creamy towers rising sudden from the Somme, the beauty of shells as they thudded in farms and copses.

One warm afternoon we marched back to a position in a clump of timber on a verdant hillside. My men—typical warriors of the new age—trench worn, alert, full of a macabre humour, trailed behind me.

Across our path rode a thing of beauty, a thing of other times. It was a young British artillery officer. He rode a satin-coated charger, was clad in immaculate polo kit. An orderly, all gleaming buttons and smartness riding another charger carrying mallets, led two prancing polo ponies.

A fierce resentment at the subordination of time, fodder, and money to the demands of sport rose in me. It seemed indecent that such a parade of privilege and inconsequence should be brought within view of my battle-weary men at such a time as this.

Out of such incidents can grow discontent and serious trouble. One Digger, looking up insolently into the face of the beautiful one, expressed our feelings in loud tones and matchless phrase.

'Look at the bastard,' he called, 'going off to play hockey on horseback.'

A laugh ran through the platoon. The officer jerked on his bit and glared at me as though he would pull up and demand redress. I laughed at him. To my disappointment he rode on without a word.

Had he stopped, I honestly think my boys would have pulled him off his horse and torn his spotless rig off him, perhaps leaving him only underpants to maintain his dignity. And I know that I would not have interfered with their pleasure.

There went one officer who would passionately proclaim the lack of discipline among Australians. But war should show no favourites.

To our bivouac among the trees came two reinforcement officers, full of anxiety to learn the ways of war.

That evening we gathered in the company mess in cheerful mood.

Just to make the newcomers feel at home I brought up the old debate, 'Should reinforcement officers be allowed to marry white women.' They sat up with a jerk, before they remembered to laugh.

One of them shared my dugout with me. We were not likely to be disturbed, so my bed was arranged for comfort. Under was a crimson eiderdown, then a fold of a great fleecy blanket. Then there was a pair of priceless linen sheets, and a further fold of the blanket— all loot from Villers. In silken pyjamas I crawled in to sleep.

This procedure completely upset all my dugout mate's preconceived ideas.

'I thought,' he said, 'that an Anzac would lie on the ground anywhere, with his tin hat on, and sleep.'

'Only when we have to,' I told him. He could not know the long tale of the months when we hesitated even to unbuckle equipment, or ever let a loaded weapon out of our reach, sleeping or waking.

Then one night the 3rd Division came up to relieve us. We

set out singing that parody that our men always sang on relief. 'In the evening by the moonlight, coming from the firing line.'

All night we marched silently along by roads. At dawn, eight abreast, we marched into our forest bivouac where the cookers waited, singing again.

That afternoon the battalion marched again, the band leading. A brave show they made, for our losses had been small, and we had received many reinforcements.

Outside Pont Noyelles we were billeted in dugouts. Battalion parades were attempted, but to our unalloyed pleasure, some long range shells came over, and they were cancelled.

The wood alongside was alive with American specialists. We visited them often. They had never been up to the line, but could tell us how everything should be done. There we met in the flesh the Yankee booster. He told us that there would be two black days in the war, the day the American planes went over the line, and the day they came back.

On 24 July came the day of the divisional sports at Allonville. Licensed bookmakers were calling the odds. Horses raced, mules raced, there were hurdle events. Someone brought me information as to every event, and I followed blindly, and in every race I backed the winner.

I reached the ground with fifteen francs and came away with pockets jammed with notes. But death was here also. Two riders were killed in a crash.

I walked home through rustling wheatfields. The forest-clad hillsides were vivid dark green. The Somme wound through a scene of peace.

Next day I was warned that I was to proceed to a rest camp, down on the coast.

21

Proud command

The sun was just peeping above the skyline when I arrived at battalion orderly room. My faithful Tom was back at my dugout strapping up the green canvas valise, beside which he would mount guard until a limber came for it.

Early as I was, there were eighteen men waiting for me. The adjutant gave me a bundle containing movement orders, rolls, and a map reference at which to catch our conveyance.

In these days, there was never any of the confusion of the early days of the war. My instructions set out clearly the times of trains and every step of the journey. To discover even the unmarked place at which the motorbuses would wait needed only reference to the ever handy map, and a moment or two of calculation on my part. The ways of wartime life were truly oiled by skill and experience.

I turned my attention to these men, who had been culled from the whole brigade. The selection for the rest camp, averaged a little over one man per company. Those chosen were the men with the longest continuous and good service in the firing line.

Quick pride was mine as I measured these men. They fell in swift and easy movement.

One speech I made, 'One thing only I ask of you. All be present when we are due to return from the rest camp. For the rest, enjoy yourselves as you like.'

'We'll be there,' they said.

Their tones were those of free men, who, in the test of the times were sure of themselves and their friends, sure too that death came but once, though it must be faced many times.

We platoon officers were always proud of our platoons, our companies, our battalions, with a consuming pride understandable only to those who endured those years. But these men were the pick of a proud brigade at the height of its fighting power in the most desperate year of the most desperate war.

I pushed out my chest as I led them across the fields.

A providential and empty lorry was stopped, and we climbed on board. The lorry took us to where several lorries were assembled that were to carry similar parties from all the other brigades and divisions. Into an empty one I piled my men.

Quietly appreciative were they as we rumbled through green Rivery, past the ripe wheat and forests of Allonville, and on to Pernois.

We piled into cattletrucks, officers and men together. The wide doors were rolled full open that we might miss nothing of the green peace of the countryside. The boys sat with their legs swinging overside, quietly watching the beauty of the moving scenes, revelling in the cessation of the months of gun-thunder that had seemed part of their lives.

It would be impossible to guess how often death had passed these men by, or how often it had taken their friends. They were reserved, not ready to make new friends, knowing how easily they would be taken from them. The strength to face the greatest tests of endurance was theirs. Otherwise they must have fallen out from their units long since, sick, shell-shocked, or mentally wrecked.

Death only, in this unending war, was all to which they could look forward. But the reaper would be met with the stoic fortitude and pride that they knew so well. As their friends had gone, so would these go when their hour came. But their testing had lasted so long, that theirs was the heavier cross.

If, from Valhalla, chosen ones are called to storm the gates of hell, these will be in the forefront, laughing as they go. Well satisfied was I to be with them, nor would I have changed places to sit with the great ones of the world. They accepted me as comrade and officer, and I was more than content.

The tang of the sea came to us when we detrained at Eu, then to march up a long hill to a tented camp. Comic disgust was on the faces of my men when civilians cheered 'Vive l'Americain!'

An English colonel greeted the officers with English courtesy, and made a short speech.

'Gentlemen,' he said, 'this is a rest camp. You will have only one duty to do—the paying of your men. If you wish to go anywhere in France, call at the office for a movement order. Now, as regards pay. Officers may draw what they please, but we regret that we are unable to allow more than five francs to other ranks. You may draw pay for your units at 8 p.m.'

This was not a rest camp. It must be heaven!

Like wild-fire round the camp ran word that NCOs and men could only draw five francs each.

While I was busy with pencil and paper, working out how much money would be needed, setting my own requirements at a thousand francs, man after man came for confirmation of the bad news.

'See what I can do,' I growled.

There seemed to be no other men bar my party from the three brigades of the 4th Division, so I was first in with a whopping great claim headed '4th Australian Division'.

With pockets crammed with bundles of five franc notes, pay roll in hand, I made my way to my tent.

The NCOs whipped up the men, glum in anticipation of a meagre pay. For many men this would be the last chance of buying pleasure. I had made precautions to ensure that they would not be stinted.

'Listen to me,' I said as they lined up, 'don't broadcast this till everyone is paid. Sergeants can draw 800 francs, corporals 700, and privates 500.'

Amazement, joy and relief showed in one mingled expression.

Stacks of notes I paid away, each man beaming as he signed the roll. Swiftly I entered each pay-book.

One man said hesitatingly, 'My pay-book is in arrears.'

Orders were strict that no more than five francs were to be paid to any man who was in debt. But could the value of these men be assessed in terms of cash? If he had his fun, my shoulders were broad enough to bear any trouble that arose out of it.

'Don't you want the blasted money?' I glared at him.

'Y-yes,' he said.

'Well sign and let the next man in.'

He scratched his signature, gathered up his pile of notes, saluted extra-regimentally, and hurried out.

I noticed that they all gave me a specially smart salute. They must have considered that such a pay, at such a time, was worth it.

Two men had not appeared for their pay. Hearing the five franc maximum, they had wandered down to the town.

I had only one eye open, before next dawn when they appeared, full of apology and anxiety. They had even lugged along a half-dressed and sleepy sergeant, to make things regimental.

'What do you want?'

'We came along to see if you could do anything about pay, sir.'

'Pay was last night.'

They launched into explanation to put me in a good frame of mind, until I had to laugh. So I sat up in my valise and reached over to my tunic for the pay sheet. 'I oughtn't to pay you. Sign there.'

In fear that I might change my mind, they scribbled their names hastily.

Reaching under my pillow I hauled out the last stacks of notes, and tossed them one each. 'Have a good time.'

They clicked their heels in a guardsman's salute, thanked me earnestly and went off. The sergeant stopped a while to tell me of the rejoicing among our men at the unexpected pay.

Blandly I returned the pay sheets to orderly room.

My duty done by the men, I was free to do as I pleased. Most of the other officers had gone into the village after paying, and had not returned.

My eyes on the distant view, I applied for and received a rail warrant for Paris.

Paris! Out of the Gare du Nord into the soft sunlight. I owned the place. Vivid and wonderful were the days and nights. On the boulevards was all the feminine beauty of the world. One walked beside me in the leafy glory of the Bois de Boulogne.

Others dined and wined with me. Others strolled with me beside the river. One took me past Boulevard St Michel, up to the glorious Sacré Coeur on the heights, where Paris as a wondrous map lay below. The Eiffel Tower reaching high steel fingers, and the Madeleine like a crouching mammoth, Notre-Dame in its ancient beauty, all mounted above the mass of the buildings.

I started out to see Paris with a pocket full of notes, a toothbrush and a set of blue silk pyjamas. After a few days, I had only the toothbrush and a few notes, so it was time to return and recuperate.

I arrived in camp at nine o'clock at night. Several officers burst in on me, 'Where have you been?'

'Paris,' I said wearily as I subsided onto my valise.

'We've only been playing hell round the villages in hired cars. Let's go to Paris. There's a train in an hour. The rest camp has been extended four days.'

But I would not budge. Rest I must have. I slept as they argued.

Early next morning they were in again. A train in two hours. Would I come? I sat up and rubbed my eyes. Would I? Too right I would!

Along I went for another pile of notes and a fresh rail warrant. We caught the train and got in a carriage full of Yankee nurses.

They fed us with wondrous things, and entertained us all the way.

The one to whom I was most partial, invited me along to a Yankee lecture that night.

My artillery mate, George Clare, was anxious to book rooms at an hotel. But I impressed on him that that was a thing one did in Paris only when ready for bed. He took my word—reluctantly at first.

That afternoon my nurse led me into a hall full of Americans. For that matter, Paris was full of Americans, all with most important jobs. If Paris had been combed out, there would have been enough men for a first-class offensive.

A Yank YMCA officer got up to give a speech. He explained that he was a veteran, had been three months in France. In fact he had even been up to the trenches, once, to see the boys. Of course, after such a prolonged stay in France, he was being sent back to dear old USA to recuperate. I gasped and pinched myself. Everyone looked serious and sympathetic.

'Hey, America,' I said to my nurse, 'getting stuffy in here, cummon out.'

She was reluctant to leave before the full story of this YMCA hero had been told. I said that I thought she had a few things to see and learn.

Around the Paris of gorgeous multicoloured uniforms and gorgeous sleek girls wandered George and I.

We fell out of one affair into another, with such rapidity that the whole period seemed in retrospect a tangled kaleidoscope of happenings.

On 5 August, as we were considering getting up to a leisurely breakfast, there came a 'Bang-wow!' The bang was the arrival of a shell from Big Bertha moving faster than the noise of the shell in travel. The 'wow' was the swift diminishing sound of the passage of the shell.

This was interesting. Each fifteen minutes a shell came, now in the next street, now miles away. There was no excitement among the populace only a strained resignation.

So we hired a gharry, and had the driver gallop in the direction of each explosion.

We were soon to learn the swift organisation, which at once, as far as possible, removes all traces of each shell burst. Only once did we come on the shell hole, still black and empty, bloodstains on the road and red splashes high up on the buildings on each side. This shell had dropped swift doom on a carriage a quarter of an hour before.

But tomorrow at dawn, our rest camp was to break up.

Reluctantly we said goodbye to Paris. After a long weary journey we landed at Eu at 3 a.m. A gale helped us up the hill. For an hour and a half we slept.

With dawn we turned out.

My NCOs had assembled my brigade party. True to their word, they were still eighteen strong. Not one of them succumbed to the temptation offered by a pocket full of money to take a few extra days, although they knew that another offensive was in preparation.

Had this been England some of them might have done so. But they were not prepared to face the jury of their peers in the line under any reproach of attempting to dodge their duty.

In cheerful orderliness we proceeded by train and lorry to where the nucleus of the brigade rested at Berteaucourt. Our battalions were in the line.

A few of the 48th officers were in the mess room of a big house when I arrived. I sighed and relaxed into an arm chair.

'I've been to Paris,' I said.

'He looks as if he does not care when Fritz gets him now,' said someone, and they all laughed.

22

The great silence

The cubs of Empire, Australian and Canadian, had smashed the unbreakable line. British, American, and French troops had taken up the chase. We knew at last that victory must crown our arms. Our fallen had paved the way to this. Our world was safe. The attacked and attacker swept so fast over the miles that we could not keep pace with events.

The battalion was training in a little village near the Somme, called Pissy.

Trained to the minute, we were issued with those things that are the sign manual of battle. Bombs were detonated. Flare pistols, extra ammunition. We dumped our packs so that we could keep up with this new war of movement.

The adjutant came to me benevolently one day and said, 'Your Anzac leave is through, and the Flying Corps is sending for you in a day or two. What are you going to do?'

I thought a bit. 'Well, I've waited for the Flying Corps so long, I shall wait a little longer.'

Last of all, we received the new maps of the faraway place where we were to pursue the beaten enemy.

Rumours of peace were in the air, but we expected peace on the points of our bayonets, heralded by our machine guns. One morning we received the word, 'Hostilities cease at 11 a.m'.

And so, at the eleventh hour of the eleventh day, of the eleventh month came the silence. London and Paris went mad, but to us, it all seemed unreal. There was a little cheering. Our men bought out the meagre supplies of the *estaminets*. No parades were held.

Our known world had slipped from us. The war might at least have waited till I started my flying training.

I walked thoughtfully down the street. A Digger called from the footpath, 'Hey—Mr Mitchell—finish stars and stripes.' That was his apt phrase for decorations and promotion.

'Yes,' I said, 'finish stars and stripes, and wooden crosses.'

Into a liberated land we marched, there to see a stunned populace who barely realised that the Prussian yoke was lifted.

The days were full of pitiful incident. Along the roads came droves of refugees seeking their homes, too often to find rubble heaps.

Hard came the frosts to bind the land as with steel.

A lorry was waiting to take a party of us back to our temporary billet from a football match. It was ready to start when a frail girl came along wheeling a pram in which was a baby and many bundles.

'I can't stand that,' said a big sergeant.

He invited her to come up into the lorry. Whether she was afraid of the big soldiery, I do not know. Oh no, she did not need a lift. She only had nine kilometres to go. The sergeant passed her up, still protesting, to other ready hands. Up came the pram. 'Dammit,' he said gruffly, 'she doesn't weigh more than a baby herself.'

Farther along we picked up an old woman and two girls. They had tramped sixty kilometres, and had twenty still to go. A little farther we stopped again, this time for a little girl with a bundle as heavy as herself.

They told us tales of forced female labour in the fields that made our blood boil. There were many sympathetic curses muttered beneath the canvas top of our lorry. We were amazed that all these refugees took it as such a matter of course.

Make no mistake. The Prussian jackboot ground these harmless civilians into the dust. Woe to the vanquished is as true today, for all our civilisation, as ever it was.

Long days we marched across unspoiled country, forest and plain.

Our welcome in each place was the welcome of liberators.

One woman said, 'I kept my wine for the first Allied troops. The Boche often hunted for it. Now it is yours.' Next morning I found her, with her husband, digging in the garden, encircled by our interested men.

Bottle after bottle came up. Many were handed to the men. Other bottles were brought in to us. We rejoiced with ceremony.

One night at a wayside halt, the skipper called me in, 'Mitch, the troops are blowing off a lot of flares in the orchard. Go down and stop them.'

Down in the orchard I found them, laughing and playing like children. Flare cartridges were being thrown on to a fire. The lit flares were shooting in all directions.

'I've been sent down to stop this,' I said, 'and this is the best way I know.'

With that I emptied the whole box on the fire. There was a wild minute of whizzing flares and laughing, dodging, men.

'I stopped them, skipper,' I said righteously.

'That's right,' he replied. 'How did you do it?'

'Put the whole flaming lot on the fire, and they all had to duck.'

'You're the worst kid of the lot of them,' he said with emphasis.

On our way to the Meuse, we passed many tell-tale sights that typified the absolute rout of the German army.

A long-snouted gun would point skyward from beside the road. About it would be a score of scuttle-shaped enemy helmets, where the crew had abandoned them and walked home. The arms and accoutrements of a vast army lay in profusion across the country.

Our long and eventful trek ended beside the mighty Meuse in the clean little village of Hastière Laveux.

The village sheltered us from the wintry blasts. No more would we fare forth, returning fewer than we set out. The bells rang of Christmas and peace on earth.

Beyond the Meuse I came to a hamlet nestling in a hollow. I stood a while outside a house listening to a piano being played. 'In the Shadows', revived many memories.

'Would I come in,' asked madame. A pretty, well-educated girl played on, then made me coffee. I came again.

The third time I would not go, though messages came by some of my men.

She was too pretty. The old soldier who would be recruit in

the new life, must needs travel in light harness. We would have much to forget and everything to learn.

The months and the battalion melted away.

The Prince of Wales came, seemed interested in us and everything there was, shook hands with all officers and went on.

Wonderful times we had, but underlying all was an indefinable sadness. The battalion, our father and our mother of unforgettable years, was drifting to pieces. The links that connected us with the unforgotten dead seemed to be snapping one by one. As each draft left, mateships were sundered, too often never to be renewed in the stress and fierce demands of civilian life.

Four and a half years after I left Australia, I again stood by the rail of a transport, steaming out of Plymouth, with men who were strangers to me.

Along the bulwarks of the great grey battleship stood the sailors who had kept the seaways of the world.

Cheer upon ordered cheer roared from them to us as they sped their brothers in arms. Cheer upon cheer answered we to our good comrades.

I stood watching as night closed over the coasts of England. Against the grey mists of distance showed well-remembered faces in an endless gallery. Those who marched beside us a while and died that our peoples might live.

They died but did not fail. We who were left must yet fight on.

Slowly, very slowly, night and distance closed over the English shores.

Strongly our ship lunged toward the Southern Seas.

Afterword

The peace was not kind to Mitch. He had lived too hard, too intensely, too close to death—and at such a formative time in his young life—for a smooth transition to the civilian world. In the infelicitous phrase of Governor Galway, he may well have returned 'with peace in his helmet and victory in his eyes', but like most of his comrades at arms, he also carried a fierce turbulence in his heart and mind. They had won the war, but at a terrible cost. And now they had to start afresh in a country that had changed immeasurably from the one that had farewelled him in 1914.

Many years later he would write movingly of broken promises from government and 'the hordes of parasites waiting to cheat and chisel' the returned man of what little he had. And though the detail of his early endeavours is lost to us, we do know that he took up one of the small soldier settler's blocks offered by the government at Mt Gambier in his home state.

There he grew potatoes and like so many others struggled to make a living with inadequate capital and limited expertise. He walked off the block in 1922 and then began a restless period in Victoria in a range of jobs, mostly selling cars and real estate, until 1926 when he travelled to Queensland. There he bought a garage—probably in the Rockhampton area—and struggled to keep it afloat for almost a decade.

It was in Queensland that he began to write, taking out his precious war diaries and weaving a narrative around their vivid imagery. In 1936 he went south to Sydney with his manuscript and found a congenial publisher in Angus & Robertson. *Backs to the Wall*, in a hard red cover, was launched with due ceremony in 1937. In the promotional whirl he signed copies 'Mitch' as well as the more formal 'G.D. Mitchell' that adorned the cover.

In later life George Mitchell described himself as a 'journalist and author'. His journalism between the wars was confined to unpaid contributions to *Reveille*, the monthly magazine of the Returned Servicemen's League, and articles in the irreverent *Smith's Weekly*. However, he was unquestionably an author with all the attributes of the born writer—the restless soul, the innate observer's persona, and the facility to distil an experience into images that retained their power long after the reader had closed the page.

In 1939 he published a novel, *The Awakening*, in which one Major Cromwell, a 43-year-old returned man from World War I now living in North Queensland, is confronted by a massive military invasion. The foreigners are not identified but are most likely Japanese. The dashing major rallies the locals into Cromwell's Commandos and, with a beautiful nurse at his side, gives a mighty account of himself as his ragtag resistance force battles south to Brisbane and thence to army HQ.

There are plans afoot to fly him to America to rouse that nation to Australia's defence. However, there is no Pearl Harbor in the offing and at the last minute the determinedly neutral Americans refuse him entry. So he remains in Australia with his troops and leads them into a final quixotic battle against the swarming enemy. The novel, it transpires, is actually Cromwell's war diaries, found at some future time when presumably the invaders have finally been driven from Australia's shores.

It is a powerful, if somewhat untamed, work and the former prime minister Billy Hughes was sufficiently impressed to write a glowing foreword in which he declared it a timely call to arms. But in a remarkable twist of life imitating art, within a few years of its publication Mitch would find himself leading a guerrilla force in World War II with all the dash and flair of his fictional hero.

As with *Backs to the Wall*, the timing of the publication militated against its success. Australia had become intensely self-absorbed. The gathering storm clouds of Europe were of small account. And the military expansionism of Japan meant little or nothing while the impregnable fortress of Singapore guarded the northern approaches.

However, there was still a rowdy minority who remembered and celebrated the Digger of Gallipoli and the Western Front and who reviled the 'Yellow Hordes'. They found voice in *Smith's Weekly*, the creation of Sydney businessman James Joynton Smith, editor Claude McKay and manager Robert Clyde Packer in 1919. It catered to the returned men and gloried in the Anzac legend. Through the 1920s and '30s it gathered a stable of outstanding black-and-white cartoonists led by the great Stan Cross and writers such as Henry Lawson, Banjo Paterson, Lennie Lower and Kenneth Slessor.

According to *Smith's* chronicler, George Blaikie, 'In the 32 years of its life it punched more noses and raised more belly laughs than the rest of the papers in Australia combined. Because of its free swinging style of journalism *Smith's* attracted the free souls of the Australian literary and art worlds to its staff. They were given pretty much a free go to demonstrate their talents, and at times the results were spectacularly brilliant.'[1]

Smith's suited Mitch to a T. And while he did not have a profile as firmly etched as some of the paper's luminaries, *Backs to the Wall* would have ensured that his contributions were treated with respect. They would also have provided him with much-needed funds while he wrote *The Awakening* as he divided his time between Sydney and his new home and garage in Taree, New South Wales.

He retained his ambivalent attitude to the military—while unimpressed with the restrictions of rank and discipline from above, he was deeply attracted to the adventure and the patriotism it offered. While in South Australia he had become a militia officer once more. In New South Wales, he became a state councillor of the Returned Sailors' and Soldiers' Imperial League of Australia (RSL). He remained in the Reserves with the rank of captain and in 1939 he edited and toured with the powerful documentary *We of the A.I.F.*, an official film on World War I. At screenings he provided a vivid commentary and answered questions from the audience.

The role of public figure attracted him and in 1938 he stood as an Independent candidate for the State Legislative Assembly seat of Oxley in his home area. He lost that time but won a thumping majority in the next election in 1941. By then he had written another publication, *Soldier in Battle*, a handbook for the front-line infantry and, more importantly, his predictions of a Japanese attack were about to be realised.

On 30 July 1941 he married a 20-year-old New Zealand-born stenographer, Thelma Agnes Bell, at St Michael's Anglican Church, Vaucluse. Mitch was 46 at the time but as full of vigour and dash as he'd ever been.

There was no time to establish a household. Called up from the Reserve at the outbreak of the Pacific War, he was given the task of training militiamen in camps dotted around Sydney. He transferred to the 13th Battalion of the Armoured Corps and early in 1942, when the Japanese bombed Broome on the Western Australian coast—with estimated casualties of more than 70—he was sent with other officers to assess the situation. His response was typical of the man. As there was a strong Japanese involvement in the local pearling industry he ordered the entire fleet of luggers blown up with gelignite.

His report canvassed the possibility of further raids and a Japanese landing in the isolated region. So army HQ, in a moment of managerial inspiration, appointed him commanding officer of the Long-Range Patrolling Group, the 3rd Australian Corps Guerrilla Warfare Unit, with a brief to patrol the thousands of kilometres of the continent's north-west.

He quickly gathered a Special Force of 60 men—mostly former stockmen from the region's massive cattle stations— together with a contingent of camels and half-wild donkeys, to criss-cross the area in a pattern of his own choosing. For the next twelve months Mitch bestrode the north-west like some antipodean Lawrence, liaising with the Aboriginal tribes and the homestead families alike.

As it happened, the Japanese stayed away. But Mitch found several suspicious indicators of enemy activity. On 7 December 1942 he reported a 'sky sign' of black stones on a white saltpan in the shape of a large figure 7 and a much smaller figure 8.

'The native guides said that this sign was not native work,' he reported. 'They also stated that at this place—Doubtful Bay—Kunmunja natives used to contact Japanese and work for them for months at a time.

'The sign was found by pure accident. There may be more,' he wrote. However, the actual purpose of the arrangement eluded him. 'I do not think an airman would need a direction sign in this area as the coast is so distinctively seen from above that any child could locate itself.'

He destroyed it anyway.

More worrying was a persistent noise in the area that resembled 'distant conveyor belt machinery'. He noted that 'it is a queer country for noise. Terrific explosions have been heard but never explained.' However, this one 'usually starts before dawn and may last for many hours.

'My first thought was that the Japs might be engaged in mining but it often seems too loud for that,' he wrote. The mystery was never solved.

According to John Pearn, who traced Mitch's activities in the book *Watermen at War*,[2] by this time 'George Deane Mitchell had the reputation of holding total disrespect for authority above him and fierce loyalty for the troops under his command. His troops were also fiercely loyal to this charismatic leader and fifty years later remember a number of battles fought (and always won) on their behalf.

'He was totally enterprising, using the system to achieve the tactical results he was called to deliver. He arranged for his wife to be at one of the isolated cattle stations which the patrol "just happened to be visiting" in the remote north-west.

'The soldiers found that odd jobs such as carrying camel-borne supplies in the roadless Kimberleys often had hidden agendas and on occasion were paybacks for support that someone had given to his small guerrilla unit. He was flamboyant, tough and always "up front".'

A son was born in August 1942. Life for Thelma Mitchell cannot have been easy as Mitch was away for months at a time. And when no Japanese invasion from the north-west eventuated he was chosen to head a new, much bigger unit, one that would operate in the front lines of the enemy's advance on New Guinea.

Once again he would be under the enemy's guns but this time he'd have an entire company under his personal command. It was almost as though his imaginary Major Cromwell had come to life. But unlike the pessimistic novel, the Americans were on side and had dealt the Japanese invasion plans a crippling blow in the Battle of the Coral Sea.

Now it was time to fight back and send the bastards packing. And Mitch would be exactly where he wanted to be—out in front, leading the charge.

† † †

No. 43 Landing Craft Company was formed in 1943 to provide inshore transport for army personnel—principally beach landings and evacuation of wounded, and the resupply of ammunition and stores for troops under fire. It would operate on the north coast of New Guinea from headquarters at a lagoon near Lae and in time it would enjoy a powerful reputation for courage and efficiency. It would also come to be known as 'Mitchell's Maniacs'.

Mitch led his merry warriors a wild ride through the front lines of battle. Fortunately, as his second in command he had the steadying hand of Captain Nigel Bowen, who would later become the nation's attorney-general and then chief justice of the Federal Court.

Also aboard was one Corporal Ninian Stephen, later governor-general of the Commonwealth. 'My own memories of the 43rd Landing Craft Company begin with Major Mitchell at Tenterfield Camp,' he wrote, 'erect in the back of a no doubt borrowed jeep, a Browning [machine gun] mounted uneasily beside him and a Luger hanging low on one hip, calling for volunteers for his new-formed unit.'[3]

Sir Ninian, remembered by his comrades-at-arms as a quiet, hard-working soldier who would be commissioned in the field as lieutenant before war's end, was sufficiently impressed by Mitch's call to step forward from the ranks. Later, another man who would make his mark on the nation, Captain [Sir] Frank Packer, would also respond to Mitch's call. Indeed, 'The Gallant 43rd' would develop such an *esprit de corps* that even today its remaining members stay in touch through their unit magazine, *Log Book*.

The foundation for this camaraderie was laid by Mitch's insistence that the unit be made up of volunteers. He fiercely resisted the army's desire to transfer men from other areas and when they insisted he invariably returned the overwhelming majority as 'unsuitable'.

The core of the new team would be the 60 men of his beloved Guerrilla Warfare Group. Next he approached another Western Australian unit, the 25th Machine Gun Regiment of Light Horse mounted infantry.

'I've got a great affinity for soldiers from Western Australia,' he told them. 'I've got the best cooks in the army; and when we're in the South Pacific we're going to live off the sea and the land, and be the best-fed troops in the whole show. Men who join me will win a lot of Military Crosses or leave a lot of wooden crosses. Who'll join me?[14]

Virtually the entire NCO complement of the regiment stepped forward as one man. However, there was still some way to go before Mitch had gathered the full establishment of 235 soldiers. The journey to Tenterfield where he so impressed young Ninian Stephen was part of his work in progress. By then he had developed the rousing speech and the flamboyant gesture that had come to characterise the man.

The Luger—a souvenir from the Western Front—in a cowboy-style holster, was no mere theatrical prop (though it was that too). On one occasion when his speech was interrupted by the persistent cawing of a nearby crow, he drew the pistol, fired from the hip and the offending bird disappeared in an explosion of black feathers.

Once he'd gathered his men—and after completing the Canungra jungle warfare course in Queensland—Mitch led them to the training area designated by the army: Coochiemudlo Island in the southern waters of Moreton Bay. To his surprise no doubt, it was an ideal base—sufficiently isolated for a tough training regime yet relatively close to the manufacturers of the landing craft in Brisbane's industrial area and to the recreational facilities of the northern capital.

It also had almost as many mosquitoes as New Guinea and more sandflies than anywhere. A favourite story that did the rounds involved a sergeant who'd had a few too many beers and fell asleep without fully securing his mosquito net. He was awakened by voices and swore he heard one giant mosquito say to its mate, 'Here's one, will we eat him in the tent or take him outside?' The second mosquito said, 'Let's eat him inside—if we take him outside the big sods will take him off us.'

The company spent fifteen weeks on the island training with the landing craft designed by army engineers and built by the Ford Motor Company. Adjustments were made as the barges went through their 'sea trials' and Mitch commandeered one as his personal flagship with a mounted Vickers machine gun.

Indeed, while his men would follow him anywhere, they also delighted in the events that punctured his more grandiose pretensions. On one occasion in the first month of training a visiting brigadier arrived to review the company. Mitch formed up the whole unit on the beach in full marching kit to demonstrate his famous saying, 'Men of Water Transport only drown as a last resort'.

Leading from the front, Mitch entered the water and struck out for a distant shore only to sink beneath the waves when his webbing, side pouches and heavy boots dragged him down. Happily his lads rescued him and thereby demonstrated 'advanced life-saving techniques', an essential element of the waterman's repertoire.

By February 1944 they were ready for action and by April the transfer to Labu Lagoon near Lae was complete. New Guineans had been employed to weave the walls of the company's headquarters, cookhouse and latrines. The town had been won back from the Japanese in the previous October, after the victories in Milne Bay, Buna and Gona. However, while the Allies had established clear air superiority, the invaders were firmly established in the area and a massive effort was underway to dislodge them.

Afterword

Within 48 hours of their arrival barges from 43 Coy were operating up to 500 kilometres away, ferrying troops and supplies to crisis points in the campaign. By now Mitch had more than 40 barges under his command, a veritable flotilla. Each had a high front ramp and straight, relatively low sides. Each was powered by two engines and carried up to 100 gallons of petrol. A flat canvas canopy protected the two-man crew from the tropical sun—and the daily downpour—and the craft became home to their crews for days and nights on end.

Dropping the ramp required nice timing. If it were lowered too early it could flood the craft; too late and it would beach it, putting undue strain on the 'kedge' anchor that had been dropped on the run to the shore and was used to drag the barge back into deep water.

Mitch's 'flagship' was one of the smaller barges but was fitted with high-powered motors that allowed him to manoeuvre through the fleet and control operations. He had a straightforward approach to navigation in the region. 'Going west,' he told his men, 'keep New Guinea on your left; going east, keep it on your right.'

Mitch's 'maniacs' quickly established an enviable reputation for efficiency and within three months two of the sergeant-coxswains were recommended for decorations for 'Meritorious Actions'.

According to company historian John Pearn, 'As 1944 progressed, greater and greater demands were made on the crews. The work was intense. Each barge, captained by its Sergeant-Coxswain with a Corporal in charge of the engines, operated independently along the coast.

'Men worked for continuous 72-hour shifts, cat-napping when possible, and then had a 24-hour break for washing, cleaning, extra rest and for writing letters home. The crews lived on the barges. The soldiers slept in hammocks slung on the craft, and all cooking was done on board.'[5]

In October, the company was given new duties, expanding their area of operations. Special training involved advanced signalling, arms instruction and open sea navigation. Mitch was in his element, commanding his flotilla like some pirate chieftain. He recruited a further 137 New Guineans as deckhands, mechanics' assistants, camp duty men and general labourers. He began a company magazine, *Barging About*, 'to be published as often as we can scrounge the makings' that leant heavily on the format of *Smith's Weekly* with cartoons and caricatures (not least of Mitch himself), serious articles from the CO, and jokes, poems and essays from the men.

Injuries were common, often from the primus stoves the crewmen used to cook meals on the high seas as they transported goods and personnel around the theatre of war. But none was wounded from enemy fire.

In late December they were called upon to undertake an epic journey for ten of the open craft several hundred kilometres to Jacquinot Bay on New Britain Island. Under the able leadership of Lieutenant Ken Ewing the voyage was an outstanding success and Mitch glowed with pride.

In March 1945 Captain Nigel Bowen led a dangerous reconnaissance expedition to the waters off enemy-held territory west of Wewak. This was part of the preparation for the big combined Operation Deluge, designed to land troops in the area and either sweep the remaining Japanese off the New Guinea mainland or capture the hold-outs. Mitch saw this as an opportunity to transform some of his barges into gunnery platforms.

He immediately ordered practice trials of the barges as launch pads for three-inch mortars. According to John Pearn, 'The use of landing craft as bomb ships had never been attempted previously by an Australian force.

'Colourful accounts of legendary Hornblower-type stories of ship-borne mortars used to attack defending castles were often recounted. Major Mitchell and Captain Bowen arranged for the infantrymen and armourers to 'bed-in' the mortars on two of the company's [barges]. All went well in training and the final co-ordinated plans for the ships of the R.A.N. and the bomb-ships of 43 Landing Craft Company were drawn up.'[6]

The target was Dove Bay and according to Mitch's own account in *Barging About*, 'The Landing Craft loaded, a crisp command and all ramps are raised, twenty-four perfectly tuned motors leap to life and shatter the still morning air with the scream of their exhausts.

'They back swiftly away from the beach, turn and once again in perfect line ahead formation ride out over the treacherous reefs bounding the lagoon, breasting the combers on the bar, pitching wildly amid clouds of spray until beyond the line of breakers. Tricky work this, one mistake of any member of the crew means instant trouble.

'They are through the reef and past the bar, and a signal comes from the Commander's craft whereupon all units move up into line abreast formation . . .'

Mitch's taskforce assembled in the darkness 10 kilometres out to sea. When they reached firing range they opened up on the enemy. According to the later Intelligence Summary, 'Accurate fire was observed on target areas, a total of 770 mortars fired during the landing of the first assault wave.' Other barges landed the troops and, 'All craft performed satisfactorily in the operation.'

According to John Pearn, 'Operation Deluge was an unqualified success and stands as the proudest moment in the battle honours of 43 Landing Craft Company.'

Thereafter the company was relegated to the more mundane tasks of resupplying troops and maintaining operational efficiency. However, this failed to satisfy Mitch's abiding quest for 'death or glory' and in May 1945 he conceived a secret plan that would bring about his downfall.

It arose from some highly dubious 'secret intelligence' that came his way from a New Guinean who reported the presence of a Japanese hold-out unit on a nearby island. Mitch's manoeuvrings with officialdom are not entirely clear. Whether he proposed an armed assault on the island and was rebuffed or whether he ignored the chain of command completely is lost in the mists of history. However, word soon spread among his men that, come what may, Mitch was planning a seaborne invasion of the tiny island with his full flotilla.

His more conservative second in command, Captain Bowen, would have been aghast at the idea and played no part in it. Just as likely, the born freebooter Captain Frank Packer would have been in it like a shot. Lieutenant Ninian Stephen's role is unknown but he was sufficiently junior in the pecking order to have escaped the consequences.

Among the men, there was a mixture of wonderment and disbelief. Indeed, the night before the proposed landing one NCO travelled to the island and nailed a sign on a prominent tree. It read, 'Sergeant X[7] was here first'.

Nevertheless, with flags flying and mounted Vickers machine guns roaring, Mitchell's Maniacs rushed ashore and demanded surrender of the occupying forces. Alas, they were met with a deafening silence. The island was completely uninhabited. The barges returned quietly and the next morning Major George Deane Mitchell MC, DCM, was paraded on the CO's carpet and relieved of his command.

It was a sad end to one of the most colourful and gallant military careers in the annals of Australia's fighting men. But he departed not just with dignity but with the strength and wisdom of all the experience of his 49 years.

'Gentlemen,' he wrote in a farewell letter to his men, 'I have been ordered to leave 43 Coy and take up a base appointment. It was my desire to remain in the services of 43 Coy until the end of the war but that cannot be.'

Now as I am about to leave, I wish to record the pleasure and pride that has been mine during my time as OC. All ranks have pulled together in comradeship. Every task given this Coy has been fully and effectively carried out. Esprit de Corps within the Coy has been of the very highest. No job, however tough, has proved beyond the capacity of the Coy.

Many of you have served with me for several years. Never have I had any doubt of your determination, endurance and loyalty. I have been most fortunate in that in all my years of war and peacetime service I have never been associated with a better unit; nor could I hope to be . . .

The war marches to its end. Soon you will enter as recruits into civil life, which many of you left as boys. Do not imagine that it will be easy. Here you have learnt to rely on and trust your comrades. If you carry that trust and good faith blindly back to civil life you will find, as we did after the last war, that hordes of parasites will be waiting to cheat and chisel you out of what little you have.

You will find that when you return a large body of people regards you as fools for risking your lives overseas, for not being clever enough to malinger out of active service. Do not let this embitter you, but rather make it strengthen your determination to fight the better. For when the war with Japan is over, the fight for Australia will be but beginning.

The profiteering and corruption you will find in high and low places will disgust you. Do not take the weak way of turning aside. You owe it to your comrades, the living and the dead, to carry on. You owe it to Australia to play your peacetime role as well as your wartime task.

It is the duty of each one of us to fight for honesty and decency, for good government, for the dignity of man, and the right of the children to grow up in a healthier, happier and wiser Australia . . .

Seek public office within your sphere, and spread your influence as widely as you may. Fight for your ideals and lead others into the fray. Do everything in your power to ensure that never again will the women and children of Australia come almost defenceless under the threat of a lustful and cruel nation. To be safe we must be strong . . .

All life is a fight, to keep on in peace as now, with zest and determination to reach the objective. Our objective is the well being of Australia, but the way is full of traps and pitfalls, the climb will be steep, long and hard. The march will demand a more enduring courage than any battlefield.

So I wish you the success you have earned, and good fortune in the fighting both of this war and of the peace to come.

He spent the rest of the war training landing craft personnel back in Moreton Bay. And when it was over, he rejoined Thelma and his son in Sydney and worked for a time for the Tubercular Sailors, Soldiers and Airman's Association. He was elected president of the Australian Water Transport Association in 1946 but did not re-nominate the following year.

He and Thelma conducted a mail order business in the Sydney

suburb of Homebush. In the early 1950s he began an association with the flamboyant businessman Hastings Deering that would provide him with a very congenial occupation for much of the decade. Deering was a noted sportsman who had been born in Sydney in 1896 and was commissioned in the British Army in 1917. He transferred to the Royal Air Force—as Mitch had tried unsuccessfully to do—in 1918 and flew in the same squadron as Charles Kingsford Smith.

After the war he studied at Oxford and on his return to Sydney started engineering and transport companies. In 1935 he became the sole distributor for the Ford Motor Company and during World War II turned part of his business over to the production of munitions.

In 1947 he acquired the Caterpillar tractor agency and bought large cattle properties in central and northern Australia. Shortly afterward he began a monthly magazine, *Hastings Deering's Ford News* in which he wrote a column, 'Faith in the Future'. And in 1952 he commissioned Mitch to embark on a mammoth expedition around Australia to seek 'the best areas' to settle the migrants who were pouring in from Europe.

Mitch and Thelma headed out from Sydney trailing a caravan and though the original mission seems to have quickly given way to an adventurous travelogue mixed with Mitch's memories of two wars, it was clearly a popular element of the magazine. He undertook no fewer than nine such series, the last ending in 1957.

In 1958 Mitch applied to join the Import Licensing Branch of the Trade Department, but it is not known if he was successful. Thelma took a secretarial position with a charity run by the radio personality Jack Davey—The House That Jack Built—and the couple attempted to resuscitate their mail order business.

However, their income tax returns suggest that money was very tight. They reveal only passing mention of their son, George Jr, who underwent three operations as a baby and later attended a school for the blind. At the time of his birth it was not uncommon for children to be seriously affected by the mother contracting German measles (Rubella), which often had devastating effects on the child.

In *Who's Who* from 1946 to 1959, Mitch listed his recreations as swimming, hiking, experimenting and writing. He died of cancer on 11 January 1961 at Darlinghurst and was cremated at the Northern Suburbs Crematorium after a service at St Michael's, Vaucluse, where he and Thelma had married. Thelma died of a heart attack in 1971.

Mitch's great legacy is the magnificent account of war on the Western Front contained within these pages. For that, and for the colour and zest he brought to the great crises of Australia's wartime history, he will be forever honoured.

Postscript

In researching Mitch's last years, I was extraordinarily fortunate in making contact—through Professor Bill Gammage—with a family who had acquired by chance a trunk full of Mitch's memorabilia. They have acted as custodians for more than 30 years but would be prepared, on application, to consider entrusting the material to surviving members of the Mitchell family. Otherwise it may be lodged with the Australian War Memorial.

Endnotes

Preface

1 G.D. Mitchell, War Diaries, 24/25 April 1915.
2 Angus & Robertson, Sydney, 1937.

Introduction

1 Weir was the son of a South Australian pioneering family from Scotland and at 49 was a middle-ranking public servant when he accepted the call. As a member of the local militia, he had worked his way up from the ranks in the Adelaide Rifles and though he volunteered for the Boer War he was no horseman and his offer was declined. Nevertheless, he continued his service in the militia and was rewarded in 1908 with the command of the Regiment. He was the obvious candidate for command of the new AIF Battalion.
2 Miscellaneous Speeches, AIF, AWM 44, pp. 310–11.
3 Miscellaneous Speeches, AIF, AWM 44, p. 311.
4 Lock, Cecil Bert Lovell, *The Fighting 10th*, Webb, Adelaide, 1936, p. 29.
5 Lock, *The Fighting 10th*, p. 30.
6 Lock, *The Fighting 10th*, p. 35.
7 Lock, *The Fighting 10th*, p. 40.
8 10th Battalion War Diary, 2 April 1915.
9 Special Order, Sir Ian Hamilton, issued prior to landing at Dardanelles, April 1915.
10 Australian and New Zealand Army Corps Order, 19 April 1915.
11 G.D. Mitchell, War Diaries, 24/25 April 1915.
12 10th Battalion War Diary, 25 April 1915.
13 The battleship *Queen Elizabeth*.
14 Names for the commanders most responsible for their defence.
15 Colonel Weir, letter from Anzac, 20 May 1915.
16 Bill Gammage, *The Broken Years*, Penguin, Ringwood, 1975, p. 51.

17   10th Battalion War Diary, 6 June 1915.
18   Typhoid.
19   G.D. Mitchell, War Diaries, 20 December 1915.
20   G.D. Mitchell, personnel file, National Archives of Australia, B2455.

Chapter 1—To sunny France

1   The *Anzac Book* was a collection of contributions from the troops on
     Gallipoli edited by war correspondent C.E.W. Bean. However, by the time
     it was published—in January 1916—they had withdrawn. Pte R.J. Godfrey
     of the 7th Field Ambulance contributed the poem.
2   The 48th was raised in Egypt in March 1916 as part of the 'doubling' of the
     AIF. About half its recruits were Gallipoli veterans, the other half reinforce-
     ments from South Australia and Western Australia.
         As part of the Australian 4th Division, the 48th had its first major battle
     on the Western Front at Pozières on the Somme defending ground captured
     earlier by the 2nd Division. It entered the firing line in two memorable bouts:
     5–7 August to receive perhaps the heaviest bombardment ever experienced by
     Australian troops, and a week later to cop another artillery pasting. The result
     was 598 casualties out of fewer than 1000 men.
         The following month they were ordered to hold the ground captured
     during the battle of Mouquet Farm.

Chapter 2—The Somme

1   The 48th was commanded by Lieutenant Colonel Raymond ('Bull') Leane
     from one of the most distinguished military families of World War I. Born in
     1878 in Prospect, South Australia, the son of a shoemaker, Leane left school at
     12 and worked for a retail and wholesale business which sent him to Albany,
     Western Australia, then Claremont where he was elected to the local council.
     He was commissioned as a lieutenant in the 11th Infantry (Perth Rifles) in
     1905, promoted to captain in 1910 and joined the AIF as a company
     commander of the 11th Battalion at the outbreak of war.
         Leane was one of the first men ashore at Anzac Cove, shortly after dawn on
     25 April 1915, and in later actions his leadership, courage and coolness under
     fire earned him the Military Cross.

Chapter 8—Bullecourt

1   Bullecourt would be a disaster of the first magnitude for the Australian troops
     of the 4th Division including Mitch's 48th Battalion. The British commander,
     General Hubert Gough—a cavalry man at heart—conceived the idea that the
     new experimental Mark I and Mark II tanks should lead the charge against the
     heavily defended Hindenburg Line.

However, in the field the tanks proved worse than useless. In desperation, the 14th Battalion's Captain Albert Jacka VC attempted to coordinate their activity but to no avail. Moreover, Gough insisted on deploying them without artillery cover that would spoil their 'surprise' value. In the result, more than two-thirds of the Australian force became casualties of Gough's 'inspiration'.

2   Though he made little of it, Mitch's action in covering his comrades' retreat then shouldering his Lewis gun and strolling back through heavy enemy fire to his lines entered AIF legend. Even C.E.W. Bean, the official historian, was impressed and used it as an example of the 4th Brigade's courage under fire. It would earn Mitch the Distinguished Conduct Medal.

Chapter 9—Lull in the storm

1   The citation for Mitch's DCM read: 'For conspicuous gallantry and devotion to duty. He handled his machine-gun with great skill throughout the operation, and was largely responsible for driving off a strong enemy counter-attack.'

Chapter 10—Back to Flanders

1   The relief model for Messines was developed by General John Monash prior to the action. It was indicative of the meticulous planning that he brought to the battles he commanded, in sharp contrast to the British generals like Hubert Gough.

2   At 3 a.m. on 7 June more than 100,000 men were lined up in battle array on a 12-kilometre front to begin the battle of Messines. The Allied artillery began its barrage but no sooner had the guns sounded across Flanders' fields than 23 mines exploded in tunnels dug under the German lines giving the Australians a running start to the battle. It would be several hours before the Germans regrouped.

Chapter 13—Relieved

1   The 'skipper' was company commander Major Harold Charles Howden, MC and Bar, aged 27.

Chapter 14—Joyous interlude

1   Philip Gibbs, official war correspondent for the *Daily Telegraph* and the *Daily Chronicle*, wrote four highly acclaimed books about the war and was later knighted.

2   Though he makes no mention of it, Mitch's return to his battalion was delayed by another rendezvous with the dreaded VD. However, after a month in hospital at Le Havre he was pronounced cured and rejoined his unit in February 1918.

Chapter 15—Backs to the wall

1   In the spring of 1918, the 48th was about to play a crucial role in blocking the main road to Amiens as the Germans launched their last great offensive.
2   Captain Lionel Carter, formerly a clergyman in Western Australia.
3   Mitch would win the Military Cross for this action. The citation read: 'For conspicuous gallantry and devotion to duty. When the enemy broke through on the right, he immediately charged with his platoon and captured about thirty.'
4   Lieutenant John Whittle.

Chapter 16—The Vin Blanc sector

1   Now that the German advance had been halted it was the Allies' turn to press their advantage. The area around Villers-Bretonneux would see much of the hardest fighting with the Australians to the fore.

Chapter 18—Slaves of the trenches

1   Australian windmill manufacturers.
2   Lt George Leslie Swan, MC.

Chapter 20—Front stalls for a battle

1   The Allied attack known as the Hundred Days Offensive would begin on 8 August 1918. On that day the Battle of Amiens was joined with III Corps Fourth British Army on the left, the First French Army on the right, and the Canadian and Australian Corps spearheading the offensive in the centre. General John Monash was in command. It involved 414 tanks of the Mark IV and Mark V type, and 120,000 men.

They advanced 12 kilometres into German-held territory in just seven hours. The German commander, Erich Ludendorff, referred to this day as 'the Black Day of the German army'.

Afterword

1   George Blaikie, *Remember Smith's Weekly*, Rigby, Adelaide, 1975, p. 2.
2   John Pearn, *Watermen at War*, privately published, 1992, p. 37.
3   Pearn, *Watermen at War*, p. vii.
4   Pearn, *Watermen at War*, p. 28.
5   Pearn, *Watermen at War*, p. 107.
6   Pearn, *Watermen at War*, p. 155.
7   Name withheld by request of the Australian Water Transport Association.